MW01146013

THE BRONCO BILL GANG

THE BRONCO BILL GANG

Karen Holliday Tanner
and John D. Tanner, Jr.

UNIVERSITY OF OKLAHOMA PRESS : NORMAN

Also by Karen Holliday Tanner
Doc Holliday: A Family Portrait (Norman, Okla., 1998)

Also by John D, Tanner, Jr.
Alaskan Trails, Siberian Dogs (Wheat Ridge, Colo., 1998)

Also by Karen Holliday Tanner and John D. Tanner, Jr.
Last of the Old-Time Outlaws: The George West Musgrave Story (Norman, Okla., 2002)
Climax Jim: The Tumultuous Tale of Arizona's Rustling Cowboy (Tucson, 2005)
New Mexico Territorial Penitentiary (1884–1912): Directory of Inmates (Fallbrook, Calif., 2006)
"Up Goes Your Hands!" Holdup at Maricopa (Tucson, 2009)

Publication of this book is made possible
through the generosity of Edith Kinney Gaylord.

Library of Congress Cataloging-in-Publication Data

Tanner, Karen Holliday, 1940–
The Bronco Bill Gang / Karen Holliday Tanner and John D. Tanner, Jr.
p. cm.
Includes bibliographical references and index.
ISBN 978-0-8061-4165-7 (hardcover : alk. paper)
1. Bronco Bill Gang. 2. Walters, William, 1869–1921. 3. Outlaws—Southwest, New—History—19th century. 4. Train robberies—Southwest, New—History—19th century. 5. Southwest, New—History—19th century. I. Tanner, John D. (John Douglas), 1943– II. Title.
F786.T365 2011
364.3—dc22

2010041005

The paper in this book meets the guidelines for permanence and durability of the Committee on Production Guidelines for Book Longevity of the Council on Library Resources, Inc. ∞

1 2 3 4 5 6 7 8 9 10

To *Jamie, Justin, Kyle, Ashley, Kelsey, Tyler,* and *Bradley*

Contents

Illlustrations

Photographs

Maps

Drawn by Paul Harden

Acknowledgments

We are indebted to all of the southwestern journalists who reported and frequently enlivened the news of the gang's depredations, to the old-timers who passed on the anecdotes that fleshed out historical skeletons, and to the court clerks who meticulously recorded the particulars of the gang's legal entanglements and thereby kept those other sources honest. We are also deeply appreciative of the efforts of so many who contributed to our effort. Our friends Jeffrey Burton and Richard Heald read much of the manuscript, made significant recommendations, and served as ready sounding boards for our hypotheses. Paul Harden, of Socorro, New Mexico, unselfishly shared the results of his significant research on the Bronco Bill gang, created maps and illustrations, and enthusiastically guided us along the Walters-Johnson flight route from Belén. Dr. Larry Ball supplied us with several important Dan Pipkin sources; Retha Amadio, Pipkin's grandniece was a generous source for Pipkin family data. Bob DeArment, Harold L. Edwards, and Howard Bryan furnished valuable encouragement. Jim Bradshaw, archivist at the Nita Stewart Haley Memorial Library, proved indispensable, as did Melissa Salazar, archives bureau chief, and Al Regensberg, senior archivist at the New Mexico State Records Center and Archives. William Creech,

National Archives, Washington D.C., and Dr. Robert J. Chandler, assistant vice president, Wells Fargo Bank, graciously provided essential assistance. Shirley Nephew opened the door into many of the mysteries that surrounded her infamous father-in-law, Rufus "Climax Jim" Nephew. Christopher A. Swingle, DO, did likewise with respect to his notorious kinsman. Dr. Jay Dew, acquisitions editor, and Steven Baker, managing editor, University of Oklahoma Press, as well as Jay Fultz, copyeditor, were instrumental in taking our manuscript and "making a book."

The authors would also like to acknowledge the following who lent their assistance:

Arizona—Tracy Hill, deputy clerk, Apache County; Wendi Goen, archivist, Arizona History and Archives Division, and Bill James, manager, Preservation Imaging, Records Management Division, Arizona State Library, Archives and Public Records, Phoenix; Toni Williams, Graham County Historical Society; Becky Ornelas, deputy clerk, Graham County Superior Court; George Hilliard and Kevin and Bev Mulkins, Tucson; Linda Offeney, park ranger, Yuma Territorial Prison State Historic Park.

California—Genevieve Troka, California State Archives, John Boessenecker, San Francisco.

Colorado—Eileen Bolger, director, archival operations, National Archives and Records Administration, Denver.

Maryland—Janis L. Wiggins, archivist, Civilian Records, National Archives and Records Administration, College Park.

New Mexico—Mo Palmer, Albuquerque Museum; John J. Vittal, senior reference librarian, Albuquerque Public Library; Debbie Macias and Betty Martin, Octavia Fellin Public Library, Gallup; Arthur Olivas, photo archivist, Palace of the Governors, Santa Fe; Dennis Daily, New Mexico State University Library, Archives and Special Collections; Jackson G. Akin, of counsel, Rodey, Dickason, Sloan, Akin and Robb, Albuquerque; Holm Olaf Bursum III, Socorro; Robert H. Weber, Socorro County

Historical Society; Professor Richard Melzer, president, Valencia County Historical Society; Hipolito Bustamante Romero, Santa Rita.

Ohio—Linda Bailey, reference librarian, Cincinnati Historical Society Library.

Pennsylvania—Donna Ernst, Lederach.

Texas—Susan Eason, archives director, Catholic Archives of Texas, Austin; Rachel Roberts, archives director, Dallas Historical Society; Lisa May, archivist, Diocese of Galveston-Houston; Leon Metz, El Paso; Patricia H. Worthington, volunteer, El Paso County Historical Society and editor of El Conquistador; Rick Miller, Harker Heights; Donaly E. Brice, reference archivist, Texas State Archives.

Utah—Janet Wilcox, former managing editor, Blue Mountain Shadows, Moab; LaVerne Tate, managing editor, Blue Mountain Shadows, chairperson of the San Juan County Historical Commission, Moab.

Who's Who

Bronco Bill Gang

James "Jim" Burnett
Ammon Edward "Ed" Colter
William "Kid" Johnson
Daniel Moroni "Red" Pipkin
William Walters (alias "Bronco Bill")

Principal Lawmen

Santiago P. Ascarate, Dona Ana County (N. Mex.) sheriff (1887–88)
A. B. Baca, Socorro County (N. Mex.) deputy sheriff
Cipriano Baca, Grant County (N. Mex.) deputy sheriff
William P. Birchfield, Graham County (Ariz.) sheriff (1897–98)
Holm Olaf Bursum, Socorro County (N. Mex.) sheriff (1895–98), superintendent, New Mexico Territorial Penitentiary (1899–1906)
Daniel Bustamante, Valencia County (N. Mex.) deputy
M. R. "Mack" Carmichael, McKinley County (N. Mex.) sheriff
Ben R. Clark, Graham County (Ariz.) sheriff (1899–1900)

Emanuel "Mannie" Clements, Jr., El Paso County (Tex.) deputy sheriff
St. George Creaghe, Apache County (Ariz.) sheriff (1889–90)
Charles Christman, Gallup (N. Mex.) city marshal
Fred J. Dodge, Wells, Fargo special officer
Creighton M. Foraker, marshal of New Mexico (1897–1912)
Fred Fornoff, Albuquerque city marshal, later captain of the New Mexico Mounted Police (1906–13)
Charles L. Fowler, Wells, Fargo special guard
William M. Griffith, marshal of Arizona (1897–1901)
Fred B. Heyn, Bernalillo County (N. Mex.) under sheriff (1905)
Thomas S. Hubbell, Bernalillo County (N. Mex.) sheriff (1895–1905)
C. H. Jennings, Wells, Fargo special guard
James A. Lockhart, Grant County (N. Mex.) sheriff (1891–94)
Horace W. "Will" Loomis, deputy U.S. marshal (N. Mex.)
Pat Lucero, Gallup (N. Mex.) night marshal
William G. McAfee, Grant County (N. Mex.) sheriff (1897–98)
Herbert J. McGrath, captain, New Mexico's Mounted Police (1918–19)
Charles Mainz, Santa Fe Railroad special officer and Bernalillo County (N. Mex.) deputy
William Andrew Maxwell, Apache County (Ariz.) deputy
Jefferson Davis Milton, Wells, Fargo messenger and deputy U.S. marshal (Ariz.)
C. E. Newcomer, Bernalillo County (N. Mex.) deputy
Frank "Pink" Peters, Grant County (N. Mex.) deputy
John G. Phillips, Grant County (N. Mex.) deputy
Robert L. "Bob" Roberts. McKinley County (N. Mex.) sheriff
Boleslo Romero, Valencia County (N. Mex.) deputy
Jesus Sanchez, Valencia County (N. Mex.) sheriff
George Adolphus Scarborough, deputy U.S. marshal (N. Mex.)
Ed Ten Eyck, El Paso County (Tex.) deputy sheriff
Eugene Thacker, Wells, Fargo and Co. special guard
John N. Thacker, Wells, Fargo and Co. special officer

Francisco X. "Frank" Vigil, Valencia County (N. Mex.) deputy
Samuel Fleming Webb, deputy U.S. marshal (Ariz.)
Harry Cornwall Wheeler, Cochise County (Ariz.) sheriff (1911–18)
Harvey Howard Whitehill, Grant County (N. Mex.) sheriff (1875–82, 1889–90)

THE BRONCO BILL GANG

Introduction

Robbing the Railroads

> "The cowboy, with criminal inclination, noted for deeds of daring, began his career by cattle 'rustling' and horse stealing, and then became a 'hold-up' of stages and trains."
>
> *William A. Pinkerton*

The calendar on the Cincinnati depot wall read Friday, May 5, 1865. Barely three weeks earlier, a divided nation had ended four years of desperate conflict. That evening, the Ohio and Mississippi express steamed out of the station on its regular eight o'clock run to St. Louis. Minutes later, the train chugged along the path of the old Cincinnati and Whitewater Canal near North Bend, the birthplace of President Benjamin Harrison. North Bend was also about to become the scene of a train robbery. Even though troops on both sides repeatedly disrupted rail service during the Civil War—most famously when James Andrews and his Union raiders seized an Atlantic Railroad train at Marietta, Georgia—the nation had yet to experience the holdup of a peacetime train. In moments, the complacency that went with that record abruptly ended.[1]

Bandits had removed a section of rail. When the locomotive plunged into the void, it "tipped over on one side, the cars following in a promiscuous smash up." The Adams Express and baggage cars went over with the engine, and the first passenger coach slammed through the end of the baggage car. Amid the commotion, two of the robbers pushed their way into each coach. Characterized by the *Cincinnati Daily Times* as "remarkably villainous in bearing and action," the bandits brandished revolvers and uttered the "vilest oaths" as they lightened the passengers' purses of money and valuables while five of their cohorts raided the express car before they all fled across the river to Kentucky.[2]

The first press reports attributed the heist to "one of the notorious gangs of cut-throat Rebel robbers." The *Times* reversed itself the next day and reported that "the band of men were not regular organized Rebel guerrillas, but a gang of desperate thieves and robbers who concocted and executed the plan for purpose of retrieving their fallen fortunes."[3]

The North Bend robbery opened a new and deadly chapter in the annals of American crime, and the extension of steel rails west from the Mississippi Valley in the post–Civil War era increased holdup opportunities. During the 1870s, Missouri's James-Younger gang turned train robbery into an art form and captured national attention, while Sam Bass and his cronies harassed trains in northern Texas. Although less often remembered today, the Rube Burrows gang carried on the practice in Texas, Arkansas, Alabama, Mississippi, and Florida in the 1880s. Even so, when special officers James B. Hume and John N. Thacker of Wells, Fargo reported the company's losses ($415,312.55) to holdups between 1870 and 1884, 97.7 percent of those robberies and attempted robberies were of stagecoaches (347 successful and attempted stage heists). In contrast, the report cited only four successful and four attempted train robberies that had cost Wells, Fargo receipts. But the cost of holdups was not measurable solely in monetary terms. In keeping with the North Bend precedent, train robbers frequently removed tracks or tampered with switches to derail trains, which often resulted in injury or death of some passengers or crewmembers. On May 23, 1889, for example, a St Louis–Los Angeles passenger train was wrecked by bandits near Sullivan, Missouri, seriously injuring all forty-five passengers. On September 21, 1892, four men were killed and thirty-five were wounded when robbers derailed an Atchison, Topeka, and Santa Fe train near Osage City, Kansas. A passenger was killed and thirteen were injured when outlaws wrecked the Houston and Texas Central near Fairbanks, Texas, on April 26, 1897. But not all deaths resulted from wreckage; shootouts between express car messengers and outlaws also swelled fatality counts.[4]

In the 1890s, particularly in the wake of the Panic of 1893, train holdups reached epidemic proportions. Cincinnati's *Express Gazette* tallied 218 robberies between the onset of the decade and 1898. Seventy-eight people died during those stick-ups; another sixty-seven suffered wounds. The frequency of train robberies continued to rise. By the end of 1899, the figures had risen to 261 train robberies, in which eighty-eight people were killed and eighty-six wounded. At the 1907 convention of the International Association of Chiefs of Police, William Allan Pinkerton, the hard-boiled son of the founder of the Pinkerton National Detective Agency, addressed the causes of that growth as he regaled his audience with tales about the nineties' foremost highwaymen—Marion Hedgepeth, John Sontag and Chris Evans, the Daltons, the Doolin gang, Bill Cook and "Cherokee Bill" Goldsby, the High Fives, the Snaky Four, and the Wild Bunch. Those modern-day Dick Turpins accounted for many of the more notorious holdups.[5]

Pinkerton first credited the gold mining camps with the advent of "the hold-up robber" and blamed the Civil War for producing guerrilla "dare-devils." After 1875, he claimed, "the cowboy, with criminal inclination, noted for deeds of daring, began his career by cattle 'rustling' and horse stealing, and then became a 'hold-up' of stages and trains." Pinkerton attributed the increase in the 1890s to the general business depression and to "the reading of yellow-covered novels." He explained: "Country lads get their minds inflamed with this class of literature. Professional thieves or designing men find among the class many who are willing to go into their schemes. The majority of these robbers are recruited from among the grown boys or young men of small country towns. They start in as amateurs under an experienced leader. They become infatuated with the work and never give it up until arrested or dead." To these causes, Pinkerton might have added that ongoing railroad construction had extended the Santa Fe, Southern Pacific, and Atlantic and Pacific railroads into the Southwest in the 1880s, and with the completion of the Great Northern in 1893, four transcontinental lines crossed the West. Stage lines proved less rewarding targets when they abandoned their longer routes to the railroads and focused on short runs between nearby communities. Express and mail cars, in turn, were more numerous—and more lucrative—to those would-be robbers.[6]

As train robberies increased, pundits offered proposals and measures designed to curb the escalation. As early as 1873, a federal statute made it a felony to rob "any mail car attached to a railway train," reflecting the fact that most bandits assaulted mail cars carrying valuable registered mail.[7] The Post Office Department also offered "liberal rewards for the apprehension and conviction of stage and train robbers, together with vigorous pursuit and prosecution of these outlaws by members of the inspector's force." Railroad and express companies posted additional rewards and occasionally employed armed guards when rumor suggested the likelihood of a holdup.[8]

Such actions punctuated William Pinkerton's assertion that "train robbery is not a profitable pursuit by any means." The son of the famed detective emphasized: "In nearly every case capture and punishment are almost certain, and death is frequently the penalty. The chances of escape are not one in a hundred, and the stealings as a rule are very small in spite of the popular belief that the train robbers succeed in getting large sums of money without being caught." An 1896 study by the *St. Louis Globe-Democrat* underscored Pinkerton's contention. The newspaper had investigated eight train robberies that netted only $840 and involved twenty-two bandits. Twenty-one of them had been killed, executed, or imprisoned. Even so, the powerful railroad and express companies continued to lobby states and territories for additional criminalization measures.[9]

Some states focused on those who derailed trains. California, for example, made train wrecking a capital offense in 1891. The Territory of New Mexico went a step further in 1887 and enacted a stiff penalty against train robbery in general:

> If any person or persons shall willfully and maliciously make any assault upon any train, railroad cars or railroad locomotive within this territory for the purpose and with the intent to commit murder, robbery or any felony upon or against any passenger on said train or cars, or upon or against any engineer, conductor, fireman, brakeman or any other officer or employee connected with said locomotive, train or cars; or upon or against any express messenger, or mail agent on said train, or in any of the cars thereof, on conviction thereof shall be deemed guilty of a felony and shall suffer the punishment of death.[10]

While this legislation temporarily forestalled train robbery in New Mexico, bandits merely shifted their operations to the Territory of Arizona, which experienced three holdups within months of its enactment.

Taking the lead from its neighbor, Arizona's territorial legislature adopted an identical measure introduced by house member Louis Martin of Pima County—a Southern Pacific Railroad engineer—and signed into law on February 28, 1889.

The new penalty failed to impress four cowboys, though they may not have been aware of it. James Shaw, John Halford, Daniel M. Harvick, and William D. Starin held up the eastbound Atlantic and Pacific no. 2 at Canyon Diablo barely three weeks later (March 20). A lenient prosecutor determined that ignorance of the law was an excuse. "It was held that as they were not aware of the passage of the act, they were allowed to plead to the alternative charge of highway robbery" and received sentences ranging from twenty-five to thirty years. Five years later, however, a less forgiving prosecution team and court rigorously upheld the statute following the September 30, 1894, holdup of the Southern Pacific's eastbound Atlantic Express at Maricopa.[11]

On December 10, 1894, a Pinal County jury convicted Frans Torén under the 1889 statute for his involvement in the holdup. The next day, Judge Owen T. Rouse sentenced Torén "to be hung by the neck until you be dead." Even so, little more than a week before the scheduled date of execution, Governor Benjamin Joseph Franklin commuted Torén's sentence to forty years' imprisonment. Although Franklin allowed that the statute "imposing the death penalty for train robbery [was] a good one" that should be rigidly enforced, he believed that "ameliorating" circumstances existed in this case.[12]

Even though Torén nearly experienced what he later described as "the undesirable sensation of a drop into—the mysterious unknown," the Arizona law failed to deter further holdups. The territory witnessed four more before the turn of the century, and three of the robberies took place in Cochise County, where Scott White, the Cochise County sheriff throughout much of the 1890s, rejected the death penalty as a viable punishment. White explained, "Train robbery had become such a popular form of outdoor sport by that time that the Southern Pacific Company began working to get a law enacted making such a crime punishable by death. Eventually they got the law, and after that there was nothing to do but try to enforce it! The law was so severe it was impossible to get a jury to convict anyone under it, regardless of the evidence."[13]

Evidence supported White's argument. On December 12, 1900, a Cochise County jury acquitted William Downing of his role in the September 9, 1899, holdup at Cochise Station. "The fact is that members of that jury were firmly convinced that the defendant was guilty of train robbery but not withstanding the Arizona statute making the offense punishable by death, they refused to return a verdict of guilty. They would not inflict the death penalty where no murder had been committed," the *Bisbee Review* editorialized. Even though the Territory's capital punishment statute carried over until the onset of statehood, Arizona never hanged a felon for holding up a train.[14]

New Mexico fared no better than Arizona. Although its capital punishment statute dissuaded train robbery for several years, the territory experienced ten holdups between 1894 and 1900. Going beyond Arizona, New Mexico Territory convicted and hanged an individual for maliciously assaulting a train with the intent to commit robbery—Tom Ketchum at Clayton on April 26, 1901. Ketchum's fate briefly halted New Mexico train robberies, but Congress enacted new legislation in July 1902 that set train robbery punishment at "imprisonment not exceeding twenty years, or by fine not exceeding five thousand dollars, or both, at the discretion of the court." With railroads firmly entrenched in interstate commerce, the federal statute trumped the previous capital punishment enactments of the territories. Shortly, on July 30, 1904, three masked bandits attempted to hold up the Chicago, Rock Island and El Paso's Golden State Limited at Logan, New Mexico.[15]

Since federal mail statute, posted rewards, energetic law enforcement, state and territory death penalties, and the tenacious Pinkertons failed to stop robberies of express and mail cars during the 1890s, other alternatives were offered. Prompted by the epidemic, General Wade Hampton, United States commissioner of railroads (1893–97), advanced several suggestions. Hampton, who had commanded General Robert E. Lee's Cavalry Corps after the death of General J. E. B. Stuart, later served two terms as South Carolina's governor but resigned in 1879 when elected to the first of two terms in the U.S. Senate. Appointed commissioner by President Grover Cleveland in 1893, the general quickly turned his attention to "brigandage on our railroads." Enjoying a reputation for resolve and tenacity, Hampton supported the enactment of "prompt and active measures to put a stop to these cowardly and murderous crimes," but questioned which actions would best achieve that end. Statutes sought by railroads and express companies had focused on capture and punishment rather than on prevention. He advocated a more proactive approach. Improved express cars, fitted with secondary doors "made of strong iron grating," would prove a serious obstacle to the desperadoes who assaulted trains, as would the addition of an armed guard to work in tandem with the express messenger. The commissioner suggested that when prevention failed and pursuit became necessary "in those parts of the country where train robberies occur most frequently, a couple of good dogs could be kept at each of certain selected stations." Then, "whenever a train is held up the dogs could be summoned by wire and in a few hours they would be on the trail of the robbers."[16]

Lieutenant John T. Knight (Third U.S. Cavalry) also pressed for preventive measures. He dissected the typical western train robbery and discovered that the express car invariably followed directly behind the locomotive and tender. Bandits would board the "'blind-baggage,' or forward platform of the [express] car next to the tender, at some small station or stopping place . . . then climb over the tender and cause the engineer . . . to stop the train. Then either the engineer or fireman, or possibly both, are made to dismount their cab and go back to the express-car, and call upon the messenger to open the door." The first step was obvious—separate the express car from the tender and locomotive. Then, with the passenger and sleeping cars coupled between the express car and locomotive, with an alarm system in the passenger cars that could be rung by the express messenger, and with two repeating shotguns mounted in a glass-front case in each car, "when the messenger sounds his tocsin of war, there would be a sufficient force of brave men at the express car to give the robbers a warm welcome."[17]

Previously, however, the editor of *Harper's Weekly* had touched on but dismissed that theme. "There is really no prevention, unless the passengers rise to the occasion, which they have never done," he cautioned. "All safeguards that have been devised for the prevention of train robbery have been overcome by the natural cussedness of man." Passenger involvement in the prevention of train robbery also raised another significant obstacle—liability. The *New York Times* similarly criticized the pro-active approach. The typical train robbery story had been repeated so frequently that "everybody except the train robbers must be tired of hearing it. One would suppose that the owners of the railroads and the custodians of the money carried in the express car would be especially weary of it, for they are the chief sufferers," the *Times* editorialized before weakening its position by concluding, "And yet they take no precautions against the repetition of it."[18]

As the debate between proactive prevention and the imposition of stiffer laws continued, so, too, did train robberies. Less than a month into 1897, robbers held up the Southern Pacific's southbound no. 14 at Shady Point near Roseburg, Oregon—the first of that year's thirty train holdups. The next year, trains that crisscrossed New Mexico suffered a trilogy of assaults at Grants (March 29), Belén (May 24), and again at Grants (August 14) when a new and deadly band of cowboys entered the ranks of southwestern outlawry—the Bronco Bill gang.[19]

CHAPTER 1

Open Spaces, Tight Places

"He was the most typical western bad man I have ever known."
Henry Brock

Pressed against the foothills of southwestern New Mexico's Little Hatchet Mountains, the town of Hachita emerged in the late 1870s when prospectors located pockets of turquoise, silver, copper, and gold in the area. Originally called Eureka for the local mining district, the town prospered in the mid-1880s. Then, like so many such communities, it declined as the ores played out. For different reasons, William "Bill" Walters, "who [boasted] the nom-de-plume 'Broncho Bill,'" and Mike [Miles] McGinnis, "who [had] not attained the celebrity of a terrific nickname," had been hanging around the deteriorating village in the fall of 1890. Little was known of Walters, save that he hailed from Texas and could sit a horse about as well as any man. Even less was known of McGinnis.[1]

On Wednesday afternoon, October 15, 1890, several discharged miners, with pay envelopes tucked in their pockets, boarded a stage for the twenty-mile ride to Separ and its railroad depot. Somehow, Walters and McGinnis discovered that one of the money-laden miners, a fellow named Jackson, carried a princely $435. With larcenous intent, the two followed the northbound stage bearing Jackson and his money.[2]

Separ already enjoyed an unsavory reputation, enhanced by recent and recurrent shootings: the previous December, Walter Birchfield, W. H. King, Pat Devine, and W. A. Bradshaw had killed Pat Hines at Separ, and only a few days earlier, a Sierra County deputy had shot one Chacon. Separ had a railroad depot, so Jackson and the other miners checked into William E. Armstrong's boardinghouse to await the arrival of the next day's trains. Still stalking their prey, Walters and McGinnis also registered and then hatched their scheme. Later that night, in the phrasing of the *Southwest Sentinel*, they "filled themselves up with Separ whiskey," yanked out their revolvers, and "chased each other around cracking their festive sixshooter." Jackson and the other frightened guests fled their rooms in panic. The two schemers dashed to the miner's room to seize his money—it was not there. Jackson had raced out in his shirtsleeves, but he had not forgotten to grab the cash. Furious, drunk, and sporting their nightclothes, Walters and McGinnis unleashed their anger on the town. They dashed to the telegraph office, where they terrorized a miner and Alice Parker, the agent. Walters "was just a kid then," recalled a longtime associate, "Salty John" Cox, in his colorful, if less than entirely reliable version of the incident. "He'd do anything just for the devilment you know."[3]

Little more than a kid herself, eighteen-year-old Alice A. Parker had come to Separ from California two years earlier to serve as the Southern Pacific Railroad agent, Wells, Fargo Express agent, and postmistress. She anxiously telegraphed dispatch after dispatch to nearby Lordsburg, another community that owed its birth to the coming of the railroad. Her tormenters soon came to terms with their failure and wandered back to the boardinghouse where they were soon fast asleep.[4]

With a resident population of less than one hundred, Separ could ill afford a city marshal and depended on the Grant

Grant County Sheriff Harvey H. Whitehill (1837–1906). Courtesy of the Silver City Museum, Silver City, New Mexico.

County sheriff or his deputies to provide at least modest law enforcement. Fifty-nine-year-old Harvey Whitehill, the county's nine-term lawman, had migrated west from Ohio to Leadville, Colorado, in 1858, before moving on to New Mexico, where voters first elected him sheriff in 1876. Whitehill happened to be in nearby Lordsburg with Robert Black, a Silver City building contractor, former mayor, and a sometime county deputy, when Parker's appeals for aid reached the telegraph office. With the eleven o'clock eastbound train about to pull out, Whitehill and Black climbed aboard and rode the twenty miles east to Separ. They arrived to discover the residents in hiding and the troublemakers still asleep.[5]

Brandishing shotguns, Whitehill and Black rudely aroused the miscreants. In spite of the scatterguns jammed in his face, Walters grabbed for his revolver. It was not a well-considered move. He was no match for the sheriff, who stood over six feet tall and tipped the scale in excess of 250 pounds. Discovering that the weapon had slipped out of his reach during the night, Walters could do little but curse the intruders and yell that they had taken advantage of him.[6]

With the westbound train not scheduled to arrive until the following evening, presumably Whitehill and Black hired a carriage and hauled Bronco and his sidekick to the Lordsburg lockup. The next morning, Benjamin Titus, the justice of the peace, ordered Walters and McGinnis held for the grand jury on deadly weapons charges and fixed bail for each at fifteen dollars. The two were soon headed to Silver City and the Grant County jail. Curiously, jail records date their commitment to October 15, at least one day prior to their arrival.[7]

Located on the first (basement) floor of the three-storied brick courthouse that loomed over Silver City's business district, the six-year-old carcel had replaced the "miserable hovel" that had contained many celebrated jail deliveries. But no lockup could successfully confine prisoners if the jailors ignored the rules

Grant County courthouse, Silver City, New Mexico. Courtesy of the Silver City Museum.

Weeks passed as Walters and McGinnis waited for the spring session of the grand jury. Meanwhile, they charmed A. Crowe, the night guard. He evidently anticipated no danger from the prisoners and eventually allowed his two charges free run of the corridor until eight or nine o'clock in the evening. Four uneventful months passed, but on Monday night, February 16, 1891, Bill decided that he had had enough of the county's hospitality. Crowe gave the two their access to the corridor until eleven o'clock. Then, as the trusting turnkey made his late night round of the cells, he came face-to-face with Walters and McGinnis. Their appearance did not surprise him, but the "handsome 38-caliber revolver" abruptly shoved his way certainly did.[8]

How the two came by the gun remains unknown. The local newspaper only reported "strong suspicions that members of a very respectable Silver City family are implicated in the rescue of the criminals." At the moment, Crowe presumably was more concerned they might use the gun. Walters and McGinnis seized his keys, opened the desk, and helped themselves to a second gun. The jailbirds then herded their keeper several miles west toward the Bremen mine on Chloride Flat before they set him free. Meanwhile, Judge James M. Lynch, out for a late night stroll, discovered the empty cells and rushed to tell James A. Lockhart, the newly elected sheriff. They returned to the jail and waited for Crowe to put in an appearance. Chagrined, disgusted, and destined to lose his job, the footsore guard arrived back at the courthouse about four o'clock in the morning. The fugitives enjoyed a five-hour head start.[9]

At sunrise, veteran deputy Herbert E. Muse enlisted the aid of townsman George Parker, and the two set out on the escapees' trail. Freckle-faced and slightly paralyzed on his left side, Muse "was a little, dried-up fella" who, in the opinion of Silver City local Wayne Wilson, "looked like some farmer from the middle west." Moreover, the sentimental deputy "could never pass a baby without picking it up and kissing it, and he'd walk along the street with a bag of lollipops and feed every kid that he ran into on the street." When trouble arose, however, Muse turned "cold as a block of ice and his eyes turned green like a cat's." He was, Wilson believed, "the most absolutely fearless man I ever saw in my life." Fortunately for Walters and McGinnis, the two eluded the deputy's catlike gaze.[10]

Muse and Parker tracked the escapees a couple of miles west to where Walters and McGinnis had been furnished horses by "a friendly guide [who] had shown them the way to the top of the [Continental] [D]ivide, and then returned to town." The pursuers stayed on the fugitives' trail northwest through the valley formed by the Big Burro Mountains on the west

Grant County's basement jail. Courtesy of the Silver City Museum.

and the Pinos Altos Range to the northeast. A twenty-mile trek brought the two-man posse to the Gila River, once the international boundary, where they abandoned the hunt. An accomplished lawman, Muse wrongly presumed that Walters and McGinnis had fled west for the safety of Arizona, barely more than twenty miles away. In fact, the fugitives had reached the Gila and separated. Walters, at least, doubled back and raced south. Later that day, after a taxing ride of about sixty-five miles, he spied the outskirts of Deming.[11]

Founded in 1891 against the backdrop of the Florida Mountains and named for Mary Ann Deming, the wife of Big Four railroad magnate Charles Crocker, the town had witnessed the driving of the spike that completed the southern transcontinental railroad junction of the Southern Pacific and the Santa Fe. It had experienced Indian raids, cowboy hurrahings, and the impact of the flotsam that railroad towns naturally attracted. It would be spared, at least for the moment, a full-blown celebration on the part of Bronco Bill. Later, a Silver City newspaper supposed that he merely congratulated "himself on the moral courage he had displayed in denying himself the pleasure of a prolonged stay at the county boarding house." He passed a few miles east of town and crossed Henry and Anna Holgate's 100 Ranch, where he helped himself to one of the former Grant County commissioner's fresh horses. "As the officers were after him when he borrowed the horse it is to be supposed, reasoning from precedents established by juries heretofore, that Bronco Bill was only acting for his own preservation," a cynical reporter for the *Enterprise* concluded, "and that the verdict would be despoiling in self-defense."[12]

Freshly mounted, Walters spurred the horse south. With the Tres Hermanas Mountains to point his way, a jaunt of little more than thirty miles brought him to Columbus, a recently emerged border crossing. He crossed the line into Mexico and reined in at Puerto Palomas, Chihuahua, the newly founded port of entry, where he penned a note of thanks to Holgate and arranged the return of the "borrowed" horse.[13]

Palomas had little to recommend it except that it stood beyond the reach of American authorities. Yet Walters remained cautious—at least temporarily. Sheriff Lockhart, piqued by a jailbreak at the onset of his term, gave Bronco good reason for vigilance. During the first week of March, the county's chief lawman spent one hundred of his own dollars and put Cipriano Baca, a Grant County deputy, on Bill's trail.[14]

Born on September 26, 1859, in California, Baca had first settled in Arizona, but the pending convergence of the Santa Fe and the Southern Pacific at Deming drew him to New Mexico in 1881. He took up the career of a lawman, and a tenacious one at that. According to an *Enterprise* reporter, Baca adopted the guise of a bill collector to hoodwink the suspicious Walters and rode south to Palomas. The newspaper neglected to describe the nature of a bill collector's guise, but assured its readers that Bronco was the Bill that Baca planned to collect.[15]

By that account, the deputy had no difficulty locating Bronco's favorite saloon, and Baca approached the wary fugitive. Mindful of Bill's affection for fandangos, the deputy invented a tale to explain his presence and offered to host a *baille* (dance) if Bronco would provide the music. "William fell in with the idea and as the matter was discussed over a long bottle of Mexican spirits visions of Mexican senoritas gaily tripping to the inspiring music of the violins floated before Bronco's uncertain vision and he became anxious," the *Enterprise* reported.[16]

Bill was known as quite a fiddler, but the saloon lacked a violin. Baca suggested that a fiddle could be found only a short ride to the north. The excited outlaw borrowed a horse, and, just for the company, Baca offered to ride with him to fetch the instrument. The two grabbed a bottle and headed just across the border to nearby Columbus. The revelers arrived and "while Broncho William was quite hilarious he was suddenly informed that his former associates were pining for his company, he was relieved of his revolvers and a pair of bracelets were slipped on his wrists. The visions of the dance faded away and the prodigal suddenly came to the realization of the fact that he was in the land of Uncle Sam and his disgust was intense," continued the *Enterprise*'s account.[17]

In contrast with the newspaper's version, the alternative account of Bronco's pal Salty John strikes closer to reality. Cox claimed that John Good tried to talk Bill into playing for a *baille* in Columbus. "No, by God, I'm afraid I'll run into old Cipriano Baca," Bill replied.

"Let that sonofabitch show up and we'll put his hide on the fence," Good assured the cautious fiddle player.

Heartened by Good's bravado, Bill grabbed a violin and rode off with Good to Columbus, where Good would host the dance. When they arrived, Good reassured him that the "coast was clear. So Bill was goin' up the steps into the big house and old Good was right behind him. Bill got up on the top step and looked right across the hall and there set Cipriano Baca. He just started to back out and old Good just threw his arms around him and caught him."[18]

Cox's account has the ring of truth about it. It is unlikely that Walters, familiar with the dark side of Grant County, would not have previously encountered or at least have gained familiarity with Cipriano Baca, one of the region's better-known deputies. Moreover, Good's presence in the region is timely. The Doña Ana County mainstay had left La Luz in December 1888 and spent about a year at Las Cruces before heading for the Deming area. Unfortunately, Cox neglected to explain Good's motivation, unless it was based on Cox's general opinion that Good "was a no good sonofagun."[19]

In the end, regardless which ruse drew Bronco Bill north of the line, Baca arrested Walters and returned to Silver City on May 9, 1891, with the wayward cowboy in tow. "Broncho had an idea that he was pretty smooth when he escaped," the *Enterprise* gloated, "but he has been ironed ever since his return. The sheriff is out a pretty penny for his capture but was bound to have him at any cost."[20]

On May 14, seven months after Walters and McGinnis had hurrahed Separ, a Grant County grand jury indicted the two on the charge of unlawfully discharging deadly weapons. Walters was in custody, but McGinnis remained at large. The court issued a warrant for McGinnis's arrest, but he continued to evade capture; the court dropped the case against him, with leave to reinstate it, on November 12, 1891. Walters, in the meantime, pleaded not guilty at his arraignment before Judge John Robert McFie. Because he was unable to hire counsel, the court appointed R. P. Barnes to represent him. When Sheriff Lockhart marched Bronco upstairs for his May 26 trial, however, Bill changed his plea to guilty and accepted a sentence of one year at hard labor in the New Mexico penitentiary. Three days later, a local newspaper speculated, "He has shown a disposition to become a bad man, but a year's reflection in the pen may change his determination." Time revealed that it did not.[21]

Bronco Bill Walters entered the New Mexico Territorial Penitentiary at Santa Fe on June 10, 1891. Six years earlier, on the evening of August 6, 1885, local society had danced and dined to the music of the Thirteenth U.S. Infantry band during the penitentiary's housewarming. Two weeks following the gala, Governor Edmund G. Ross declared the penitentiary open. Yet, it had many faults.[22]

Built some three miles south of the plaza of Santa Fe, the prison was two miles from any supply of water, four miles from any source of stone, and twenty miles from any coal mine that might provide convict employment. In the opinion of a committee of legislators, the location met "neither the letter nor the spirit of law." Constructed on a foundation of small stones, the walls of the main building continued to settle at an uneven

New Mexico Territorial Penitentiary, Santa Fe. Courtesy of the New Mexico Department of Tourism Photograph Collection, image no. 1541, New Mexico State Records Center and Archive, Santa Fe.

Dr. Gotthold A. L. Neeff, standing in the interior of the main cell-block, New Mexico Territorial Penitentiary. Courtesy of the New Mexico State Records Center and Archives, Adella Collier Photograph Collection, image no. 32747, Santa Fe.

rate and were out of plumb. The iron in the grates, bars, and cell doors had been in use for at least forty years before purchased and was old, rusty, and "entirely useless." The penitentiary's management record was little better. The first warden, James E. Gregg (1885), diverted funds to furnish his own quarters and to provide for his family's living expenses. Investigation found that under his replacement, Thomas P. Gable (1886–87), "the institution simply changed in name but not in value; it was the same horse but a new and informed saddle."[23]

Prison records document that Walters (inmate no. 485) was a twenty-two-year-old native of Austin, Texas, who stood five feet, nine inches tall and weighed 138 pounds. The unmarried cowboy had brown hair, blue eyes, a light complexion, and sported five large burn scars above his right knee. Both of his parents were dead, which probably explained his assertion that he had been on his own since the age of eleven. Literate and a user of tobacco, he claimed to be temperate, yet attributed his crime to drunkenness. Lastly, Bronco listed D. H. Hunter of Silver City as his closest relative or friend.[24]

Eight years older than Walters, Drewry H. "Drew" Hunter, the son of Andrew M. Hunter (superintendent of the Montezuma Mining Company at Mogollon), was a native of Concho County, Texas. What his relationship with Bronco might have been cannot be established with certainty, nor is there evidence that the Hunters were the "prominent family" the Silver City press suspected of having aided Bronco's escape. Like Bill, however, the Hunters were no shrinking violets. On May 1, 1891, the *Enterprise* had information "that old man Hunter and son of the Upper Mimbres, one day last week commenced shooting at George Nye, who returned the fire killing a horse that one of the Hunter's was riding. Nye then took to the hills." The newspaper provided no further details, but local residents soon learned that a shooting had taken place between the Hunters and Nye at the latter's ranch on April 24. Later in the month, the Grant County grand jury indicted the Hunters for assault to commit murder. Deputy Muse arrested them without resistance, and they were bound over for trial. Little more than a week later, and the day following Walters's conviction, a jury believed testimony that "tended to show that Nye had fired the first shot" and acquitted Andrew Hunter. The prosecutor decided not to proceed (*nolle prosequi*) with the charge against Drew and discharged both. Walters's connection with the Hunters, it would seem, was based on nothing more than his brief association with them when the three stayed at the "Lockhart Hotel."[25]

Penitentiary records reveal that Bill obeyed the rules. Ten months after he entered prison, on April 26, 1892, he obtained an early release under New Mexico's good time policy and headed south. He spent at least a portion of the next two years in Mexico working for Akron, Ohio, native Israel H. King, longtime secretary of the Grant County Stock Association, one-term New Mexico territorial senator, and owner of the Half Three C Ranch on the lower Mimbres River near Deming. Aptly described as "a little red headed fellow," King suffered from weak lungs and had sought New Mexico's outdoor life on advice of his physicians. The former schoolteacher, attorney, and senator also owned the sizable X outfit on the Casas Grandes River south of the border. At one time or another, Walters cowboyed on both ranches, but he was with some Half Three C hands when he first encountered Henry Brock, the future ranch manager of the vast Diamond A spread in southwestern New Mexico's boot heel.[26]

Henry Brock—like King, an Ohio native—had gone to work for a cattle-feeding ranch in Kansas in 1888. He abandoned Kansas for New Mexico in 1890, landed a job at the Diamond A as a horse wrangler, and rose through the ranks. He recalled that it was 1894 when he first saw Walters in the company of King's foreman, Henry Coleman (real name Street Hudspeth), and other of King's hands at a Deming sporting house. Later that year, Bill left King's employ and took a job with the Diamond A.[27]

Founded by wealthy investors George Hearst, James Ben Ali Haggin, Addison Head, and Lloyd Tevis, the Diamond A Ranch enjoyed a well-deserved reputation for harboring dubious characters. "I just asked them what their traveling name was—what name they wanted their checks made to," Walter Birchfield, the one-time ranch superintendent, explained. "At least half of the people in the country then were not going under their right name. You could trust any of those cowpuncher outlaws if he was working for you—they'd do anything for you." Salty John Cox, himself one of those dubious characters—he had been arrested for smuggling stolen cattle from Mexico—

agreed that the Diamond A "was out there to raise steers but they was raisin' outlaws mostly." Cox was on the mark; in addition to Bronco Bill, the Playas Valley ranch at one time or another employed High Five gang members George Musgrave, Bob Hayes, Code Young, and other hard cases such as Tom Capehart, Fenton Smith, and Tom Darnell.[28]

Significantly, in spite of Walters's known presence in the Hachita area in 1890, Brock steadfastly insisted that Bill "never had worked for the Diamond A before he got in the pen [1892]" and dated his arrival: "I first met Bronco Bill in 1894 when he first worked for the Diamond A." Walters "came out of Mexico when he came to us on the Diamond A Ranch," Birchfield added, "and he came out afoot."[29]

Years later, Brock still remembered an early encounter with Bill. "He came by Cow Springs and I was over there and he came up to me. I was building a kitchen on the house there for the company, it was the company's ranch, and he came around to the house and he was a hard-looker. Just as soon as ever you looked at him that would strike you about bein' a pretty tough lookin' man but he usually always was just smiling." On another occasion Brock reflected, "He was the most typical western bad man I have ever known. He was cool and daring, tough but not mean, and absolutely without fear." Bill "was a good worker, and you could trust him as long as he was working for you," added Birchfield. "He wouldn't steal a thing. He'd kill a man once in a while, though. He was anything in the way of a ranch hand—he was a *real* ranch hand. He'd wrangle horses, cook, clean out mudholes, punch cows—anything."[30]

Birchfield assigned Walters and a cowboy called only "Sage-Brush Bill" to the Diamond A's Lang Ranch in the Animas Valley on the Mexican border. Bronco Bill and Sagebrush Bill were soon at odds.

Sagebrush always managed to get in before Walters, cook a meal only large enough for himself, and then toss out any that was left over—a serious breach of cowhand etiquette. Bill would then ride in and have to fix his own. One day, Bronco calmly yanked his six-gun and urged Sagebrush to cook up a second meal. "Sage-Brush cooked a splendid meal," recalled Birchfield. The hungry Walters bolted down the supper and then turned to his partner and uttered, "This camp ain't big enough for both of us. I guess one of us will have to move and it ain't gonna be me."

Sagebrush agreed and fled to the Diamond A headquarters at Ciénegas, forty-five miles northeast. In his rush, the thoughtless cook even forgot to take his outfit. Birchfield listened to the frightened cowboy's story, then rode down to the Lang Ranch.

"I guess you're going to fire me," mumbled Walters, "but I just wanted to teach him to cook."

"Not a bad idea," replied the experienced superintendent. "We need good cooks."

The two reticent men then sat and stared at each other for a time before Birchfield broke the silence. "No, I'm not going to fire you or him either. He wants to work and so do you."

With that, Birchfield rode off, but later reflected, "Sage-Brush was a good cook, who would fix a meal for anybody, and clean up too, ever after that."[31]

It seems, however, that Walters sought more out of life than wrangling, cleaning, punching cows, and training cooks for the Diamond A. He drifted north to Silver City where, on November 30, 1895, he was convicted in a justice court of carrying a deadly weapon and sentenced to a fifty-dollar fine or sixty days in jail. He was released at the end of January 1896. Less than a week later he turned up at Cooney, a mining camp in the Mogollon Mountains of Socorro (now Catron) County.[32]

Named for James C. Cooney, who had discovered silver ore on Mineral Creek, the thriving settlement attracted miners, merchants, swindlers—and Bronco Bill, who, surely desperate, broke into John Johnson's saloon. The *Silver City Enterprise* reported wryly, with a Cooney dateline of February 12, 1896:

> We feel our camp is on the move, as John Johnson's saloon was burglarized a few nights ago. The thief crawled up through a back window. Not having the combination of Johnson's strong box, he whittled his way with a razor which the boys claim Johnson scalped a . . . preacher with when in Texas. The loss was very light—one rifle, one sixshooter and $1.10 in money. Johnny, who is a law abiding citizen and doesn't believe in stealing, especially when he is the loser, notified our live deputy sheriff [Cipriano] Baca, who acted quickly and had the rogue inside bars before he had time to move beyond Mule Springs.[33]

Although the report failed to name Walters, another account disclosed that it was Bill who had been collared by his old nemeses. "Bronco Bill, a hard character not unacquainted with penitentiary customs, was brought in [to Silver City] from Cooney Saturday [February 15], charged with robbing John Johnson's saloon." Several days later, Holm Olaf Bursum, the Socorro County sheriff, traveled to Silver City, gathered Bronco along with some other reprobates from the Mogollon Country, and headed to Socorro, the county seat.[34]

Originally named Pilabó by the Piro Indians, a Puebloan group in the fertile Rio Grande Valley, the site was rechristened Socorro in 1598 by explorer Juan de Oñate, who led the Spanish push to settle in the upper Rio Grande Valley. Oñate chose the name, meaning "succor," after the Piros fed his party of starving colonials. Although not located on the Santa Fe Trail—Socorro was astride the Camino Real—the community profited from the arrival of the trail in Santa Fe in the early nineteenth century, and the post–Civil War discovery of lead and silver in the district supplemented the area's agricultural and livestock enterprises. It was a flourishing town to which Sheriff Bursum hauled his prisoners. The county courthouse stood

Socorro County Courthouse with attached jail, Socorro, New Mexico, ca 1895. Courtesy Palace of the Governors Photo Archives (NMHM/DCA) negative no. 14804.

at the south end of Court Street at the intersection with Church Street. Behind it, connected by a narrow corridor, was the jail. The two-story, tin roofed, octagonal-shaped building had barred windows; the scenic view of the Magdalena Mountains to the west encouraged Bill and his cellmates to take exception to their confinement.

The moon shown bright during the early morning hours of Friday, February 28, as Walters and nine other prisoners slipped past the sleeping guard. Socorro citizens had often complained that prisoners were "generally allowed to go about as they pleased, without guards, especially those in for murder." But these prisoners had located a key and an axe. They knew "just where to get aid and in what direction to go,

Socorro County Sheriff Holm O. Bursum (1867–1953), ca. 1885. Courtesy Palace of the Governors Photo Archives (NMHM/DCA), negative no. 75478.

there is no doubt but they had help from outside," the local newspaper judged.[35]

At daylight, officials discovered the vacant cells. News of the breakout reportedly caused little surprise among the town's disgusted residents. Sheriff Bursum, who was in another part of the county rounding up a couple of other desperate characters, returned later in the day. He and his deputies soon collared nearly all of the escapees, most of whom had wandered west to Magdalena and brazenly checked into the local hotel. But Bronco Bill had stolen J. N. Wiley's horse and headed south. The veteran jail breaker eluded Socorro's lawmen.[36]

CHAPTER 2

Bronco's Luck

"The old west ain't what it used to be. Such shooting makes us feel sad and forlorn."

Silver City Enterprise

Bronco Bill fled to Deming after his Socorro "jail delivery" on February 28, 1896. Whether he rode there on the horse he had rustled or arrived as a stowaway on the Santa Fe train, as Salty John later recalled, is uncertain. Regardless, he reached familiar haunts. Prudence required that he continue south into Mexico and make himself scarce—evidently that was his original intention. "But he had a girl there in Deming," Cox revealed, "and he got off there and Big Sarah was her name." Walters holed up in Sarah's tiny one-room adobe throughout most of the month of March and had "a hell of a time," he later boasted to lawman Jeff Milton. While Bill and Sarah cavorted, local officials, alerted that Bronco was somewhere in their village, waited for Walters to reveal himself. Just after midnight on April 1, Bill rewarded their patience. The lawmen learned that he had retreated to his girlfriend's after a whiskey-buying trek to Burrell Quimby Musgrave's saloon. Deputies Tex Cushing, John Phillips, and Pink Peters cautiously approached Big Sarah's adobe.[1]

"The sleeping citizens of Deming were startled from their slumbers by the rapid firing of guns and pistols" that Wednesday morning. Cox described the outburst: "John Phillips, and a little Texas fella called Tex, and Pink Peters [reached the] 'dobe house and he was in there with her and it had a door and a window on the front side. Well, they found Bill in there and they called him to the door and went to shootin' too. He had a Short's 45 and had it in his overcoat pocket and he whipped 'em and run 'em off." The *Deming Headlight* provided a more detailed but somewhat variant account.[2]

Veteran Deming lawman Frank "Pink" Peters, Deputy John G. Phillips, and night watchman Tex Cushing, armed with a Wells, Fargo sawed-off scattergun, rushed the "retreat" and saw Bronco dodge around the house. The threesome dashed forward, cornered their prey in a lot near the Cabinet Saloon, and Phillips called for Walters to surrender. Bronco spurned the deputy's demand and turned his revolver on the lawman. Barely fifteen feet away, Phillips "leveled his firearm at 'Broncho' and turned it loose." While Walters and Phillips exchanged lead, Peters raced around the house in an effort to cut off Bill's escape route. Then he, too, started shooting.[3]

The *Silver City Enterprise* entertained its readers with news of the battle:

> Wild William the invader of the peace of Deming was generalissimo in charge of his own forces and also impersonated the rank and file of his army. The contending forces came upon each other within the shadow of the walls of the Cabinet saloon, the contestants were only fifteen feet apart. The official army opened fire on the enemy who deployed his force, single file, in the front rank, making a gallant resistance and at times assuming the aggressive, directing his fire principally against the Philip's brigade which occupied a position on the left wing of the attacking army.

> Philips was ably supported by the night watchman who opened fire on the enemy with his Wells Fargo shotgun battery. The army of Wild William, being short on field pieces, was compelled to retreat after fifteen shots had been fired.[4]

Phillips claimed that his fourth shot struck Bill, who "reeled and turned half around, but in turning started to run." A fifth round from the deputy's revolver missed the fleeing outlaw. While Phillips and Peters reloaded, Bronco made good his escape. The *Santa Fe Daily New Mexican* added that Phillips's fourth shot struck Walters as he mounted his horse, "and he reeled as if badly hurt, but he put spur to his horse and got away." The *New Mexican*'s mention of Bill's escape on horseback also confirms the outlaw's own account later provided to Jeff Milton. "They notified him that the house was surrounded. Old Bill told me he had his horses out about four hundred yards from there, [']and I knew nobody would find my horse and next morning just before daylight [Phillips] just stepped out and I just threw that door open shooting both ways and . . . everybody run. And I just run on off there and got on my horses and got away.[']"[5]

Walters's story seems the most accurate. Rather than advance, the deputies evidently retreated, and subsequent physical records do not reveal that Bill carried any gunshot scar. The *Enterprise* caustically lamented:

> It is really too bad that disgrace should be brought upon our county and territory by such poor shooting at close range. Our people, even our desperadoes are degenerating to the level of French or Italian duellists. While there may be some excuse for the bad aim of the officials, there can be no excuse for the shameful marksmanship of a bad man who carried such a suggestive sobriquet as Bronco Bill. His nerve in standing

> off the three officers was all right, but his pistol practice, missing all three of them, makes us weary, "The old west ain't what it used to be. Such shooting makes us feel sad and forlorn."[6]

Whether Cox's brief and unadorned retelling, the *Headlight*'s story, Walters's own account, or even the *Enterprise*'s facetious tale is the more accurate—Bronco Bill escaped apprehension.

From Deming, Bill raced south toward the border and sanctuary at Israel King's X Ranch in Chihuahua. It is also probable that his horse broke down during the flight and he could rustle no other. "Well, then he come on into Mexico," John Cox remembered. "He walked in down there, that's when he come on down there and went to work for me when I was runnin' that outfit." Bill was safe, but only briefly. A dangerous dispute between King and Mexican authorities soon involved Walters, Cox, and the rest of King's cowhands. It was not the first such confrontation. The previous November 1895, Mexican authorities had arrested the rancher, his foreman Henry Coleman (whose real name was Street Hudspeth), and ranch hand John Ward at Ascensión, Mexico. They claimed that two Mexican steers had strayed into King's herd. Authorities temporarily held them at Palomas. Now, at the onset of 1896, six Mexican-owned calves meandered in with the herd as King and his hands drove X-branded cattle north toward the international line.[7]

When a cowboy spotted the wayward stock, King properly went to the local rancher, paid fifty dollars for the calves, and received a bill of sale. Even so, as the herd drew within fifteen miles of the border, Mexican soldiers suddenly appeared and arrested a couple of King's men—Henry Coleman and John Reed—as rustlers and detained King as a witness. The soldiers took the three to Ascención, where King posted their bail. The trio pledged to appear at Ciudad Juárez on Thursday, April 2, and was released.[8]

King, Coleman, and Reed returned to Juárez on the day of the hearing and found the border town's citizens in the midst of celebrations leading toward Easter Sunday (April 5). Judges, lawyers, and court officers, engaged with religious duties, were too busy to attend to their secular responsibilities. The Mexican jailor was on duty, however. He seized Israel King and his cowboys and threw them into his *calabozo.* Within hours, El Paso policeman John Selman, Jr., the son of the infamous gunman and lawman John Selman, was tossed in with them. In an elopement attempt, the younger Selman and the fifteen-year-old daughter of El Paso's prominent José Maria Ruiz had crossed into Juárez. Their effort to find a government official—in this instance, one able to perform a marriage ceremony—was no more successful than King's. The girl's mother, opposed to the marriage, had better luck. She appealed to the Juárez mayor, who, joined by two policemen, located the couple, foiled their plan, and jailed young Selman.[9]

With the nearest judge at Chihuahua City, and with no one to extend the bond or approve a new one, King, Coleman, and Reed languished in Juárez's "dungeon of filth" throughout most of April. In the meantime, Louis M. Buford, the U.S. consul to Paso del Norte America, Mexico, traveled from El Paso to Chihuahua City on April 17, in an effort to secure their release but learned from the governor of Chihuahua that "enemies of Mr. King in [Silver] [C]ity have made every effort to procure testimony which would be an obstacle to his release." The *El Paso Herald* provided meager details: "It will be remembered that he and his cowboys voluntarily went to Juárez from this side of the river to answer to some charges which had been made against them at Ascención." King had been "detained at a house that in no way resembled a jail," the newspaper continued, "until two Americans showed up and testified against his character. He was then shifted to the jail." The *Herald* did not reveal why King had enemies, or why they sought to keep him detained, but implied that his release was not imminent. While still vague, the *Deming Headlight* added that the two men were O. P. (Orson Pratt) Brown and E. C. Houghton, and that they carried an affidavit made by O. R. Gruelle—one of the two men from whom King had bought the X outfit in Mexico—that implicated King's men as rustlers. The two had urged Mexican authorities to hold King and company "fifteen or twenty days while they hunt for evidence."[10]

John Cox filled in most of the remaining blanks. "King was a good man," Cox judged, "but he got this fellow [Henry] Coleman" to oversee his ranch near the Mormon colony of Colonia Díaz (northwest of La Ascención across Mexico's Casas Grandes River). "Coleman was nothin' but an outlaw and he was robbin' those Mormons, stealin' 'em blind." Coleman's actions had also fostered serious animosity toward King from some of the Mormon ranchers on the New Mexico–Arizona side of the border. They now had an opportunity to vent that anger.[11]

With King and some of his hands in jail, Cox later disclosed that the rancher's young wife, Mary Kephart King, turned to him for help. Even though he was only nineteen at the time, she placed him in charge of some six thousand head that remained in Mexico. "They got Coleman and all the outfit in jail but me," he related, "and then I was runnin' the outfit and I was gatherin' a herd of cattle." In addition to Cox and Bronco Bill, King employees Jack Smyth, Rastus "Rusty" Graham, Rex Myers, and Ray Castro remained at the Chihuahua ranch. Shorthanded, they had corralled about a thousand head, mostly large steers, about fifteen miles south of the border and started to drive them north toward King's Deming ranch. "The Mexicans had sent word that we'd never cross the line with those cattle, they'd arrest us before [we crossed]. We built corrals and we'd hold 'em in the corral at night and knowing they was gonna try to arrest us we'd roll up our beds and carry 'em out on some hill half a mile maybe from camp."[12]

Mexican law decreed that any unbranded calf or maverick two years old or older belonged to the Mexican government.

King's herd had many freshly branded yearlings from the Casas Grandes ranch, and Saul Moore, King's cook, also had one of his own Rafter Cross brand yearlings in the herd. There were no mavericks on the drive. A potentially dangerous incident nevertheless arose at the corral when Steve Maestas, a Mexican soldier from Ascensión, tried to seize the burnt yearlings. Although Maestas had no legal cause for the confiscation, Cox hesitated to take any action that might make matters worse for King, Coleman, and Reed.

As Maestas started to cut out the steers, Cox noticed Walters beginning to laugh:

> Bronco Bill he was one of these men when he got mad he'd laugh like hell, you know. I saw him asettin' off to one side and laughin' like hell. Every time that gendarme Steve Maestas cut one of those fresh-branded yearlings I'd go and try to talk him out of it. By God it was ours but by God we couldn't raise no fuss about it because our outfit was in jail. And I saw Bill alaughin' and I thought he was laughin' because I was lettin' that damned Mexican run over me like that. I went up and I said, "What are you laughin' at Bill?"
>
> He said, "There's one fresh-branded yearlin' that black sonofabitch will never cut."
>
> I said, "What one is that?"
>
> He said, "That Rafter Cross yearling of Saul Moore's. If he ever starts out with him I'm gonna roll him."
>
> Now whether that Mexican [heard Bill,] he never did try to cut it. Whether he overlooked it I don't know but old Bronco Bill woulda killed him just as sure as, yeah. [Bill] was a goodnatured, hardworkin' devil, always in a good humor, but a tough, hell to drink. And he'd drink any damned thing that would make a man drunk but he was a good worker. He cooked for the outfit and stood first guard every night

> around them cattle and not a word outa him, you know. Oh, he was a working' sonofagun and good-natured but . . . I tell ya he was hell to drink and when he got drunk he'd do any damned thing but still alaughin'.[13]

So long as they remained with the herd south of the line, Walters, Cox, and the others faced danger. The morning they left the corral, Cox spotted four riders and assumed they were Mexican soldiers. "Bill, yonder they come," he hollered.

"By gollies that's right. Let's get out there in the mesquite," Walters shouted back. "Let's get out there. We can whip the Mexican government."[14]

The X Ranch's six cowboys galloped their horses through the mesquite brush and sacaton grass to a favorable site, where they dismounted and prepared to make a fight. But as the distant riders approached, King's hands recognized them as friendly Mexican customhouse men. Cox, Walters, and the others drove the steers north to Palomas without further problems. Albert Lindaur, a Palomas merchant, met them as they rode toward the port of entry. "There's fifty men left here this morning goin' to the river after you," Lindaur warned.

"They haven't had much luck arresting us yet," Cox boasted. Then, a sudden realization that the soldiers awaited reinforcements before they made a move quashed his bravado. Cox, Bronco Bill, and the four others heeded Lindaur's warning and decided to stampede the herd toward the border, still four miles to the north. Some Mexican soldiers attempted to cut them off, but King's cowboys outrode them. Cox later recalled, "That horse I was riding, Old Doc, ran that night, ran over the roughest ground I ever rode over with his tail sticking straight up. And he never once stumbled. He was as scared as I was, and they never overtook us." King's outfit on the New Mexico side of the line met Cox's crew and took the cattle across "in spite of the Mexican police. There wasn't any fences."[15]

Later in the month, the Mexican government finally released King on $7,000 bond. Seriously ill, he never recovered his health. After an eight-week bout with pleuropneumonia, he died at his Deming home on Friday night, June 13. Meanwhile, Henry Coleman and cowboy John Reed remained in the Juárez jail. In the opinion of John Cox, Coleman's actions had justified his continued incarceration. Coleman "was just robbin' those Mormons and they got 'em in jail in Juárez." Again, Cox's revelation did much to explain King's difficulties with the Mexican authorities and more to explain Coleman's. Nevertheless, Mary King, while caring for her sick husband, urged Cox, Walters, and some other King's hands to break Coleman and Reed out of the Juárez *calabozo*.[16]

In May 1896, "a maneater [killer] from Texas named Sam Murray" and Henry Coleman's younger brothers, James Roy and Claude Bennett Hudspeth, arrived in El Paso to join Walters, Cox, and Saul Moore in planning the break. They made an unlikely sextet. Samuel H. Murray, the "maneater," would later return to Texas and add to his string of killings. In contrast, the Hudspeths were upstanding community fixtures. James Roy had served as sheriff of Bandera County and as a deputy United States marshal. Younger brother Claude would go on to serve one term in the Texas House of Representatives (1902–1906) and twelve years in the Texas Senate (1906–18) before his election to six successive terms in the U.S. House of Representatives (1919–31). For now, their focus was on freeing Coleman.[17]

As the plan came together, Cox returned to Deming to gather some more information. He had warned Walters, "Now Bill, don't you go downtown. Goddamnit you." Unable to resist the temptations offered by the city on the Rio Grande, Walters ignored Cox's admonition and headed downtown. It was a mistake.[18]

Socorro County officials, meanwhile, had not forgotten their wayward escapee. On May 26 they received news of

Bronco Bill's presence in El Paso. Delancey D. Freeborn, a Socorro bookstore owner, filed a complaint before Henry R. Harris, justice of the peace of Socorro County's precinct 1, alleging that the previous February 28—the day of the Socorro jailbreak—Walters stole J. N. Wiley's seventy-five-dollar horse. Harris issued a fugitive warrant for Walters's arrest.[19]

The next day, Walters was at 222 South El Paso Street, hoisting a few beers at the Senate Saloon. Local lawman "Mannie" Clements spotted him. Emanuel Clements, Jr., was no stranger to hard cases and their violent ways. His father, the late Emanuel "Mannen" Clements, Sr., had been a dangerous gunslinger; his three Clement uncles—James, John "Gip" Gipson, and Joseph Hardin—were cousins of gunslinger John Wesley Hardin; and his brother-in-law was the infamous James Brown "Killin' Jim" Miller. Clements sought out Deputy William J. Ten Eyck, who, in turn, obtained a warrant for Walters's arrest. The two then headed to the Senate and confronted the luckless cowboy. Calmly, Bill asked that they read the warrant. He was told that a warrant would be read after he delivered up his guns. "I ain't got no guns," he asserted disingenuously.[20]

"We'll see about that," countered Ten Eyck, who knew Walters's reputation. The deputy seized Bill by the wrists while Clements yanked one six-shooter from Bronco's waistband and a second from inside Walters's trousers at the rear. Only then did Ten Eyck take time to read the warrant before he and Clements marched Bronco off to jail.[21]

When Harry M. Dougherty, the Socorro County district attorney, learned that Walters was in the custody of the El Paso sheriff, he applied to New Mexico's governor, William Thornton, for a fugitive requisition. Four days later, the governor signed the requisition, addressed it to Governor Charles A. Culberson of Texas, and nominated Holm Bursum as agent to travel to El Paso and take custody of the errant badman.[22]

Cox, meanwhile, returned to El Paso on May 29. The next day, as Sheriff Bursum sat in Socorro and awaited the governor's requisition, the effort to break Henry Coleman out of jail began to unfold. Bill's arrest had pared the party down to Cox and four cronies, Murray, Moore, and the two Hudspeths. Unknown to them, Consul Buford had gotten word of the planned attempt. To avoid international complications, he passed the information to Ranger Captain John Hughes and El Paso mayor Richard F. Campbell and also notified Juárez officials.[23]

Cox rented a saddle horse from El Paso's Star Stables, and, on the Sunday afternoon of May 31, the would-be liberators crossed the Rio Grande into Juárez. When they reached the *calabozo,* Cox tossed one end of a rope over the twenty-foot-high wall that surrounded the jail and tied the other end to his saddle horn; he planned to haul Coleman up and over the barrier. Regrettably, the livery stable horse was not a "cow pony," and when Cox put the spurs to him, he refused to pull the load. As the horse reared, and as Coleman dangled from the other end of the rope, the forewarned guards started shooting—two bullets struck Cox's stirrup. At the first sound of gunfire, the two Hudspeths, along with Murray and Moore, beat a hasty retreat. Abandoned by the others, as well as by his skittish horse, Cox later claimed that he had to fight his way back to the American line alone and on foot.[24]

A half-century later, his recollection of the experience remained vivid:

> And they was right there and we was to fight our way out. So I had two sixshooters. I had one for myself and one for Coleman and the one I had for Coleman was in my pants. Pretty soon someone shot at me. I was stooped down and this horse alungin', he wouldn't pull, that new sixshooter went down my britches and fell on the ground. I stepped off to get that gun and

> this sonofabitch shot at me again and I guess he shot between me and the horse, Anyway the horse whirled and jerked loose from me and there I was afoot. Well I started then to the river, three-quarters of a mile I guess, it felt like a mile and a half. Well, I expected to meet these goddamned bastards every step, you see, because that was the understanding.[25]

Saul Moore eventually stopped and waited for Cox to catch up; they got no help from the other three. "Them goddamn wood-beatin' maneatin' Texicans now they hadn't done a damned thing but run," Cox fumed. Later, with more than a dash of false bravado, one of those "maneatin' Texicans" asserted: "With Coleman we would have been six strong with plenty of ammunition and would have whipped any twenty five soldiers or policemen they could have sent after us. We didn't bank on doing any running and we would not have experienced any difficulty had not some patriotic American [Consul Buford], fond of licking the boots of Mexican officials, given us away to the Mexican and American consuls."[26]

The El Paso press fully reported the news of the abortive escape effort, and, in the El Paso jail, Bronco Bill undoubtedly learned the details of the adventure he had missed. Two days after the failed break, Sheriff Bursum received the requisition for Walters and set off for El Paso to take the fugitive into custody. And what of Coleman and Reed? Some months later, a Mexican court found the two guilty of rustling and sentenced them to eight-year terms. On Friday night, November 20, 1896, Coleman finally escaped without the help of either Bronco Bill or Salty John.

During their months of imprisonment, Coleman and Reed had befriended trusty Jim "Santiago" Dowell. Six years into his own thirteen-year sentence, Dowell handled the cell keys. With the trusty's help, Coleman made an impression of the key to the cell door and sent it to El Paso friends. From it, a key was made and smuggled to Coleman in a bottle of medicine. At one o'clock in the morning, when "everything was as quiet as a grave," Coleman's cell door swung open. The two climbed a ladder to scale the wall and then dropped down to the street on the northwest side of the jail. A sentry hollered out, "There goes Coleman." Amid the confusion that followed, prisoner Presidio Vasquez also managed to sneak away. Coleman and Dowell slipped across the Rio Grande three hours later. John Reed, "who lacked the nerve to make the effort," remained in the "Juarez jug." Mexican authorities had released the other King cowboys, Adams and Little, some weeks earlier. Bronco Bill Walters should have been as lucky.[27]

CHAPTER 3

Strange Ways of Justice

"He only gave me twenty days to get outa the Territory."

Bronco Bill Walters, referring to Judge Bantz

On June 18, 1896, the day the Republicans nominated presidential standard-bearer William McKinley in St. Louis, the cell door of the Socorro County jail again slammed shut on Bronco Bill Walters. Several weeks later, another William—William Jennings Bryan—held Democrats spellbound with his impassioned "Cross of Gold" speech and won his party's nomination. As the nation focused on the political scene, Walters could only gaze out at the nearby Magdalena Mountains and the freedom they represented.[1]

A. B. Baca, a Socorro County deputy, filed a burglary complaint against Walters in Justice Henry Harris's court on August 8. Harris listened to convincing testimony from John Johnson (the Cooney burglary victim) during an August 28 evidence hearing, bound Bronco over for a December term trial, fixed bail at $250, and handed Bill back to Sheriff Bursum's custody. More months passed as the nation elected McKinley, and the Ohio governor packed his belongings in preparation for his move into the White House. The Socorro County lockup, meanwhile, remained Bronco Bill's home.[2]

Walters appeared before Humphrey B. Hamilton, the presiding judge of the Fifth Judicial District Court on December 9. Bill waived arraignment and entered a plea of guilty to the single charge of petit larceny "of a rifle, the property of one John Johnson." Dr. Charles G. Dungan, the Socorro County physician, testified that Walters was in very weak condition. "His health is being impaired by his close confinement and if allowed to remain where he is any length of time may result fatally." Judge Hamilton evidently found the doctor's warning unconvincing and ordered Bronco's continued confinement. Three days later, the judge sentenced Bill to thirty days' incarceration from that date—December 12, 1896. Curiously, the Socorro County grand jury never heard the horse theft charge, even though it had provided the justification for Bronco Bill's extradition from Texas.[3]

On January 11, 1897, Sheriff Bursum unlocked a cell door and released Walters. In spite of Dr. Dungan's gloomy prediction, Bill remained very much alive, but his freedom proved short-lived. William G. McAfee, the newly elected sheriff of Grant County, waited outside with shackles in hand. He immediately arrested Bronco and hustled him to Silver City to face the next Grant County grand jury for having, in the words of the *Deming Headlight*, "enlivened this city [Deming] some months ago by shooting at Deputy Sheriff Peters and Phillips several times." More months of confinement followed in the Grant County jail as Walters awaited the district court's spring term. On May 24, a grand jury finally indicted Bill on two counts of assault with a deadly weapon with intent to murder Deputy Sheriff John Phillips while the latter was "in the legal exercise and discharge of the duties of his said office." Two days later, Walters appeared before Judge Gideon D. Bantz for a bail hearing, only a formality in light of Bill's meager resources.[4]

A native of St. Louis, forty-two-year-old Gideon Diaphonous Bantz had opened his Silver City law practice in 1886. Nine years later, President Grover Cleveland appointed him an associate justice of the New Mexico Territorial Supreme Court and presiding judge of the Third Judicial District. Eulogized in 1898 as a judge who "meted out strict justice to the unfortunate criminal, but tempered it with mercy and pity as far as consistent with duty," Bantz showed Bronco neither mercy nor pity. He set the penniless outlaw's bail at $250 on the one charge and $150 on the other.[5]

On Monday, May 31, Judge Bantz subpoenaed Pink Peters and Tex Cushing to testify. The following Friday, Sheriff McAfee ushered Bronco into Silver City's county courthouse, where Bronco entered a plea of not guilty. Texas-born Thomas S. Heflin, the county's district attorney, presented the territory's case. Only recently named to the prosecutor post for Grant and nearby Sierra County by Lorion Miller, the acting governor, Heflin called Peters and then Cushing to the stand. Each testified that they "were confident" that Walters was the attacker.[6]

Bill's attorney, Francis Joseph "Frank" Wright, described as busy and successful, had been practicing in Silver City for sixteen years. The crafty advocate seized on that opening. He confronted both prosecution witnesses and forced them to admit that, although confident, they were "not absolutely positive that 'Broncho' was the man who did the shooting behind the adobe walls." Walters then took the stand on his own behalf, emphatically insisted that he was at Lordsburg at the time, and naturally denied responsibility for the crime.[7]

After the defense finished its presentation, Bantz instructed the jury following closing arguments. Although the judge focused on the difference between an assault without excuse and self-defense, the distinction was of little import—Walters had maintained that he was not there. Either he was—or he was not. The critical instruction read, "If the defendant was not present at the time the crime in question was committed then he was of course not guilty. The burden is on the prosecution to show that he was present." The members of the jury returned, and the foreman, George D. Jones, reported that

Heflin had failed to meet that burden; Bronco Bill was not guilty. Having been given the benefit of the doubt, Bill "wended his way joyfully down the street, a free man again." But, he was not out of the woods.[8]

The evening following his June 4 acquittal, Walters was rearrested on a perjury charge, "it being claimed," the *Silver City Independent* reported, "that he was undoubtedly in Deming the night of the affray." Prosecutor Heflin's failure to convince a petit jury of that fact proved significant; the grand jury failed to return a bill of indictment. Walters was discharged from custody with orders that he "quit the territory." All accounts indicate that he followed instructions. Bronco Bill had spent close to thirteen months in El Paso, Socorro, and Silver City jails on an unindicted horse larceny charge, a petit larceny conviction for which he received a thirty-day sentence, and an assault charge that resulted in an acquittal—justice moved in strange ways.[9]

Salty John Cox provided Walters's own voice: "I was out there at the 76 Ranch southwest of Deming and he [Bill] come out and I saw he had hell in the make and he said, 'John, they tried me for stealin' that horse . . . and I had no lawyer only what they give me and I beat that. When they tried me for shootin' at Pink Peters and Phillips and that Tex, the night watchman at Deming, and couldn't prove that and then,' he said, 'he got mad and he only gave me twenty days to get outa the Territory.'"[10]

Bill returned to New Mexico's boot heel region and apparently wandered between the Diamond A Ranch in the Playas Valley and Mrs. King's ranch in Old Mexico. An event six months later raises the question: did he meander elsewhere?

On the night of Thursday, December 9, 1897, Texas-born outlaws Dave Atkins, Ed Cullen, Will Carver, and Tom and Sam Ketchum attempted to seize the Southern Pacific's no. 20 train at Steins Pass, New Mexico. Because lawmen had expected a holdup, Eugene Thacker and Charles H. Jennings, Wells, Fargo special guards, rode in the express car with the messenger, Charles J. Adair. As the desperadoes moved against the train, a Jennings-fired bullet removed the top of Cullen's head. Mixing wisdom with discretion, the other four bandits fled.[11]

Was Bronco Bill involved in the Steins Pass robbery effort? Neither circumstance nor evidence supports such a contention. Even so, there were multiple efforts to link him to that fiasco. Six months later, for example, the *Silver City Enterprise* reported that Bronco Bill organized a band to liberate from the city's jail the alleged Ketchum gang confederates Leonard Alverson, William Warderman, Walter Hoffman, John Vinnedge (alias Cush), Tom Capehart, and Henry Marshall, who were arrested for holding up the train at Steins Pass. "He came up from the south with this band," the *Enterprise* claimed, "crossing the railroad between Separ and Lordsburg. The officials here were notified and had a warm welcome awaiting the gang[;] they scented the danger and shied off into the Burro mountains, going thence via Frisco and Eagle creeks to the Black River."[12]

The newspaper must have assumed that its readership suffered from short memories. Six months earlier, when the *Enterprise* first reported a rumored plot to capture the Grant County jail, it attributed the scheme to "six desperate men . . . in sympathy and collusion with the Black Jack [Christian] gang," but not part of the "original bandit organization." Bronco Bill (who was never associated with the Black Jack–High Five gang) was unmentioned. No other contemporary news account reported the anecdote or linked Walters to the Ketchum gang. Yet veteran lawman Jeff Milton, then a Wells, Fargo messenger on the New Mexico and Arizona Railroad run from Benson through Nogales (and on to Guaymas aboard the Sonora Railway Company, Limited), was later thought to have given credence to Bill's involvement in the holdup.[13]

Born in Florida at the onset of the Civil War, Jefferson Davis Milton had an assortment of lawman experiences as a

Texas Ranger, a range detective, a deputy collector with the Customs Service, and as the police chief of El Paso. Arizona marshal William Griffith had appointed Milton a field deputy just prior to the Steins Pass robbery; he took the oath on December 6, 1897, at Nogales before U.S. Commissioner Frank J. Duffy. Milton later claimed to have sought arrest warrants for Bronco Bill, Bill Johnson, and Red Pipkin before Duffy at Nogales on February 6, 1898—almost two months before any train robbery attributable to Walters and his fledgling gang and before the offering of any rewards, the only inducement for an independent hunt.[14]

On what grounds would Commissioner Duffy have issued warrants for any of the three? No report contemporary with the Steins Pass holdup mentioned Walters as a suspect. Neither did the accounts link the actual robbers—Dave Atkins, Will Carver, and Tom and Sam Ketchum (known as the Snaky Four)—to the holdup. On the contrary, the press focused entirely on three topics: the death of Ed Cullen; the identities of suspects Alverson, Warderman, Hoffman, Vinnedge, Capehart, and Marshall; and official acknowledgment that the holdup was not committed by the Black Jack Christian gang. Also, there is no evidence that Walters, Johnson, and Pipkin had yet met, let alone joined forces; in fact, there is considerable indication that they had not. Milton could have secured only warrants of a "John Doe" variety that he could fill out as needed during the pursuit of the Steins Pass culprits.[15]

The practice of issuing John Doe warrants, subpoenas, and even indictments was not uncommon. William Burr Childers, the U.S. attorney for New Mexico, wrote John N. Thacker, Wells, Fargo's special officer on February 13, 1898: "If you need any blank subpoenas wire me and I will send you some after the indictment [of Alverson, Warderman, Hoffman, Vinnedge, Capehart, and Marshall] is returned. These subpoenas are dated the 15th. I have the subpoenas dated in the advance of the indictment so that they will reach you by Tuesday." Yet three months after Walters's capture, Marshal Griffith confirmed that the warrants specifically named Walters, Johnson, and Pipkin. Events, as they unfolded, would provide a basis for understanding Griffith's assertion.[16]

With warrants in hand, Milton later claimed to his biographer, J. Evetts Haley, that he had gathered a posse of "Sam Webb and Scarborough—think I had three men." They would ride in quest of Walters, Johnson, and Pipkin.[17]

Two years older than Milton, George Adolphus Scarborough was born in Louisiana, though much of his lawman career had played out in Texas, where he gained considerable notoriety for the 1896 killing of John Henry Selman. The next year, Milton had persuaded Scarborough to relocate and join in the effort to capture the various gangs of train robbers running rampant in New Mexico and Arizona. Scarborough moved to Deming, secured a deputy's badge with the U.S. Marshals Service, and waited his chance. That opportunity came in the wake of the Steins Pass holdup. But, did he join Milton on this alleged hunt for Walters? Milton told of his posse's arrival at Steins Pass after the February 15 sinking of the USS *Maine.* Two days after the sinking, however, U.S. Attorney Childers wrote to Wells, Fargo's special agent John Thacker, "Scarborough is here [Silver City]; I will keep him here." Given the respective notoriety of the two Scarboroughs, this nonspecific reference to Scarborough and his significance to the trial would almost surely be to George, the father. Subsequent events suggest that the Scarborough who rode with Milton was George's son Ed. Young George Edgar "Ed" Scarborough, the oldest of the of the deputy's seven children, had ridden previously with Milton during a sojourn into Mexico seeking the Steins Pass bandits.[18]

Samuel Fleming Webb, the posse's third member, a native of Grass Valley, California, had lived for a time in Julian, California, before settling in Arizona. He acquired ownership of the Phoenix *Arizona Gazette* in July 1889 and for a time served as customs collector at the Nogales port of entry. He took his oath as a field deputy under Marshal Griffith on December 16, 1897.[19]

Milton's account to Haley asserted that the three trailed Walters through the Chiricahua Mountains to the San Simon ranch where the outlaws had a couple of fresh horses waiting. "When I got to Mulberry Pasture [in the San Simon Valley] old Bill had found out we was after him and he had cut straight across the mountains and gone in to the headquarters and stayed all night there," Milton explained. Presumably warned, Walters had crossed the Peloncillo Mountains into New Mexico and headed for the Diamond A headquarters at Ciénegas, in the Playas Valley. "I hit his trail again and followed him into these headquarters," Milton continued. At the Diamond A, one of the cowboys who knew Milton well took him aside and said, "'He's got two horses here. He has been riding like thunder to get here to get them horses.' I says, I will beat him to it. I'll take them myself. So I took them."[20]

Milton and his posse took the trail again the next morning. Focused on the immediate task of apprehending Walters, and cut off from access to breaking national news, they were unaware that growing tension over the Spanish role in Cuba was about to draw the United States and Spain into conflict. They followed Walters and his cohorts toward Steins Pass. That evening, Milton's party camped about three to four hundred yards west of the settlement with the hillside to their backs. "We got there before dark, and were looking for a camp, and asked for a telegram for me, and the fellow said, 'Gracious alive, man!' And he talked about the *Maine* being blowed up [on February 15], and I said, 'Hell, that will be war sure!'" Milton also learned that Southern Pacific officials had been trying to reach him. They wanted him to head for Silver City to testify at the trial of train robbery suspects Alverson, Warderman, Hoffman, Vinnedge, Capehart, and Marshall. "We went on and camped there [at Steins], and Broncho told me afterwards he thought we had quit him. We would have got him sure the next day," the lawman concluded. Milton claimed that Bill later told him, "I guess I was pretty lucky. I stayed there a day and a night."[21]

Milton's account leaves much to question. Were he and his posse on the chase as a result of instructions received from Marshal Griffith? Griffith's papers contain no such written instructions, and any such order, written or verbal, would have put the marshal out of compliance with normal Department of Justice policy, reconfirmed on February 16, 1898, in response to his December 28, 1897, inquiry: "In case a railroad train is stopped by robbers and a robbery of the express car attempted, the mail being unmolested beyond its detention, is it my duty to attempt to capture the robbers, or should I leave it to the local authorities?" Attorney General John W. Griggs replied, "You should not undertake to make any arrest of such train robbers until you receive process commanding you to make an arrest, and that you should not employ a posse until specially authorized by the Department." No authorization was forthcoming in the matter of the Steins Pass bandits.[22]

Curiously, barely a month after Milton claimed to have been tracking Walters and his cohorts throughout eastern Arizona, the lawman expressed only modest interest in Bronco when cowboy Bill Martin of the Diamond A, searched for four horses from that Playas Valley ranch—horses for which Bill had neglected to pay. Martin tracked the rustled mounts from the Mexico line to Colonel Joseph H. Hampson's vast Double Circle Ranch on Eagle Creek (twenty miles northwest of Clifton, Arizona).[23]

In 1883, railroad contractor Hampson had purchased a small spread on Eagle Creek that grew into one the largest in ranches in Arizona. Described by western writer Frank M. King as "the most beautiful ranch in the West," the Double Circle supported Hereford stock that became its distinctive trademark. It also harbored many an outlaw amid its immense and rugged terrain.[24]

Martin headed to Clifton, south of the Double Circle, and telegraphed Milton to meet him. The lawman traveled to hear Martin's story, evidenced little interest, and returned to Nogales on the next train. Undeterred, Martin returned to the Double Circle's horse camp on Black River and recovered the Diamond A mounts. Milton's actions in mid-March are inconsistent with those of a deputy hunting a man that he later claimed to have chased through the Chiricahua Mountains and across the Playas Valley to Steins Pass only a month earlier.

On September 13, 1898, Marshal Griffith submitted a requisition for fees earned by Milton. Attorney General Griggs had expressly forbidden Griffith from employing a posse without authorization. When that permission finally came, New Mexico's Marshal Foraker, not Marshal Griffith, received it. Still, Griffith sought expenses, and, aware of the Department of Justice's parsimonious nature, he prepared the attorney general: "This submission is made because of the peculiar circumstances surrounding the case which may require some explanation." A lengthy history of the events that led to the death of Johnson and the capture of Walters followed. Significantly, in defending Milton's expenses, Griffith stressed that Milton claimed "mileage expense to serve warrant from Nogales, where he received the warrant from the commissioner [on February 6], to the point of arrest [on July 30] *by the nearest and direct route* [authors' emphasis]. He really traveled hundred miles after leaving the R.R. at Geronimo, instead of the 52 claimed, going around the mountains and entering them from an entirely different direction." Griffith's explanation was correct in one respect—reconciling the "the nearest and direct route" (some three hundred miles) that required almost six months to traverse (February 6 to July 30) certainly did present a "peculiar circumstance."[25]

Deputy Marshal Milton had been on the trail of Steins Pass suspects and some rumor probably tossed Bronco Bill's name into the mix. When the deputy did travel, albeit briefly, to Clifton in March to seek him out on a possible New Mexico territorial charge—rustling—he gave the matter little attention. But Walters, Johnson, and Pipkin's involvement in subsequent holdups and Milton's later success in bringing the gang to bay most likely justified, at least in Griffith's mind, stretching the story back to February in an effort to secure recompense for unauthorized expenses and possibly to add weight to the lawmen's claims for rewards. Significantly, although Griffith's tale lengthened the hunt for Walters by many months, the marshal never attempted to link Bronco Bill to the Steins Pass holdup and its aftermath.[26]

Even so, on April 26, 1901, the day of his hanging at Clayton, New Mexico, train robber Tom Ketchum did attempt to implicate Walters as one of the Steins bandits:

> I desire to communicate with you by this letter some facts which I deem to be of interest to the people through their president and perhaps be the means of liberating innocent men. There are three men in the Santa Fe Prison serving sentences for the robbery of the United States mail at Steins Pass, New Mexico in 1897. They are Leonard Albertson [*sic*], Walter Hoffman, and Bill Waterman [*sic*]. They are as innocent of the crime as an unborn baby. The names of the men who did commit the crime are Dave Atkins, Ed Cullen, Will Carver, Sam Ketchum, Bronco Bill and myself.[27]

Cullen, Carver, and Sam Ketchum were dead and beyond the jurisdiction of any secular court. Dave Atkins was under bond in Tom Green County, Texas, awaiting trial on a murder charge. That left Bronco Bill. Why would Ketchum incriminate Walters when, at the same time, he exonerated Alverson,

Hoffman, and Warderman, of involvement? A *Western Liberal* editorial, published as Ketchum and Walters awaited trial for their respective offenses, provided a clue to a likely explanation: "Last Saturday the doctors at the penitentiary amputated Tom Ketchum's right arm, above the elbow, this being necessary to save his life. If owing to alibi witnesses or crooked jurymen or Oliver Lee[,] luck Ketchum and 'Broncho Bill' should be turned loose both would have to practice shooting with the left hand before they could resume their original occupations."[28]

Ketchum had suffered a buckshot wound in the right arm during his August 16, 1899, holdup of the Colorado and Southern south-bound no. 1 near Folsom, New Mexico. Officials transferred him by train to Santa Fe on August 23. The next day, they confined him for safekeeping at the New Mexico Territorial Penitentiary, where surgeons removed his gangrenous limb on September 2. During twenty months of confinement (August 24, 1899, to April 23, 1901), Ketchum remained at the Santa Fe prison. He was taken to Las Vegas for his November 15, 1899, trial on a federal indictment of delaying the U.S. mail, convicted, and returned to the Santa Fe penitentiary. He remained there until taken to Clayton, in Union County, on September 3, 1900, to stand trial on the territorial charge of train robbery. Convicted, he was back at the territorial penitentiary by September 13. So he was absent from the penitentiary for less than two weeks, and, for much of that time, he enjoyed at least some access to the general inmate population.[29]

For most of those same twenty months, the penitentiary also housed Bronco Bill Walters, who entered for safekeeping on August 7, 1898, and only occasionally left when officials periodically hauled him to Socorro County for hearings related to his forthcoming trial. The two captured train robbers and known killers shared a similar disability—severely wounded at the time of his capture, Walters had permanently lost the use of his right arm and Ketchum had much of his right limb removed. The tempestuous Bronco Bill and the surly Ketchum were otherwise no more alike than oil and water. By that time, however, Bronco Bill had killed two New Mexico deputies and a Navajo tracker following a highly successful train robbery at Belén, while Ketchum, so far as New Mexico officialdom was concerned, had slain no one in New Mexico—he was wanted on murder charges in Arizona—nor had he gotten anything other than buckshot in his most recent attempt to heist a train. Yet, following their respective trials, only Ketchum would be sentenced to hang. Certainly, he had grounds for a grudge; he likely sought to even the score.[30]

Ketchum biographer Jeff Burton reached much the same conclusion. In a letter to the authors, he wrote: "I always attributed TK's eagerness to implicate Bronco Bill to spite-and-malice: Bill had robbed a train and murdered his way out of the noose, whereas Tom himself had not only failed to rob a train but had failed to insure his neck by murdering one of the train crew. Your adoption of the same view is itself evidence, of a kind, particularly as you introduce something that didn't occur to me—the point that the two men would have seen a lot of each other in prison, and would have got on together very badly. (Whoever did get on well with T. Ketchum?)"[31]

New Mexico's Governor Miguel Otero (1897–1906), probably influenced by Ketchum, later identified Walters as a member of Ketchum's gang and asserted that "Broncho Bill was left in charge of the 'Robbers' Roost'" at Turkey Creek Canyon in the Taos Mountains near Cimarron when the others stopped the Union Pacific, Denver and Gulf train near Folsom, New Mexico, on September 3, 1897. Otero further claimed that Walters, "disgusted with camp life," left the others in the late spring of 1899, prior to their July 11 assault on the Colorado and Southern (the renamed Union Pacific, Denver and Gulf). The governor's contentions notwithstanding, all evidence indicates that Bronco Bill was at the opposite end of the territory throughout the second half of 1897. Furthermore, Otero, governor at the time, assuredly was aware that Walters had

New Mexico governor Miguel A. "Gilly" Otero (1859–1944). Courtesy Palace of the Governors Photo Archives (NMHM/DCA), negative no. 50610.

been in New Mexico's custody since August 1898, fully one-half year prior to his alleged abandonment of the Ketchum gang at Turkey Creek Canyon.[32]

Ketchum's influence on some contemporaries extended beyond Otero. It evidently affected Walter C. Hovey (alias Hoffman) as well. Years after having been convicted of post office robbery in the aftermath of the Steins Pass holdup, Hoffman recalled: "We had been at Santa Fe for about two years when William Walters, better known as Bronco Bill, was ambushed by officers in Arizona. His right arm had been shot off and he was captured and brought to prison. Shortly after his capture he made a statement that he, Ed Cullen (who was killed at Steins Pass train holdup), Bill Carver, Dave Atkins, and Sam and Tom Ketchum were responsible for the train holdup. Not long after Bronco Bill's arrest, Sam Ketchum was captured."[33]

Like Otero's account, Hovey's is crammed with errors. In truth, New Mexico Territorial Penitentiary received "Hoffman, Walter (alias Clarence Walter Hovey)" on September 28, 1898 (as inmate number 1160). Foraker had escorted Walters to the hospital ward at the penitentiary on August 6, 1898—almost two months *prior* to Hovey's arrival, not two years after. Sam Ketchum's arrest followed that of Walters by almost one year. Hovey's chronological sequence prompts much doubt, as does his claim that Walters's arm had been "shot off." What remains is Hovey's allegation that Bronco made an incriminating statement. Interviewed from his hospital bed "shortly after his capture" and before Hovey's admission, Walters remarked, "'Well, my lawyers will look out for me,' as [he] handed the reporter the business card of a Solomonville attorney." It is not credible that Walters (even were he part of the Steins Pass outfit), represented by able counsel (Humphrey B. Hamilton, his former convicting judge, and the controversial Elfego Baca), would implicate himself in one capital offense while his attorneys labored at length (to change the venue and reduce the charge to second-degree murder) in order to save his neck in another.[34]

In spite of later assertions and innuendo, there is no basis for the claim that either Walters or his later associates participated in the abortive Steins Pass robbery—the evidence suggests the opposite. What is certain is Walters's relocation from New Mexico's boot heel region to the White Mountains of

Arizona Territory shortly after 1897 became 1898. As Diamond A cowboy Martin had reported, Bronco Bill reached Hampson's Double Circle Ranch by March, about three months after the Steins pass holdup.[35]

CHAPTER 4

Black River Toughs

"I won't be arrested."

William "Kid" Johnson

Founded in 1879 around Henry Springer's trading post, Springerville, the self-styled gateway to Arizona's White Mountains, is situated in Round Valley along the headwaters of the Little Colorado River. Only fifteen miles west of the Arizona–New Mexico border in Apache County, the area (at its founding, part of Yavapai County) could support a considerable livestock industry. It extends to Graham County and the nearby valleys of Socorro (now Catron) County, New Mexico. To tap that grazing resource, as well as the rich lead and zinc deposits of New Mexico's Magdalena Mountains, the New Mexican Railroad Company constructed a twenty-seven-mile trunk line from Socorro across the western edge of the Rio Grande Rift to Magdalena. Completed in October 1884 and later leased to the Santa Fe, the railhead served as a powerful magnet. Cowboys and herders began to drive thousands of head of cattle and sheep over the 125-mile Beefsteak Trail from Springerville to Magdalena's stockyards; briefly, Magdalena was second only to Chicago as a livestock shipping point. Yet the very economic rewards that motivated ranchers to develop a stock business also encouraged rustlers to plunder it.[1]

The depredations of the "Gila monsters," a group of outlaws headquartered north of the trail in New Mexico's Datil Mountains, spawned the Cattlemen's Protective Association during the first week of December 1882—almost two years before the railroad's completion. The association had one goal: to exterminate rustlers. At San Jose on the Pecos (San Miguel County), lawmen captured rustlers who had stolen a team from the Calhoun brothers' ranch on the Jornado del Muerto, near Nutt. The next several months witnessed even more success as various members of the John Kinney gang, including its leader, found their way into official hands. All the same, the rugged and isolated setting of the area continued to provide a haven for desperadoes on the lam and also produced the members of Bronco Bill's gang—notably Bill "Kid" Johnson, Ammon "Ed" Colter, and Daniel "Red" Pipkin.[2]

Like so many Texas families, the Johnsons had their roots in Tennessee. At a time now long forgotten, William Thomas Johnson (1833–1906) and his wife, Ann Brinkley Johnson immigrated to Texas and settled near Gatesville, the county seat of Coryell County. Their son, Albert Haywood "Ab" Johnson, was born November 28, 1855, only one year after the county was organized out of Bell County. Twenty years later, on December 16, 1875, Ab Johnson married Wisconsin native Emeline Catherine, the daughter of Thomas and Sophronia Steele of neighboring McLennan County, and they soon headed about eighty miles west to Brownwood, the county seat of Brown County, where the Johnsons started raising horses and children.[3]

On a feeder line of the Western Trail at the geographic center of Texas, Brownwood numbered little more than one hundred residents in 1875, but that number soon grew by one with the birth of Ab and Emeline's first child, named for paternal grandfather William. Second son Asa Albert "Ace" followed on July 10, 1879, and Alice Mary joined the family on March 12, 1882. Greener pastures beckoned, however, and the Johnsons bid Texas farewell in 1883 and hauled their freight to Luna Valley in Socorro County, New Mexico, less than forty miles southeast and across the line from Springerville. County records indicate that Albert Johnson purchased land in Socorro County on October 30, 1883. On their Blue River spread, the Johnsons continued to raise horses and welcomed a third son, Charles Henry (born July 27, 1888). But tragedy struck the family on April 13, 1896, when the mother, Emeline, died. Her death had a certain impact on the oldest boy, William "Kid" Johnson, who quickly turned into a hard case.[4]

Apache County stockman Evans P. Coleman (1874–1954), who spent his youth cowboying on the Blue and Little Colorado rivers, grew up with Kid Johnson. Born on a ranch near Pioche, Nevada, on February 12, 1874, Coleman came with his family to Arizona in 1880 and developed into an "early-day cowboy, humorist, and a friend of bad men and sheriffs alike." Coleman recalled that, Johnson, during the winter following his mother's death, "got into a little cattle stealing scrape over on the border."[5]

"I won't be arrested," Johnson avowed when it became evident that New Mexico authorities were going to catch up with him and that successful prosecution would likely follow. His friends feared that he would be taken alive only if he could not get to his gun. Irish native St. George Creaghe, the soon-to-be sheriff of Apache County, and Albert H. Pratt, a wealthy and well-known cattlemen of the area, counseled Johnson to "stand your trial and if convicted you wouldn't stay long." The Kid remained adamant and fled south.[6]

He sought refuge in some of the most beautiful but forbidding country in the West, Arizona's Black River region sprawled between Apache and Graham counties. Before leaving, he confided to Coleman, who then worked for the Black, Keiner, Hearst, and Wiley Y Ranch, that he did not think that lawmen from New Mexico would venture into such an isolated part of the country; even if they did and captured him, they would then have to face the difficulties of extradition. Kid Johnson hired on with Joe Hampson's Double Circle outfit on Eagle Creek, where Ed Colter, a member of one of Apache County's pioneer families, soon drifted in.[7]

A cross-continental trek had brought his father, James Gilbert Henneger Colter (born December 28, 1844, as Coulter), to Apache County from Wallace Bay, Cumberland County, Nova Scotia, Canada. He was joined by James D. Murray and James Powell. The migrants reached New Mexico and learned of a new region that had just opened on the Little Colorado River and of the possibility of raising barley for nearby Camp (now Fort) Apache. After they paid one-half of the food as toll for crossing the Navajo Reservation, they settled in Nutrioso Valley, just south of Round Valley.[8]

With grass belly-high to a horse, and streams that formed the headwaters of the meandering Little Colorado, the agricultural and stock potential of the area was obvious to James Colter and his party. In March 1875, Melvin Jones had established squatter's rights near the south end of the valley, hardly two miles from present-day Nutrioso. Four months later, Colter bought those rights from Jones. Tucked away near the northeast foot of Gobbler Peak and along a creek that now bears Colter's name, the land was prime for planting. The Nova Scotia emigrant raised a good crop of barley that year; the next year he introduced the area's first threshing machine.

Others soon found their way into the area. On their trek west from Arkansas, the Rudd party had met Henry Springer when they stopped in Albuquerque for supplies; he urged them to point their wagons toward Round Valley. Dr. William Mann Rudd (ca. 1827–1915), his wife Elizabeth Catherine (1836–1933), their two daughters, Rudd's brothers Ben and Jim, Jim's family, and the Bush family arrived on the afternoon of August 25, 1876. As they corralled the wagons and cooked dinner, people gathered around to see the "New Comers." Melvin Jones and Jim Colter often traveled the few miles north to Henry Springer's store. On their next trip to Springer's, they took a detour to meet the Rudds.[9]

Smitten by the doctor's sixteen-year-old daughter, Rosalia ("Rosa"), Colter all the way back to camp kept repeating, "Gosh but she's a pretty girl," or, "Gosh darn it if I've ever seen her like." The next Sunday, Colter dressed up in his very best and went to call on the southern belle. Before long, they were engaged, and, according to Jones, "Jim kept sober all that time . . . though usually he was a heavy drinker." Jim and Rosa married at Springerville on February 20, 1877.[10]

Edward F. Bowers, the sheriff of Yavapai County, shortly named Colter deputy sheriff for the Round and Nutrioso Valley regions. "It was about three hundred and fifty miles from Prescott, and I had to assess property and collect [taxes] as far as Clifton, which was the first mining camp opened up," Colter recalled. "I had to travel through Indian country all the way; it was all Indians that day, you know. I always travelled in the night; mostly on horseback with pack animals; we would make fires to cook a little coffee, etc., and then I would put them out and move camp. When I laid down I would lay down in another place from where I had had my fire." Colter continued to raise stock and barley and contracted to provide barley to Camp Apache at nine dollars per one hundred pounds.[11]

In 1878, Erastus Snow, an apostle with the Latter-day Saints Church, encouraged the Mormons to begin the colonization of the upper Little Colorado River. Soon after the birth of the Colters' first son, Fred, on February 2, 1879, prominent Mormon colonist William Jordan Flake came to Nutrioso from Snowflake to buy wheat. "Why don't you buy the place and raise your own wheat?" questioned Colter. The idea appealed to Flake. Over the next hour the two struck a bargain; Flake took title to the land, its improvements, and all equipment in exchange for three hundred head of cattle to be delivered the following November. On their arrival, the Colters drove them across the Arizona line to nearby Keller Valley and the small settlement of Alma, New Mexico.[12]

Located at the western base of the Mogollon Mountains along the San Francisco River, Alma had started to emerge as an agricultural-based community when James C. Cooney, formerly a guide and scout at Fort Bayard, led a party of prospectors to nearby Mineral Creek and located the region's first mining claims. Now committed to stock raising rather than farming or mining, Colter filed on a quarter section of government land and ran his stock on a portion of the site that later became the renowned WS Ranch. It was also here that the Colters joined a battle against one of the Southwest's best-known Apache raiders.[13]

Mimbres Apache chief Victorio and his followers had bolted the Mescalero Reservation near Fort Stanton, New Mexico, about the time the Colters made their trek to Alma. Following several skirmishes with the army, and a brief flight into Mexico, Victorio and his band returned to southwestern New Mexico. On April 28, 1880, they attacked a group of miners on Mineral Creek. Jim Cooney and Jack Chick rode to warn the settlers in Keller Valley. Alma's miniscule population raced to John Roberts's ranch and barricaded themselves within the house. The siege continued throughout the night and the following day. "My father and Uncle Jim Murray were wounded in battle and hundreds of livestock were killed," young Fred Colter later related. "The Indians were finally driven off."[14]

The threat of repeated attacks prompted Jim Colter to move his family into Silver City. In the meantime, on March 8, 1881, the Santa Fe tracks converged with those of the Southern Pacific Railroad at Deming. At that time, Colter "had butchershops at Deming, Silver City, in the mines, and the beef contract for Fort Bayard, nine miles out of Silver City." Jim and Rosa's family grew along with his expanded business interests. The

Colters returned to Keller Valley, where their second son, Ammon Edward "Ed," was born on November 14, 1882. Soon after, in the spring of 1883, James H. Cook, representing Harold C. Wilson of Cheltenham, England, began to buy up land in the valley.[15]

Cook bought Colter's 160-acre ranch on March 9, began to burn the stock with the WS brand (Wilson and Stevens), and thereby christened the WS spread. With the proceeds of the ranch sale, Colter later claimed that he established Silver City's first bank. Colter, however, soon was on the move again. On June 29, less than three months after the sale, he and his family left for Los Angeles, California, then visited his parents in Nova Scotia. They returned to Grant County by January 1884, and spent two weeks at Hudson's Hot Springs. A month later, Colter negotiated the purchase of a transfer business at El Paso, but the peripatetic Colter family soon left El Paso and settled in Newton, Kansas, where Colter farmed and raised livestock. In November 1884, Colter returned to Silver City for a short visit. "He has purchased a huge tract of land five miles from Newton," the *Enterprise* reported, "and has determined to make an Eden for his declining years." The last three Colter children were born in Newton.[16]

Melvin Jones remembered that Colter planted corn on the Newton farm that grew into the finest stand the new Kansas farmer had ever seen. James borrowed all he could to buy more land, but the next crop failed, and he nearly went broke. Even so, he managed to borrow yet more money, experienced a second failure, and, owing "everyone in town," lost everything but two carloads of horses that he sold in Mexico for a good price.[17]

About 1891, following the Kansas debacle, the Colters returned to Apache County, where James and Rosa separated. He left the area. Word of him occasionally reached Rosa and the family—he had gone to San Francisco; he was raising wheat in Canada; he was developing real estate in Los Angeles. Rosa worked as a seamstress and dressmaker to keep the family clothed and fed; the boys also worked to supplement the family's income. Fred, a future Arizona state senator, finished elementary school and hired on as a wrangler for the 24 Ranch, owned by the English firm of Smith, Tea, and Carson. A few years later, he went to work for Bill Phelps's inverse B Bar P Ranch (with a brand the inverse of the name), one of Apache County's largest cattle spreads. During the summer of 1898, eleven-year-old Bert Colter, destined to also serve in the Arizona state senate, signed on as a wrangler for Walter Baird at the W Slash spread in the hills twenty-five miles east of St. Johns. Ed Colter continued in school and also worked the range with schoolmate Evans Coleman. But circumstances would soon explain why neighbor Melvin Jones remembered young Ed as "the second oldest [boy that] they did not speak of."[18]

During the winter of 1897–98, Evans Coleman related that Ed Colter "committed a little misdemeanor . . . which, had he answered to the Court, would have perhaps cost him $2.50 or $5.00 fine." In the fashion of Kid Johnson, fifteen-year-old Colter insisted, "I won't be arrested. No officer can arrest me." He saddled a horse and rode south about one hundred miles into the Black River country. "It was an out of the way place and he was quite sure he could work for an outfit during the summer and not be molested," Coleman later explained. It was the isolation of the region that had attracted Colter, as it had Kid Johnson. That remoteness also proved a magnet for another Apache County lad who was drawn to Bronco Bill Walters—Red Pipkin.[19] The background that gave rise to his outlawry deserves a look.

CHAPTER 5

Bringing Up Red

"Not worth two whoops in the petrified forest."

Evans Coleman

Tennessee native Aser Pipkin returned from the Mexican War in 1848 and, after more than forty years' residence in the Nashville region, resolved to build a new life elsewhere. He packed up his wife, Margaret, and their son and surviving daughters and pointed his team west for Marshall County in northern Mississippi. Three years later, probably lured by the advance of the cotton frontier into the area, the family headed farther west to White County, Arkansas, and still later settled at nearby Pigeon Roost Creek (near the settlement of Hickory Plains) in Prairie County, barely thirty miles north of Little Rock. Here, their son, James Knox Polk Pipkin, met and married Emaline Octavia Yarber and started a family.[1]

By 1860, Prairie County's population had pushed beyond eight thousand; slaves accounted for about 25 percent of the total. Not surprisingly, when Arkansas passed an ordinance of secession on May 6, 1861, Prairie County stood in sympathy with the Confederacy. Young James Pipkin left his wife and two infant sons, Aser and John, to enlist in Lieutenant E. C. Kirk's company of Colonel Allan R. Witt's Tenth Regiment of Arkansas

Cavalry, formed during the summer of 1864. Most of the men had served with the Tenth Arkansas Infantry. In August 1864, Jefferson Davis authorized Major General Sterling Price, a Mexican War veteran and former governor of Missouri, to lead an expedition to Missouri in a bid to relieve some of the Union Army pressure on Atlanta. With 12,000 mounted infantry, including Witt's Cavalry, Price began his raid into Missouri on September 19. His attacks along the Missouri River toward Lexington and Kansas City, pro-Confederate regions of Missouri, drew more recruits. Most of the guerilla bands (including those of Bloody Bill Anderson and William Quantrill) also joined the column. Still vastly overmatched, Price and his Confederates withdrew from Missouri following an engagement at Westport (October 23, 1864).

Unlike most of Price's units, Witt's Cavalry did not retreat into northeastern Texas. By the onset of December, it had returned to Arkansas. Within two weeks, the Federals captured Lieutenant Kirk, Sergeant Pipkin, and many other soldiers from the company during a skirmish in Woodruff County. Confined in Little Rock from December 14, 1864, Pipkin remained a prisoner until May 7, 1865, when he returned to his family at nearby Pigeon Roost Creek. He farmed for the remainder of the decade, during which time three more sons, Price, Polk, and Richard, joined the family. Still another son, Joseph, was born in 1873.[2]

In 1874, Henry G. Boyle and John D. H. McCallister, elders in the Latter-day Saints Church, established "a most successful mission in Prairie county, Arkansas, baptizing some eighty souls." The Pipkins, who joined the church on April 3, were numbered among the Mormon converts. "The missionaries converted my father and grandfather and they and my grandmother and two boys were baptized the same day," recalled one of James's sons. "The neighbors learned of the baptism and they gathered to cuss and swear at the missionaries and throw rocks at them."[3]

Daniel Moroni Pipkin, James and Emaline's seventh surviving son, joined the family on February 14, 1876. Emaline died only four months later on July 28. A month following her death, the redheaded infant, his widowed father, his grandparents, and his older brothers—Aser, John, Price, Polk, Richard, and Joseph—accompanied many of the other recently converted Mormon families when they packed up and headed west to St. George, the county seat of Washington County, Utah. "Converts from Alabama, Georgia, and Tennessee all met and left in 1876 for the West, mostly Utah," Polk recalled. "There were about 100 families and they travelled mostly with ox teams although there were one or two horse teams in the train. We had to put iron shoes on the oxen before we could start over the Rocky Mts. At night we would circle the wagons so the front wheel of one wagon was against the back wheel of the next so as to form a corral. We would cook and light fires in this corral. If the ground was hard," Polk continued, "the people would dance after supper. We had a couple of fiddlers in the company. We had night riders to look after the herds, but sometimes the Mexicans or Indians would raid and steal some of the oxen. One of my father's oxen died and we had to break an old black cow to work. The leaders of the Church sent word where all the saints would settle."[4]

Mormon efforts to colonize within the lower valley of Arizona's Little Colorado River began with James S. Brown's 1875 scouting expedition into Apache County (a region that became part of Navajo County after 1895). The next year, colonists founded Ballenger Camp (later renamed Brigham City), St. Joseph (preceded by nearby Allen's Camp), Obed (near St. Joseph), and Sunset, the northernmost of the settlements. All were near present-day Winslow. The Saints soon called upon the Pipkin clan to leave St. George for Sunset and its communally oriented United Order. On their arrival, the Pipkins donated all the property to a common fund and submitted to the single-minded and frequently overbearing leadership of Mormon Battalion veteran Lot Smith. The Sunset colonists used rock to construct apartments within a wooden stockade, worked together in the communal fields, and ate at a common table. The Pipkins established two households near the north end of the compound's west wall. Red moved in with his grandparents while his father and brothers lived in the adjoining apartment.[5]

Some applauded the community style of life, but Smith's authoritarianism led to discontent among others. Sunset settler William McClellan described the fort's living conditions as "unnecessarily poor & niggardly—our houses very uncomfortable with little or no hopes for better—as every energy is bent gathering around us large herds of horses and cattle." Smith's explosive temper heightened the dissatisfaction. Red's father, the assistant postmaster, complained to McClellan that Smith had threatened some of the folks with physical violence. Smith's autocratic leadership, accounting irregularities, the area's poor soil, and irrigation difficulties all occasioned the quick failure of Sunset and its United Order.[6]

In 1882, the Church authorities called the Pipkins and several other families to abandon the largely deserted compound at Sunset and head for New Mexico. Extremely displeased with the distribution of the Order's assets, Aser complained, "I had taken two good yoke of Oxen one good wagon & one horse beside many other things to [*sic*] numerous to mention for which he gave me three young steers & one little old ox not worth $20 the steers unbroke & so wild that I could not manage them . . . & for the horse I never got anything at all and for a good wagon which could not have been bought anywhere in this country for less than $125 it was appraised in at $55 for which I got a wagon which is of no use only for the Old Iron & this is in keeping with the whole Settlement if it can be called a Settlement." The obstreperous head of the Pipkin clan refused to sign a receipt for the useless wagon, and as the family was about to pull out, Smith "run in before my horses with an Iron wagon Rod in his hand swinging around saying that I would sign it before I left I told him if force was his game to pop his whip." At the end of the set-to, Pipkin did sign, although he remained disgruntled. "I do not consider I had anything like a fair Settlement," he grumbled, "but that has nothing to do with the Gospel." Lot Smith's temperamental nature eventually cost him his life. He was gunned down in Tuba City, Arizona on June 21, 1892. After having dedicated six years to the failed enterprise, however, the Pipkin clan had long since moved east into New Mexico.[7]

By 1876, Latter-day Saint missionaries Ammon M. Tenney and Robert H. Smith had reached Zuni pueblo in Valencia (now McKinley) County. Lorenzo H. Hatch and John Maughan replaced them early in 1877, spent time at Pescado (Fish Springs), and wintered at San Lorenzo. Ernst Tietjen and Luther C. Burnham soon founded the nearby villages of Savoia and Savoietta, but lack of proselytizing success at Zuni disappointed the settlers. A smallpox epidemic in 1878, followed by Indian difficulties in 1880, plagued the villages and the Saints temporarily abandoned the sites. The failure of the Sunset and the Brigham City colonies encouraged the Mormons to again colonize among the Zunis. The Pipkins and other immigrants settled about six miles south of the abandoned Savoia and founded the village of Navajo (renamed Ramah in 1884) on August 7, 1882.[8]

James Pipkin opened a post office almost immediately. Soon, the forty-four-year-old widower also married Sarah Levira "Vira" Lewis (1870–1960), a woman barely fifteen whose family had reached Ramah in 1882 by way of Alpine, Arizona. Vira was also in love, but not with James. Rather, she favored his son, John, and, evidently, he returned her love. Nevertheless, she married his father, and their first child, Arthur Isaiah Pipkin, was born on December 6, 1885. Emaline (born 1887), Ella Bertha (1889), and Josephine (1891) soon followed. But all was not well in the Pipkin clan.[9]

In October 1884, John Pipkin, distraught over the loss of Vira, committed suicide. A serious drought and a shortage of rations in 1886 were followed by legal problems in 1887. U.S. postal officials found that postmaster Pipkin had defrauded the government and closed the post office. Although the St. Johns High Council took no action against Pipkin, it disfellowshipped him on June 16. There were still more troubles on the home front.[10]

A journal left by Vira's brother, Samuel Edward Lewis, suggests that domestic problems had begun by the end of 1888, when Lewis went to the Pipkin home to see his sister, "who was in trouble." Little more than a year later, during the March 17 celebration of Ella Bertha Pipkin's first birthday, Vira had a confrontation with her stepson. Her brother wrote, "My sister, Vira, came to my house after dark, having traveled about 8 miles with a babe [Ella Bertha] on her arm; she claimed that her husband's son hurt her so she fled for help." Fourteen-year-old Red is the unnamed but obvious culprit; the older boys were out of the household. He probably fostered deep-seated resentment over his father's marriage to Vira (little more than five years his senior) and his brother's suicide. Perhaps his half-sister's first birthday celebration only aggravated Red's bitterness and led to the violent outbreak.[11]

James Pipkin's problems continued. In August, Ella Bertha drowned. Then, in October, Vira asked her mother, Sara Jane, and her younger brother Joseph to take her into their Arizona home. Pipkin, accompanied by his sister Nancy's stepson, Joseph Wilford Hatch, chased after his despondent wife. In turn, Vira's brother Samuel, accompanied by Ernest Tietjen and William H. Bond, pursued Pipkin and Hatch. The three parties converged on October 26, 1890.[12]

Vira's brother Samuel described the encounter:

> Circumstances led me to get two men and follow my folks. We followed about forty miles to the crossing

> of the Zuni Wash. We suddenly came upon two saddled horses standing near the road; we halted a few minutes to ascertain where the men were. In a few minutes we heard three shots and a man cried out. Then we heard the words with awful oaths; "Then you will give up then will you?". Then the screams of women cried out. In a few minutes we saw two men approaching with pistols in hand. When near by Brother Teitgen [*sic*] called for them to hold up their hands; they demanded the same thing. Brother Teitgen threw his pistol to the ground. They then opened fire on me. Brother Teitgen picked up his pistol and both parties soon emptied their pistols at a very close distance, but no person was hit. My horse was killed and Brother Teitgen's horse was wounded. As soon as the firing stopped, Pipkin and Hatch mounted their horses and fled. I then went to the place where the first firing was heard and there I found my brother, Joseph, shot and dying. We put him in the wagon with the other effects and started for Ramah.[13]

The Lewis family buried Joe on October 29. News quickly reached Ramah that St. George Creaghe, the Apache County sheriff, had that day mistakenly shot and killed Ira Stearns Hatch, believing that he was the younger brother Joseph Wilford Hatch. Samuel Lewis was arrested for using a gun on Pipkin and Hatch and hauled to nearby San Rafael. He was later released. Lewis, in turn, brought charges against Pipkin and Hatch. Under the impression that Joe had "killed a man by the name of Pitkin," a Gallup deputy took Hatch into custody in December. When the Arizona sheriff failed to respond, Hatch, too, was released. No charges were brought against Pipkin or Hatch, but Vira soon divorced James. The Pipkins left Ramah in 1892 and headed to Olio (now Kirtland), New Mexico. Red, however, was long gone.[14]

Amid the chaos, violence, and resentment that had become his life, Red fled from his dysfunctional family about 1890 and returned to the Apache County region. Old-timer Evans Coleman recalled that Mr. And Mrs. William Crabtree who, along with Claire Vance Peery, had the XO spread about twenty miles northeast of Walter Baird's W Slash Ranch, took in the youngster, whom they judged to be about eight years old and an orphan. At least fourteen and with a family, he evidently did nothing to correct their opinion.[15]

Light complexioned and freckled, Pipkin was distinguished by his red hair. He matured into a fellow of average height (five feet, seven and a half inches), weighed slightly more than 150 pounds, and was, at least in the judgment of some, decidedly self-centered. "I never saw anyone so good to anyone as Crabtrees and Bud Jones [Zuni Salt Lake rancher] have been to that boy," related Coleman, "and he doesn't appreciate it a bit." He continued, "Last spring [1896] when they needed a man badly on the round-up, 'Red' just up and quit." Mrs. Crabtree labored over his cooking and washing. "She says: 'Poor Red, he is an orphan. He came to us when about eight years old, and we have taken care of him ever since. If we sent him away he might go bad. He almost joined an outlaw band last year [1895], but I went out and brought him home and Bill and Mr. Jones talked him out of going.'" A disgusted Coleman groused, "Say, isn't that a mother spirit for you? And 'Red' about 20 years old and her worrying and fussing over him and he not worth two whoops in the petrified forest."[16]

Although he may not have felt indebted to Mrs. Crabtree, Red was devoted to the ladies. At the end of April 1896, several dozen cowboys and ranchers from Apache (Arizona) and Socorro (New Mexico) counties pooled their efforts in a large roundup. They finished east of Salt Lake in Socorro County in mid-July. Three and one-half months in the saddle had worn them out, and with the last calf branded and the final cow tallied, the self-styled "Salt Creek Pool" decided to take a fishing trip to White River on Arizona's Apache Reservation. Pipkin, Bud Jones, V. A. Word, the Crabtrees, Walter Baird, Mr. Bradley, Bill Blevins, George Phelps, Claire Peery, and Jim Claybrook joined in the adventure, along with Bud Jones's daughters, Ruthie and Isabell, Coleman's sister Susie, and Lizzie Jenkins. Evans Coleman served as the cook; Luther Hulsey was the horse wrangler. From July 19 through July 25, the party caught 2,445 fish. Red, who spent most of his time paying attention to the ladies, landed a meager thirteen. One day (July 23), Susie Coleman, George Phelps, the Jones sisters, Red, and Lizzie Jenkins rode off to Benjamin Slade's ranch near Eagar, about ten miles east of the camp. On the return trip, Red, the Jones sisters, and Lizzie Jenkins rode off on their own. "Well," Evans Coleman later recounted, "'Red' is considerable taken with Ruthie and of course for a joke he and Ruthie lose the two little girls. It is also cloudy and raining some. 'Red' and Ruthie rode into camp. Mr. and Mrs. Crabtree had just unsaddled and turned their horses into the remuda."

"Mr. Crabtree said, 'Red, where are the little girls?"

"'Red' said, 'They are alright, we left them back there."

"Mr. Crabtree told 'Red' he had a notion to whale him with the double of his lasso," but concern for the girls' welfare dictated that he sidestep the urge. Crabtree ordered Pipkin to get right back on his horse and go out and find Isabell and Lizzie. Red rode off, not so much worried about the girls, in Coleman's opinion, but rather about Crabtree's rope. "If they find the girls," Coleman opined, "Mr. Crabtree is more apt to go over 'Red's' withers with the double of that McArty [*sic*] just from sheer joy than anything else." Crabtree, meanwhile, had grabbed his Winchester and fired three rounds in rapid succession to draw the others in. The resultant hunt was successful. Walter Baird rode in with the girls later that night. Red evidently avoided a lashing.[17]

Pipkin next "blowed into Springerville" and fell in with the likes of Ed Colter and Kid Johnson. Red "wanted to be real bad, shot things up" in town, resisted arrest, and fled south. He hired on at Peter and Mason "Mace" Slaughter's P Lazy S Ranch on the forks of the Black River. The Slaughter brothers had trailed a herd west from Texas into Arizona in 1880, homesteaded the headquarters ranch near Alpine, and eventually leased the Paradise Ranch and the Reservation Ranch from the U.S. Forest Service and the Bureau of Indian Affairs. Their range extended south to Joe Hampson's Double Circle spread on Eagle Creek. Pipkin readily developed a close friendship with Monterey "Monte" Slaughter, Peter's oldest son, and through the younger Slaughter, he also established close ties with Monte's friend, local stockmen J. Allen Chitty, a twenty-eight-year-old Alabama transplant.[18]

Sometime later, Pipkin ventured farther south and signed on to cowboy at the Double Circle Ranch. Hampson's foreman, Sid Moore (alias Ef Hilman), was a morose man always depressed over something. Thirtyish and going bald, he soon abandoned the Double Circle to join, first, Van Musgrave's gang of Grant County (New Mexico) horse rustlers and, eventually, the notorious High Five gang. Moore introduced Red to Van (alias Theodore James), to younger brother George Musgrave (alias Jeff Davis, Jess Johnson, Jesse Miller, etc.), and the Christian brothers, Will (alias Black Jack) and Bob (alias Tom Anderson).

By the spring of 1897, the twenty-one-year-old redhead was hanging around the High Fives and stood at the threshold of major outlawry. Then his career suffered a setback. A posse ambushed and killed Black Jack Christian in Cole Creek Canyon on April 28, 1897, and the surviving High Five members fled into Mexico. They left Red behind, but Pipkin was not entirely without friends. Within the next year, he joined up with one of them—known to locals as "Red" Burnett, but known as James Burnett to officials of the U.S. Department of Justice.[19]

Springerville's residents thought Burnett, a drifter in his early twenties, had a criminal record and he was "a very rough fellow." Horace W. "Will" Loomis, a deputy U.S. marshal from

New Mexico, later learned that Burnett was also believed to be a deserter from the navy. Burnett, too, was soon in trouble, and although it was over a minor offense, he feared that authorities might learn something of his past. Probably having nowhere else to go, Burnett found his way to the Black River country, where he was joined by another hard case who made a futile attempt to hide his identity behind the alias Bill Andrews, but who was known to lawmen throughout southern New Mexico as Bronco Bill Walters.[20]

CHAPTER 6

Fiasco at Grants

"Get me away from here; we can't finish this job tonight."

Ed Colter

The life of the cowboy, with long days in the saddle followed by lonely nights alongside a campfire, offered little chance for upward economic mobility. Barely more than migrant workers, many ranch hands sought a better life and pondered the means to secure it; the old cowboy saying of "a million dollars in a million days" did little to satisfy the expectations of Bill Johnson, Ed Colter, James Burnett, and Red Pipkin. William A. Pinkerton had complained that many train robbers "start as amateurs under an experienced leader." Bronco Bill Walters, no stranger to outlawry, may have introduced the others to the prospect of life on the outlaw trail. Equally possible, considering his reputation as one who had listened to the owls hoot many a night, the others may have sought him out. In either case, the five decided to rob a train. "Bill Johnson was going," Evans Coleman reflected. "[Walters] told Ed and Red that they had better stay out. This Burnett was a hard hombre, and it didn't make any difference to him." In spite of Bronco's caution, all five agreed to hold up the Wells, Fargo express car on the Santa Fe road.[1]

The fledgling gang members gathered their gear. Johnson, who had worked for the Double Circle outfit the previous year, picked out five of the best horses from the ranch's Black River remuda; the boys helped themselves to the mounts as well as provision for several weeks. This bit of larceny was ill-advised; outlaws generally did not rustle from local ranchers. John N. Thacker, Wells, Fargo's special officer, explained why. "The great trouble we experience in endeavoring to secure the conviction of this class of criminals is the lack of support on the part of the cattlemen. If we had their support," the detective continued, "we would be able to clear this country of these criminals in a remarkably short length of time, but as it is we are working at a great disadvantage." By rustling Joe Hampson's stock, Bronco Bill and his gang broke a cardinal rule and jeopardized their relationship with the hands that rode for the Double Circle brand.[2]

The five rode into the hills east of St. Johns and into New Mexico, where they set up camp along a small creek that emptied into the Carrizo Wash, just below Walter Baird's W Slash Ranch. Familiar with the layout, young Colter slipped in to the ranch and helped himself to some Giant powder. Well-mounted and now stocked with explosives, the five continued northeast into midwestern New Mexico's Malpais (bad country) region.[3]

Settlers did not call the area Malpais unfairly. Cattle, wagons, people, and railroads avoided the vast lava flow whenever possible. The thousands of square miles of isolated ruggedness appealed to outlaws on the prowl as it deterred ranchers and farmers. The Bronco Bill gang crossed in anticipation of a significant payday, unaware that John Thacker, a Wells, Fargo special officer, had been warned that Bill was coming, and "thought he might be after the Santa-Fe Pacific road, so he put guards on the trains." A greeting party awaited the gang's arrival.[4]

The Santa Fe Pacific's westbound no. 1 chugged out of Albuquerque a few minutes before nine o'clock on the evening of March 28, 1898. Fifteen minutes behind schedule, it pulled into Grants, New Mexico, thirty-five minutes past midnight the next morning. Originally known as Grant's Camp, then Grant's Station, and eventually just Grants, the small station with little more than a few adobe houses, a depot, and a telegraph office, had acquired an unenviable reputation: it was a good place for a holdup. The previous November 6, George and Van Musgrave, Bob Christian, and Sid Moore—the High Five gang—had successfully assaulted the Santa Fe Pacific near the little railroad siding and ridden away with a stunning $90,000, the greatest loss ever suffered by that line.[5] Walters and his crowd looked forward to a similar haul.

As the train approached the depot and stopped to take on water, B. A. Workman, the engineer, climbed down from the cab, glanced at the track, and saw that the engine had not stopped where he wanted it. He stepped back to the gangway to call to the fireman, Judson Lathrop, to pull the engine a bit farther forward. Before the words were out of his mouth, two men who had leaped into the cab shoved Winchesters in his face. "*Cuidado!*" (Look out!), one of them shouted. The clicks of the rifles' hammers resonated in the engineer's ears; the interlopers were serious.

Charles Renno, the brakeman, emerged out of the darkness, and Workman cried out, "Go back; we're held up." Inside the cab, as the two robbers accosted Lathrop, Workman slipped out, ran inside the depot, and reported the holdup to the agent. As the engineer reappeared, engine no. 110 started to move down the track. Unable to reach the engine, Workman jumped on one of the moving cars just as the two robbers in the cab began shooting. One held the muzzle of his rifle so close to Lathrop that the fireman's face was powder burned. Already standing on the platform, conductor Charles Berry dashed behind the depot to avoid the flying bullets. As the frightened conductor made himself scarce, three more heavily armed robbers appeared, riding on the rear of the engine. They unholstered their six-shooters and added to the barrage of bullets.

The Santa Fe Pacific continued west along the tracks as Walters, Johnson, Pipkin, Colter, and Burnett kept up constant gunfire in the direction of the passenger and express cars. About one mile west of Grants, they ordered the train stopped. As it came to a halt, the five bandits turned their attention toward the express car. Inside, a surprise awaited them. Although it is uncertain whether it was by intent or loose tongue, Red Burnett had forewarned officials of the holdup plan. Prudently, Wells, Fargo had assigned special guard Charles L. Fowler to ride with the express messenger, Charles C. Lord. Described by one newspaper as "dead game," the Texas-born Fowler was a longtime guard with the express company. Lord was already a veteran of this sort of thing—he had been in the express car five months earlier when the High Five gang had robbed the eastbound train at Grants. Fowler and Lord had bided their time as the train moved forward. Now, as it came to a halt, they threw open the door, and Fowler, rifle in hand, jumped to the ground. He and Lord returned the bandits' fire; the resistance caught the robbers unaware.

Fowler put a bullet through the arm of Ed Colter. "I'm shot," the young outlaw cried out, "Get me away from here; we can't finish this job tonight." By another account, "The robber screamed when he fell, and one of his cohorts cried out, 'It's no good tonight boy!'" The four outlaws grabbed their wounded companion and fled south, back into the rugged Malpais. Walters and Johnson later talked to Apache County rancher Evans Coleman. According to Coleman, "When they went to go into the mail [express] car, old Fowler, the messenger, met them with a gun. I was pretty well acquainted with Fowler, he was the biggest bragger you ever saw, but he would fight. They said, 'He met us at the door, and we fought there and he run us out and we got down under the car and fought. And finally Ed Colter left his post and come in there pretty close and Fowler shot him.'"[6]

For their success in thwarting the gang's assault, both Fowler and Lord were later "watched" (presented testimonial watches) by Wells, Fargo. President John J. Valentine acknowledged Lord's "heroic conduct" in both the March 29 robbery and the earlier November 6, 1897, holdup. But, during these critical moments, as the gang raced away, Fowler and Lord were not considering future awards and citation from the company; there were outlaws to catch.[7]

Fowler followed the luckless bandits a short distance on foot. Unable to get in another effective shot, he walked back to the train and spoke to Workman, "All right; they have left; and I think I shot one." The engineer then whistled for his fireman, and, failing to get a response, backed the train to the depot. When it stopped, conductor Berry rushed out, and he, Fowler, and Workman surveyed the scene. At first glance, the attempted raid had accounted for little more than a bullet-riddled express car and the train's headlight shot to pieces; the booty had remained untouched. Fowler and Workman then went to look for the missing fireman. In no time, they discovered Lathrop as he crept toward the train. He had caught a bullet in the leg.[8]

Workman, who sported a hefty bump on his head, evidently pounded by one of the revolver-toting bandits, was later asked, "Did one of the robbers shoot Lathrop or was he hit by a stray bullet from the guard?"

"That question I can not answer positively," the engineer, replied. "There was considerable shooting going on and bullets flying in all directions." When Lathrop hobbled up to the engine, he confirmed that Fowler had been shooting under the cars. The fireman probably was struck by one of Fowler's bullets. In the end, it mattered little whose bullet struck the unlucky fireman. Lathrop's condition remained serious for some months.

As Workman and Fowler loaded Lathrop into a tourist car to be attached to an eastbound freight train, conductor

Berry wired news of the holdup attempt to trainmaster Allen at Gallup. Allen organized a posse and started after the bandits at daylight. Meanwhile, brakeman Renno took Lathrop's position in the cab, and the westbound train pulled out of Grants. It stopped briefly at Blue Water to take on Will Gibson to relieve Renno, then continued on to Gallup. In the forenoon, the eastbound freight train, bearing Lathrop, reached Albuquerque where the fireman was hospitalized. Dr. P. G. Cornish, Sr., assisted by a railroad physician, Dr. Elder, removed a bullet lodged just below the knee of his right leg. Lathrop's sister, Nora Putnam, rushed from Pleasant Valley, Arizona, to nurse her brother. She returned home a week and a half later, but his condition remained serious for several more weeks. Yet he ultimately recovered and survived another half-century.[9]

As Lathrop underwent surgery, Santa Fe officials brought out a special train for Fred Fornoff, Albuquerque's city marshal. The Maryland native was experienced at chasing Grants robbers; he had headed up a posse following the High Five's successful heist the previous November. Fornoff rode west to Grants, where he joined a second posse that Fowler had organized. Meanwhile, A. G. Wells, the Santa Fe's vice president, announced that in addition to the standard Wells, Fargo reward of $300, the Santa Fe would offer $500 each "for the capture of any part or all of them, dead or alive."[10]

In the late 1890s, lawmen and journalists attributed almost all train robberies committed in southern Arizona or New Mexico to the Black Jack gang. Typically, the *Silver City Eagle* blamed them for this Grants robbery and chided the El Paso press:

> It is unfortunate that the reported extermination of the Black Jack gang could not have been postponed for a few days. It is a matter of some perplexity just who the El Paso newspapers and correspondents can make responsible for the recent hold-up at Grants since

> Black Jack met his death so prematurely at their hands. Newspaper enterprise is always to be commended but it is to be regretted that the territories should be cut off from the ever prolific source of sensational news as Black Jack and his gang of border bandits. Train robbers from now on will gradually drop out of popular favor.[11]

Elsewhere, an early report that appeared in the *Los Angeles Daily Times* pointed toward "the same outlaws who left Salt Lake [New Mexico] three weeks ago," who had raided Gallup only ten days earlier, and had cleaned out several gambling parlors, including that of Pete Kitchen and John Kennedy, of hundreds of dollars. The report was wrong. Wells, Fargo, in possession of inside information, revealed the gang member's correct identities almost immediately; employee L. A. Cameron recorded the terse details in his notebook: "Grants, N.M.—2nd time—Attempt made to hold up no. 1 at Grants, N.M. Mch 28/98 about midnight. Guard Fowler shot and wounded one man. Lord, mess. saw 2 men—nobody hurt. Everything OK. 5 robbers in holdup—Bronco Bill's gang."[12]

The oral traditions of the Zuni Indians, living some sixty miles west of Grants, provide some sparse insight into the gang's path of escape. One tradition says that the five outlaws, evidently, crossed the Malpais to reach Towayalane, east of Zuni Pueblo, where they camped above some fields by the Corn Cob Ridge. That the Zunis recognized Red Pipkin and assumed that he led the gang is unremarkable, considering his family's one-time residence in nearby Ramah. The rest of the saga, including tales of a confrontation between the Zunis and the outlaws, the gang's flight toward the mountains about Nutria, their capture by troops from Fort Wingate, and their subsequent trial and conviction are not born out by documentation and are presumably based upon convolutions and embellishments.[13]

Special Officer John Thacker took up the chase. The veteran Wells, Fargo detective had tracked California bandit Charles E. Boles ("Black Bart") for eight years before he captured the illusive duster-clad outlaw in 1883. In the 1890s, Thacker's region of investigation had shifted to the Southwest. On April 4, only a week after the attempted holdup at Grants, Thacker reached Geronimo, Arizona, in the company of a five-man posse led by Jeff Milton, with Sam Webb and one of the Scarboroughs certainly numbered among the five. They knew whom they chased. Bronco Bill's gang had rustled horses from the friendly Double Circle Ranch. Some of the ranch's cowboys had given officials the bandits' names—William "Bronco Bill" Walters, Bill "Kid" Johnson, Dan "Red" Pipkin, Ed Colter, and Jim Burnett. They were labeled by the *Graham Guardian* as "one of the worst gangs of desperadoes that ever went unhung." Adding to the hyperbole, the *Guardian* wrongly identified one Ed Leonard as a member of the gang. [14]

Thacker returned to Bowie, but not before he gave Milton and the posse orders to ride as rapidly as possible to Hampson's Eagle Creek ranch to intercept the prey. The morning following the departure of the Milton posse, Thacker learned that Fowler's posse had tracked the bandits from Grants to William Baxter Slaughter's ranch. An aggressive foe of rustlers, Slaughter (1850–1929), a brother of Red Pipkin's friends Pete and Mace Slaughter, had settled in New Mexico's American Valley (approximately a dozen miles north of Aragon in western New Mexico near the Arizona border).[15]

Thacker notified Graham County deputy Ben Clark in Clifton of Fowler's whereabouts and sent word to Geronimo, Arizona, to have a rider catch up with the Milton posse to share the news. Meanwhile, on April 9, U.S. Marshal Creighton M. Foraker telegraphed U.S. Attorney General John W. Griggs to seek authorization to hire "for sixty days one good man as posse on train robbery cases at five dollars a day." Governor Miguel Otero sent an accompanying telegram urging the attorney general to approve Foraker's request. General Griggs authorized the request later that day.[16]

The Fowler-led posse stayed on the outlaws' trail and tracked the gang from Slaughter's ranch to the W Slash Ranch, forty miles east of St. Johns. Evans Coleman recalled:

> I come to the [W Slash] ranch one evening, and as I come down the trail to the ranch, I see a man riding off about half a mile away. I asked at the ranch, "Who was that fellow who just left here." Walter Beard [*sic*] and two or three others said, "Just don't ask. It was none of your particular business. You don't want to know who it was." I said, "Well, all right."
>
> The next morning I left there to go down on Eagle Creek to get a bunch of saddle horses and Walter and Henry Thompson and Primie Coleman took the wagon, and went out toward American Valley to commence work. I took the horses and went out and a posse came and picked [Deputy Andrew] Maxwell up and was out on the trail after this man. They had robbed a train and they knew who it was. Next morning after we left the ranch there was a "long H" saddle horse drifted in there. We took this horse and a pack horse marked "W slash."[17]

Walters and his band had not stolen any stock from the W Slash, and the hands, unlike the robbed cowboys at the Double Circle, offered the gang the usual type of protection. The Fowler posse reached Baird's ranch and found Baird, Prime Coleman, and "some of the other boys." Folwer charged, "That W Slash outfit is aiding and abetting this bunch. You let them have that outfit."

"I didn't know that they had any outfit," Baird fired back. "If you are looking for trouble, you can get it right here. We are not backing down. Don't accuse us any more. If one of those boys comes here and wants to stop, they can stop, or if they want a horse, he can get it. The railroad ain't backing us up."[18]

Prime T. Coleman, Evans's older brother, recounted the story to newspaperman Roscoe G. Willson many years later. By his account, he and Walter Baird were there when the Fowler posse rode up and asked if they had seen the outlaws. Coleman replied that they had been there the previous evening, had eaten, and then rode on. He referred to Colter as "Ed Something," told Fowler that the outlaws had left a wounded member of the gang on a ranch not far from St. Johns, but intentionally neglected to provide Colter's last name or information that he had been taken into the hills by one of the ranch hands, V. A. Word. Some time later, brother Evans added that Word was "kind of a lookout" for Bronco Bill and Johnson. "I have tried to write a character sketch of this man. So far I have not succeeded. He was a dangerous man, and a very peculiar one."[19]

Fowler and his posse rode on, but soon one of Fowler's Indian trailers reported, "There's only four men in the bunch now. One of them [the wounded one] turned off here, like he was going to Springerville."

Deputy Andrew Maxwell of Nutrioso, who rode with Fowler's posse, knew the local boys. A Nevada native who later served a term as Apache County sheriff (1927–29) and was reputed to have been the county's only sheriff to take a bullet, Maxwell told Fowler, "That one that went to Springerville is likely Ed Colter."

"We don't want him. It is Bronco Bill and Johnson that we want," Fowler replied.[20]

Evans Coleman later explained, "Ed Colter was taken care of by friends, and since he was just what we called a boy, they gave him a chance to get out of the country, which he did. If he was ever heard from again, I don't know it." Bert Crosby afterward revealed that he and Jesse Slade were unloading barrels of whiskey brought in from Magdalena soon after the holdup, and they saw Colter in an old adobe house in east Springerville. Years later, Colter's sister Maude disclosed to Milo Wiltbank, a member of a pioneer Round Valley family, that her grandfather, Dr. Rudd, took care of Colter until he recovered sufficiently to ride. Then, "brother Fred drove her and her mother out to Coyote [Coyote Hills near Springerville] to tell him good-bye."[21]

Milo Wiltbank, a member of a pioneer family in Eagar, Arizona later offered several variant and sometimes convoluted observations. He erroneously claimed that Henry Mott was one of the Grants bandits. Mott was a "trapper, fence builder, ranch hand, loner—who had little to say and said that in a very few words.". At his death, Mott supposedly left a map and a story of the Grants holdup and confessed to being one of the bandits, also implicating Colter, whom (Wiltbank said) they left wounded in Springerville. Wiltbank further claimed that Mott and one of the other train robbers, who had been shot through the lung, were overtaken by darkness after leaving Colter. They camped that night and buried their loot of "at least $12,000 in gold and other valuables" in Lee Valley, near Greer.[22]

Wiltbank's account does not stand under scrutiny. There was no loot secured in the Grants holdup on March 29, 1898, and there was no report of involvement on the part of Henry Mott. Wiltbank, moreover, specifically named "local boys" Ed Colter, Bill Johnson, and Red Pipkin, so the mysterious Henry Mott must assume the role of either Bronco Bill or Jim Burnett. He certainly was not the former, and no account identifies him as the latter. Finally, there were no reported wounds from this robbery other than that suffered by Colter. Wiltbank's account adds some vague details more in keeping with Walters's and Johnson's return to Apache County following a later fracas. Wiltbank remarked that he did not know what happened to the wounded Colter, but added, "I am sure several years ago [ca. 1970s] we, my wife and I, saw him in Albuquerque. Although Colter was not the name he gave us, he asked us as we sat in the airport about things that only Ed Colter could have known of or about." Colter, if it were he, would have been almost ninety years old at the time.[23]

As Colter recovered at Coyote Hills, Fowler and his men continued to pursue their primary quarry—Walters and Johnson. From the W Slash Ranch the posse headed in a southwesterly direction, crossed the border into Apache County, and rode on to the Black River basin, where the trail forked. One branch headed down the draw and the other followed the ridgeline down. Deputy Maxwell knew that Harris Miller had a camp on the river where he wintered some of his Half Box N horses. Warily, they followed the upper train down the ridgeline. Their caution proved well advised. Someone had slipped word to Bronco Bill and his band that the posse was near. Walters, Johnson, Pipkin, and Burnett saddled up and headed up the trail that ran through the draw. They intended to ambush their followers before they reached the fork. By the time the outlaws got there, the posse had passed by safely. Maxwell recounted that later on they did get near the fugitives. He fired a few rounds at Pipkin; a couple of bullets came close enough to force Red to weave and dodge, but the outlaws rode on unchecked.[24]

The posse continued on their trail as it headed toward Eagle Creek and the Double Circle Ranch, but when Walters and his band reached the Big Prairie, they turned south across the Nantanes Mountains. The lawman's jaded horses could not keep up the pace set by the fresh mounts of the outlaws. Fowler concluded that Bill and his band were bound for Mexico and that further chase was futile. The lawmen turned back.[25]

The movements of Walters and his gang during the next several weeks remain uncertain. Pipkin evidently took flight to Mexico, where, according to later reports, he found "great social attractions." Bronco Bill and Kid Johnson later told Evans

Coleman that there was also an effort to ambush them farther south in Arizona. The time frame is imprecise and the identity of the bushwhackers is unknown, but according to Kid Johnson, "We were somewhere in the south part of [Arizona] and made a holdup and was going up the creek, with ridges on each side." Johnson continued, "We was jogging up that creek and the first thing we knew they was crossing fire on us, and we turned back. We had good horses and sure riding them and we didn't stop to fight and they were on a bluff shooting all around us, and we crossed a creek and my horse fell to his knees, and that was all that saved me. There was a bullet went right over my shoulder and hit the water ahead of me."[26]

"Where is Burnett now?" Coleman asked.

"We don't know," replied Johnson, "But we'll bet he doesn't tip any more officers off."[27]

Tipster Jim Burnett was never heard from again, With Colter and Pipkin gone and Burnett eliminated, Bronco Bill and Kid Johnson doubled back into the Black River country and hid—but not for long.

About three o' clock on the afternoon of April 20, two masked men dressed as cowboys held up the Geronimo, San Carlos, and Globe stage about five miles south of Geronimo near Oliver C. May's ranch on the San Carlos Apache Reservation. As one of the bandits demanded that the driver, Alexander, produce the express box, his partner ordered the passengers out of the stagecoach. He demanded that the six passengers—Mack Grimes, Harrison Smith, P. Smith (a railroad conductor), Mrs. Franklin O. (Grace) Mackey and her daughter, and W. S. Zeniga—"pungle" (pay up or contribute). Alexander evidently convinced them that there was no express box on board; the mail and the express remained unmolested. The passengers dug deep into their wallets and purses to produce a total of five dollars. Walters and Johnson refused to take the meager loot, but did accept two oranges before permitting the stage to go on.[28]

Graham County Sheriff William P. "Billy" Birchfield, ca. May 1898. Courtesy Graham County Historical Society.

That evening, word of the holdup was telegraphed to William P. "Billy" Birchfield, Graham County's sheriff. "There is a general belief that the robbers are a part of Broncho Bill's gang of bandits," the *Arizona Bulletin* reported. As Walters and Johnson were known to be in the Black River country, the "general belief" was well reasoned. Birchfield sought assistance from Lieutenant Sedgewick Rice, the San Carlos agent, then rode to the scene of the holdup. A number of seasoned Apache trackers sent by Rice met him there. They readily located the robbers' trail—it led north, directly into the Black River country. For the next several days, Birchfield and the Apaches followed the tracks of the two highwaymen; then the trackers lost them amid the hoofprints of a large herd of cattle. The Birchfield posse turned back, yet the *Graham County Guardian* assured its readers that "officers know who the robbers are and that they will be captured." The newspaper was only half right. Walters and Johnson avoided capture. They headed for the security of New Mexico's Mogollon Mountains and laid low.[29]

CHAPTER 7

Belén and Beyond

"I throwed my gun back and hit him right between the eyes."
Bronco Bill Walters

Nuestra Señora de Belén (Our Lady of Bethlehem), on the west bank of the Rio Grande, traced its origin to 1740, when the Spanish government founded the settlement as a buffer against the attacks of marauding Apaches and Navajos. Although farming and sheep ranching were the mainstay of the area, the 1880 extension of the Santa Fe's rail line from Albuquerque to San Marcial heralded the emergence of Belén as a transportation hub. The railroad's presence also marked out the place as a potential target for train robbers. Bandits struck that mark in the early morning hours of May 24, 1898.[1]

The Santa Fe's southbound no. 21 steamed out of Albuquerque on schedule and pulled into Belén at fourteen minutes after one o'clock in the morning. When the train stopped, station agent J. J. Ringo stood on the depot's platform ready to load express packages. To his surprise, the cars suddenly lurched forward and started to move down the tracks. James Connors, the perturbed conductor, signaled the train to stop, but engineer Tait (dubbed variously Tate and Taft) ignored the signal. Unknown to Ringo and Connors, two masked bandits—

Bronco Bill and Bill Johnson—had mounted the engine, turned their revolvers on the engineer and his fireman, and ordered the train moved ahead. Several shots in the direction of the cars told the conductor that the robbers controlled the train, and he made no further effort to halt it. The courageous Connors jumped aboard and rushed through the cars warning passengers.[2]

About three miles down the track, the two outlaws ordered Tait to stop the train. As the engine came to a halt, Connors dashed ahead toward the engine, "but beat a hasty retreat when a bullet sang its deadly song in the close proximity of his face." As Connors fled, Ed W. Hiscock, the Wells, Fargo express messenger, secreted the waybills and some other valuables and then reached for his rifle. Inside the mail car, clerk Sampson remained calm, even though a few bullets crashed through the walls. The outlaws hurriedly uncoupled the engine and express car from the rest of the train and then ordered the engineer to pull ahead. Another mile passed before Walters and Johnson again yelled to Tait to stop the engine. Many newspapers later relied on the Associated Press account that placed the holdup almost three miles south of Belén. Others fixed the location at two miles; yet another reported the distance as about four miles. An examination of the topography along the route argues the accuracy of the latter account, that of the *Santa Fe Daily New Mexican.* About four miles south of Belén, hills to the west stretch toward the tracks and offer an observation point for a lookout, as well as a measure of cover for escaping bandits.[3]

As the engine again came to a standstill, Red Pipkin, returned from Mexico, probably stood guard nearby in the darkness. Most lawmen later believed he was one of the Belén robbers, and his presence would explain how Walters and Johnson reached the depot when their horses were hobbled four miles to the south. The three likely had ridden to Belén. Pipkin then took the horses south, leaving Walters and Johnson to board the train. Otherwise, the two would have had to walk those miles to town—a dreary prospect for a cowboy.

Whether or not Pipkin was present, he was certainly unseen by Tait and his fireman as Bronco and the Kid herded them back to the express car and demanded entry. Inside, Hiscock, fearing for the safety of the two railroad men, unbolted the door. As the bandits entered the car, messenger Hiscock fled, running the mile back up the tracks. After passing the uncoupled train, he came upon the brakeman, accompanied by a correspondent for the *Albuquerque Morning Democrat* who happened to be a passenger on the ill-fated run. The three continued back toward Belén on foot.[4]

Engineer Tait, meanwhile, mindful of the damage Giant dynamite could do to the express car, urged the two outlaws to remove the large iron safe before blowing it. Congenially, they hauled the safe to the open door and shoved it to the ground. The *Democrat*'s correspondent described what happened next. "At 2:10 a terrific explosion greeted our ears, telling us that the safe had been blown up." Later, investigators learned that Walters and Johnson had placed dynamite on top of the safe, covered it with mud "to make the downward concussion greater, and then lighting a fuse followed." The two robbers, along with the engineer and fireman, stood back as the fuse burned toward the dynamite. The explosion "came soon after, and then all the miscreants had to do was to place their hands in the safe and take what they wanted." They bypassed the United States and Mexican bonds, many of which were scattered by the explosion, and tossed much of the silver to the two railroaders. Throughout the robbery, which lasted an hour and a half, "the desperadoes showed themselves to have cool heads, taking things as easy as if there was no fear of arrest or death." With their saddlebags filled with cash, Bronco and the Kid "threw a shower of silver on the seats of the cab," then, in the early morning darkness, they dashed to where

Pipkin held the horses and fled southwest toward Sierra Ladrónes (Robbers Mountain).[5]

The outlaws had covered little ground before the coins became a weighty problem. They halted near a small hill west of Bosque and went to work. Walters later claimed that they buried three of the sacks of coins atop that hill. A mid-1990s discovery of 332 Morgan silver dollars on top of a small hill near West Mesa may lend credence to Walters's assertion.[6]

As Walters, Johnson, and Pipkin disappeared into the night, the passengers reached the safe and found that "one side had been blown out completely and the other sides were considerably bent." Wells, Fargo informed the press that the robbers had blown the local safe and estimated the loss at the standard $500. An Albuquerque newspaper retorted, "Others, however, have reason to believe that it was one of the express company's richest safes, and that several thousand dollars went along with the robbers." Passengers insisted that the silver in the engine's cab well exceeded the $500 reported by Wells, Fargo, and the *Democrat* opined that the "regulation '$500' [was] about as close to the correct figure as the public will ever get, unless the men who did the job make a report." Walters, one of those "who did the job," later claimed they had seized about $20,000.[7]

Even though the engineer, fireman, and mail clerk reportedly "described the men very accurately," the descriptions were sketchy at best. "Both were smooth faced and apparently about 20 years of age. They wore canvas coats and dressed like cowboys." One, a light-complected "American" answered "closely to the description of [George] Musgrave." But in the spring of 1898, train robber George Musgrave—light-complected, three days shy of his twenty-first birthday, and well over six feet tall and two hundred pounds—was known to be a fugitive in Chihuahua, Mexico. No description of Kid Johnson has surfaced, but brothers Asa and Charles Johnson were tall, with medium builds, and light-complected; the description probably fit Kid Johnson. The other bandit, portrayed as dark-complected and reported by some as half Mexican, probably described Bronco Bill, notwithstanding later prison records that described him as having "brown hair, blue eyes, a light complexion." Most who knew Walters, including sheriff and later prison superintendent Holm Bursum, described him as dark-complected. At five feet, nine inches, moreover, the slender Walters should never have been mistaken for the much larger Musgrave. No one recalled a medium-sized, light-complected and freckled redhead. Pipkin, the gang's likely wrangler that morning, would have escaped the eyes of onlookers.[8]

Conductor Conners telegraphed accounts of the holdup to Albuquerque trainmaster George E. Ayer and Fred Fornoff, the city marshal. Equally busy, messenger Hiscock wired details of the heist to W. F. Powars, the Wells, Fargo and Company's express agent at Albuquerque. Powars, Deputy C. E. Newcomer, and Thomas McMillen, the Albuquerque stationmaster, left for Belén on an early morning southbound freight. Powars returned to Albuquerque that evening with the dynamited safe. Meanwhile, the enriched robbers continued their southwest flight.[9]

A number of hours after the robbery, Walters and Johnson reached Puertecito, southwest of Belén on the Rio Salado, after about fifty miles of riding. They stopped at the trading post and post office of Anastácio Baca. Whether Pipkin remained on guard outside the small settlement or had already left the two is uncertain. Prime Coleman, a Black River country acquaintance of Pipkin's, insisted that the redheaded outlaw had "split off from them during the previous night." Red could, however, have reasonably accompanied Walters and Johnson to Puertecito before separating from them and continuing on his own, perhaps to his father's residence at Ramah (little more than sixty miles northwest).[10]

Fifty-eight years later, Sister Juanita Baca (a teacher at Albuquerque's St. Vincent's Academy) recalled there were only two outlaws at her father's Puertecito store. "I walked into the store while the two bandits were talking to my father. They were dressed in cowboy clothes, and each of them had a big money belt around his waist. One of them kept looking out the door to see if anybody was coming," she remembered. They bought sardines and crackers and some feed for their horses, she added. While they were there, her father sent her to see her mother, and she realized that he wanted her out of the way. When she stepped outside, her eyes wandered toward the men's horses and the pair of thick pouches that hung from their saddles. "The men came out and fed their horses, then went back into the store and ate their sardines and crackers at the counter," she continued. "One of them paid for the food from a large roll of bills. I was sure their money belts and saddle pouches were filled with money." According to John Cox, Walters and Johnson also bought a barrel of wine. Bronco Bill rolled it out into the street, seized a hammer, and knocked out the barrel's head. He grabbed a dipper and offered a drink of wine to everyone who strolled by. "There'll be some people on our trail any time now," Walters accurately surmised before the duo mounted and headed west. They skirted the Navajo settlement of Alamo near the northern base of the Galinas Mountains and continued along the Rio Salado as it cut between Table Mountain and Tres Hermanas Mesa. Once they cleared the pass, they continued toward the river's junction with Alamocita Creek.[11]

Matias Sanchez, an Albuquerque resident who owned sheep ranches in Socorro County, traveled northeast from his ranches to his home on the afternoon following the robbery. He passed two strangers on horseback near the Angelito (now the D Cross) Ranch, west of the Navajo settlement at Alamo. "The men were between 20 and 30 years old and undoubtedly Americans," Sanchez informed authorities. "They were well mounted, one riding a strong looking gray horse and the other striding a dark bay horse of equal strength and endurance. They wore

Francisco X. "Frank" Vigil, the chief deputy sheriff of Valencia County. Courtesy of Tibo Chavez, Belén, New Mexico.

guns strapped to their backs and wore cartridge belts well filled with cartridges. They wore the ordinary costume of cowboys or ranch men."[12]

Several posses pursued the not so ordinary cowboys. Charlie Fowler, the Wells, Fargo guard, gathered a group to ride south from Albuquerque. Socorro deputies Cipriano Baca and Henry Dreyfuss rode north to take up the chase, as did their boss, Sheriff Bursum, whose horse gave out near

Puertecito. At Los Lunas, Francisco X. "Frank" Vigil, the well-connected chief deputy sheriff of Valencia County, joined the hunt with his cousin, Daniel Bustamante, a blacksmith from nearby Los Chávez.

No one questioned Vigil's bravery; descendants have learned that "no tenía meido de nada" (he wasn't afraid of anything), and only Bustamante was willing to ride with him in spite of wife Sabrina's appeals for him to stay. "He had to go because of his friendship with Vigil," his grandson explained. "He had a very close relationship with Vigil." In their haste, Vigil and Bustamante failed to arm themselves with anything more than revolvers, a serious oversight when going up against seasoned desperadoes with rifles.[13]

The two Valencia County deputies located the fleeing outlaws' trail with little difficulty and followed it to Puertecito, where they learned that they were hot on the trail. They rode on to Alamo and recruited several trackers, including Vicente Wuerro and Juan Capitano, likely one and the same as Capitan, boss of the nearby Morley Ranch sheep outfit and later subpoenaed to testify at Walters's trial.[14]

Later in the afternoon, Walters and Johnson left the Rio Salado and rode along Alamocita Creek across Ada McPherson Morley's vast Swinging W Ranch, where they crossed trails with young William Raymond "Ray" Morley. Known for his legendary strength as well as his celebrated pranks, twenty-two-year-old Morley was scheduled to enter Columbia University to study engineering. He later earned a place on Walter Camp's 1900 and 1901 All-American football squads. He stayed to coach the 1902 football team, but abandoned both engineering and coaching in order to develop his Drag A Ranch in the Datil Mountains. Eventually, the ranch "comprised about two hundred 640-acre sections to which he held title by patent or by perpetual lease, and possible treble that number that he controlled by virtue of the location of the watering places or by National Forest permits."[15]

Deputy Daniel Bustamante and his bride, Sabrina, on their wedding day. Courtesy of Palomino Photo Collection.

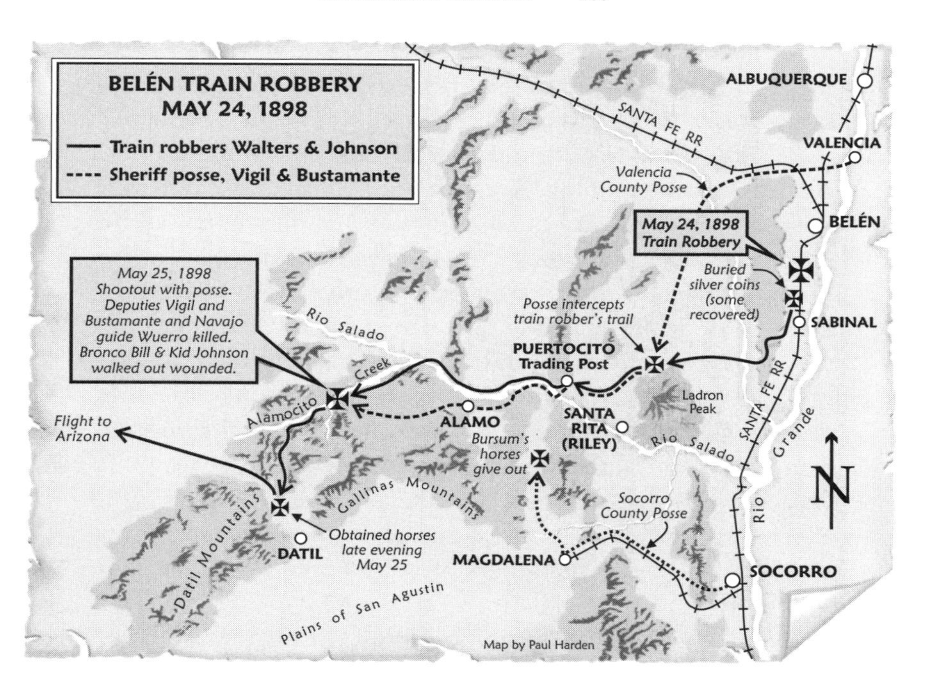

Like most ranchers, Morley welcomed outlaw and lawman alike as long as they did not bother him or his stock. His chuck wagon was at the creek, and Walters and Johnson joined him for supper. Morley later recounted that they had the "goddamndest lot of money. Each of them had big saddle pockets and they was just stuffed full of money." The fugitives left the camp about sundown and continued along Alamocita Creek about three miles to a grove of cottonwood trees—on the Morley family's Los Esteros ranch. They stopped near the head of a small arroyo amid mesquite and piñons. A small wash was immediately to the west, and more mesquite and piñons stood beyond. They unsaddled and hobbled their horses at a rock outcropping about three hundred yards to the north; the only nearby source of water had a stand of grama grass. Walters and Johnson walked back to camp and settled in for the night—

it had been a long day beginning in the wee hours of the morning. "We figured on getting up before daylight and going on, but we slept until sunup," Walters later told Evans Coleman.[16]

Vigil's Navajo trackers did their job and located the bandits' camp that same evening. According to Wuerro's descendants, they saw the fugitives hobble the horses and stash two more sacks of coins into a rock crevice on the north side of the outcropping before they rode back and apprised Vigil and Bustamante of the camp's location. In order to strike at sunrise, the posse continued on and camped that night at the west end of Table Mountain, about five miles west of Alamo. Early the next morning (May 25), the posse approached the outlaws' camp from the southeast along an unnamed arroyo. Accounts vary as to what happened next. Walters later related his version to several acquaintances. Navajo trackers provided their accounts to official inquirers, members of the lawmen's families, and to the press.

Vigil and Bustamante cautiously left the arroyo and crept west through a thicket of mesquite and piñon to a position about fifty yards south of the outlaws' campsite. According to Daniel Bustamante's nephew Alfredo, his uncle then ordered Capitano, Wuerro, and a third scout to sneak around the camp and seize the outlaws' horses and rifles. As the deputies watched, the Navajos slowly moved north of the encampment, snatched the hobbled horses, and hid them farther north and out of sight on the opposite side of the rock outcropping. Walters told a different story: "[W]e took our bridles and went down to get them [the horses]. We had our pistols on." The saddles and rifles remained behind at the campsite. By his account, he and Johnson got the horses and started back. One fact is certain: the Navajos had the horses at the end of the confrontation.[17]

Alfredo Bustamante related to Socorro County historian Paul Harden that Vigil and Bustamante now disagreed on how to approach Walters and Johnson; Alfredo's uncle believed it rash to attempt to apprehend Walters and Johnson with insufficient men and weapons. Circumstances resolved the issue. With the horses secure, the Navajos had started south again. When Vigil questioned the action, Bustamante replied that they were now going for the bandits' rifles leaning against a fallen log. Believing that it would not look good if they had to shoot unarmed outlaws, Vigil vainly motioned the Navajos to stop. Unable to catch their attention, he suddenly jumped up, began to wave a piece of paper to suggest a warrant, and yelled down at Walters and Johnson to surrender. It proved a fatal mistake for the pistol-toting lawman. Although he and Bustamante fired as the outlaws dashed to their Winchesters, the distance rendered their shots ineffective.[18]

"We turned our horses loose and run to get our saddles. We run and they run," Bronco Bill recalled, "We just had a running fight. We was shooting and so were they." The two outlaws finally reached their Winchesters as a bullet grazed Walters across his hip. They brought the rifles into action and drove the deputies back with deadly intensity. A bullet from Johnson's gun struck Vigil between the eyes. The valiant deputy died instantly. Walters fired several shots in Bustamante's direction. From the north, the Navajos had also joined the fray, and the outlaws found themselves in a crossfire. Then one of Bronco's bullets found its mark, killing Bustamante.[19]

The two bandits jumped over the dry creek bank, and Johnson suddenly went down, shot through the neck. Bill readily recognized that his partner could not have fallen victim to one of the deputies' bullets. "I knew someone was behind me shooting at me, and this shot I got through here [the hip] come from in front of me [from Bustamante]. But this one (in the shoulder) come from behind me. Two or three shots were fired from behind me," Walters judged.[20]

He glanced down the creek about fifty to seventy-five yards away and spotted one of the Navajo trackers who had taken cover behind a nearby log. Wuerro was just ready to shoot when Walters shouldered his Winchester and snapped off a shot. "I throwed my gun back and hit him right between the eyes," he later revealed. "And then Johnson come to, and they quit fighting and I grabbed him and got him up. We took our guns and went across this wash. We stood there and watched them come and get our horses and put our saddles on and load these men on and go." In fact, the surviving trackers only took the horses; they left the bodies where they had fallen.[21]

Years later, Pipkin summed up the shooting to one-time Diamond A Ranch foreman Henry Brock. "Bronco chattered right along and got up close to the deputies, then opened fire and skadooed." In a more complete account, Walters later confided to Evans Coleman, "I grabbed [Johnson] by the collar and helped him up, at the same time picking up his Winchester and handing it to him, and somehow we got hold of the money, and I half dragged and carried Bill across the little wash, by which time he was able to navigate for himself. We climbed a little hill, and about 150 yards from our saddles we sat down. The posse had got all the fight they wanted." As Walters had revealed that he had watched the Navajos "put our saddles on . . . and go," the trackers may have had "all the fight they wanted." The trackers also retrieved the two sacks of coins—reportedly one thousand coins, which were divided among the families and used for poker chips.[22]

When silence finally returned to the valley, Vigil, Bustamante, and Wuerro lay dead. Johnson was a bloody mess on account of his neck wound. Walters had suffered a flesh wound in his hip and another bullet had struck his shoulder blade and exited at the top of his shoulder. The trackers had seized the outlaws' horses and fled from the carnage. From Magdalena, Capitano telegraphed the news of the battle. Newspapers throughout the Southwest quickly spread the news of "The Awful Sequel" to the Belén robbery.[23]

In Lordsburg, Don H. Kedzie, the editor of the *Western Liberal*, eulogized the bravery of the deputies while regretting their tragic miscalculation:

> When the train was robbed on the Santa Fe last week all the deputy sheriffs in central New Mexico went after the robbers. Among them were Frank X. Vigil and Dan Bustamante of Valencia County. There is no newspaper published in Valencia County and these officers were not posted on the ethics governing train robbers and sheriffs in New Mexico. They supposed it was the duty of a deputy sheriff to arrest a train robber. They did not know that all a deputy sheriff was expected to do was to follow a train robber at a respectful distance till he got into an "inaccessible mountain country" and then come back and tell about it. In their ignorance they got a couple of Indian trailers and went after their men. Twenty-four hours later they discovered the train robbers' camp, surrounded it and called on the robbers to surrender. In the melée that followed Vigil, Bustamante and one Indian were killed, the other Indian captured the train robbers' horses and returned with the news that the train robbers escaped. Deputy sheriffs from other counties who understood the business, followed the train robbers to the "inaccessible mountains" and then returned home. It is queer how many mountains in this country are inaccessible to officers and are open highways to train robbers. Vigil and Bustamante are highly spoken of as competent officers by those who knew them. That they were brave is shown by the way they went to their deaths.[24]

Kedzie was less than fair in his criticism of deputies. Historian Larry Ball, in his study of New Mexico and Arizona sheriffs, examined the lack of economic incentive provided lawmen by many counties. Meager salaries made the risk of life and limb a poor exchange when chasing deadly fugitives, as the fate of these intrepid deputies proved.[25]

As the surviving Navajo trackers raced southeast to Magdalena with news of the battle, Bronco Bill and Johnson, both wounded, fled southwest on foot. Bonifacio Lopez, who lived near the site, carried the news of the shooting to Belén. When Sheriff Bursum learned of the battle he started in a buggy, drawn by a couple of good mares, with the intention of getting horses at Puertecito. "Word got out that I was after men for Spanish-American War, & when I got to Puertecito, all men gone—took to the country. Had to come back [to Socorro], put saddle horses in train[;] got to Magdalena, & took out for the trail." The Socorro County Sheriff, joined by a party from Belén, reached the site and found the bodies "lying where they were shot down and it is believed that they were killed outright."[26]

Numerous questions arose concerning the disposition of the remains. The *Citizen* reported accurately, "The dead bodies are now at Santa Rita." The next day, May 27, 1898, the *Albuquerque Morning Democrat* reported that the bodies of Vigil and Bustamante would be taken to their respective homes for burial, but Wuerro would be buried at Santa Rita. A day later, on May 28, the *Citizen* reported that Vigil and Bustamante had been buried the previous day at Belén. In fact, Wuerro's body was returned to his family at Alamo, and the group from Belén took the remains of the two lawmen to Santa Rita (now Riley), the home of Bustamante's parents, and buried the bodies side-by-side at the Santa Rita Church. Bustamante's resting place remains there.[27]

Eslavio Vigil, prominent in Bernalillo County's Republican affairs, raced to Los Lunas expecting to find his brother's body and was incensed to learn from Valencia County sheriff Jesus Sanchez that the body had been buried at Santa Rita without consultation with the family. Several days later, two men hired by Vigil's widow retrieved the deputy's remains for reburial in the Vigil family plot in Albuquerque's south valley. Taking the wagon road that went over a pass in Ladrónes

Grave of Deputy Daniel Bustamante (1864–1898) at Santa Rita. The marker was carved by his grandnephew, Hipolito Bustamante Romero. Photograph by the authors.

Mountain and to Veguita, the two men, wearing bandanas over their noses, carted Vigil's decomposing body across the New Mexico desert. After they crossed over to the east bank of the Rio Grande, they stopped for dinner at the village of Valencia. As the two ate their meal in the cantina, several residents complained to the local priest of the dreadful smell emanating from the decaying body in the parked wagon. Quick to respond, the priest ordered that Vigil's body be buried immediately at Valencia's old Chapel of Sangre de Cristo, directly across the street from the cantina.[28]

While the press busied itself with the location of graves, Sheriff Bursum took out after the killers. He was convinced that he was hunting three men—"Bronco Bill, Pipkin & another."[29]

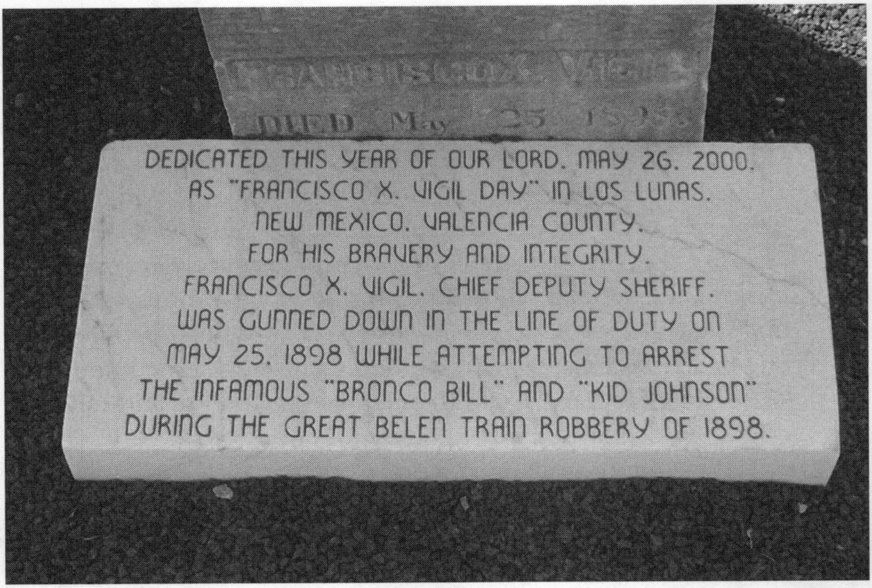

Grave of Francisco X. Vigil at Sangre de Cristo Catholic Church, Valencia. Photograph by the authors.

During the morning following the fatal gunfight, Ray Morley again met Walters and Johnson as they fled south. He later told John Cox that "Kid Johnson had on a comparatively white shirt and he was shot through the . . . he wasn't killed at all, he was just creased, and he was the bloodiest damn thing, that blood had run all over him. One said, 'Morley, we've got to have some horses, we're afoot.'

"So I see," Morley replied. "Now I'm stayin' down at old Datil. You come down there tonight, I'm stayin' in a horse camp down there. The [V] Cross [T] is stayin' up there at the Swingin' [W] Ranch," Morley continued, "but you come to my camp and when you knock on the door, you throw down on me because no tellin' who will be there and I don't want 'em to say I give you fellas the horses."[30]

Morley's nephew, Norman Cleaveland, provided a variant version of what actually happened. Walters walked up to the Swinging W's ranch house and asked for a horse, saddle, and Morley's hat. Later, Ray's older sister Agnes arrived and, upon hearing the story, chided her brother for having aided and abetted a train robber. Surely the law would soon be on him. Moreover, when they captured Walters, he would be wearing Morley's hat. A short time later, Morley spotted an approaching horseman leading a saddled horse. Agnes agreed that it was undoubtedly the sheriff and counseled that Ray had best flee. She promised to leave food for him daily at an agreed upon site—Pyramid Rock. Morley then jumped on a horse and rode off. The rider turned out to be their cousin, Orrin McPherson, the frequent victim of Morley's practical jokes. He and Agnes "were beside themselves with joy to think of poor Ray hiding in the hills. And indeed they saw to it that sufficient food was left daily at Pyramid Rock to keep him from coming out of the hills because of hunger. After several days [Agnes] relented and left a message that all was clear. Shortly a very weary and bedraggled brother Ray showed up."[31]

Almost one-half century after the shootout, and twelve years after Morley's death, Bursum confirmed accounts of Morley's assistance. "I took trail, trailed them all day, but had traveled on their course all night. Wasn't 30 minutes behind them when found where somebody had br[ought] in pack horses from somebody in the Datils. They then had such advantage on me that I had to let them go." Bursum heard "a year or two later" that "Ray Morley supposed to have sent them horses."[32]

Speculation continued, meanwhile, as to the identities of the remounted outlaws. The *Albuquerque Citizen* confidently insisted, "When the Belén train robbers are captured, if ever, they will be found to be Pedro Garcia and Joe Evans, two well known desperadoes." Locals had spotted Garcia and a companion, according to the report, at Manzano (twenty-six miles east of Belén) ten days previously. More recently, Garcia and Evans had been camped near Progresso, almost sixty miles east of Belén, and next had been seen riding along the railroad tracks near Rio Puerco on the night before the holdup. There were fatal problems with the *Citizen*'s conclusion. It neglected to explain the two alleged outlaws' easterly movements away from Belén, only to have them suddenly reemerge west of the settlement. Additionally, but perhaps understandably, the newspaper identified the wrong Kid Johnson. At least a decade older, three-time loser and housepainter Joe Evans, alias Ben Masters, alias Kid Johnson, was *not* Bill "Kid" Johnson of Luna, New Mexico.[33]

The *Citizen* attempted to correct itself the next day when it revealed that "less than two months ago" Garcia had written a letter "from somewhere down in Texas on the Mexican border" to a woman in Laguna, New Mexico. The newspaper further reported that Tom Hubbell, Bernalillo County's sheriff, believed the two desperadoes were young cowboys, known throughout New Mexico and western Arizona as "Kid" Johnson and "Kid" Swingle. Hubbell was half right.[34]

More emphatic in its reporting, the *Morning Democrat* maintained:

> Both the robbers are now believed to be Americans, one undoubtedly being the notorious "Kid Johnson" with the other thought to be "Kid Swingle," a recent acquisition to the ranks of New Mexico's bad men from the neighborhood of Springerville, Arizona. Both of these young men are said to have been seen near Belén the night before the robbery. The fact of their having lost their horses does not signify very much as there are a great many good horses in the neighborhood in which they were last reported and Johnson is perfectly acquainted with every foot of the region.

> His father, with whom he is said to be on bad terms, is a resident of Luna valley nearby. Men who will hold up a train and kill three men are not apt to walk any great distance in a country where there are plenty of horses.[35]

The *Democrat* also got it half right; it identified the correct Kid Johnson, a fact confirmed by Deputy Cipriano Baca. "Just returned from chasing robbers," he telegraphed Creighton Foraker, the U.S. marshal. "Will Johnson, son of Ab Johnson, of Luna Valley, is one of the robbers. Lost trail fifteen miles west of Datil." As for G. S. "Kid" Swingle (alias Montana Kid, Claude Preston, and C. W. Johnson), the mysterious highwayman who had enjoyed a brief but successful criminal career in the late 1880s, he and Bronco Bill Walters were not one and the same.[36]

On Sunday night, May 29, John N. Thacker, Special Officer Fred J. Dodge, and Charles H. Young gathered at Superintendent Powars's Albuquerque office and discussed the clues at hand. Dodge, an intimate of Wyatt Earp's, was then posted to Kansas City. Young, the division agent out of Denver, had served previously as Wells, Fargo Express Company's local superintendent and agent in Albuquerque. Thacker, who had just returned from Magdalena in an effort to correctly identify the robbers, shared his findings. All agreed that the robbers would be brought to bay only if the pressure was maintained. Thacker and Dodge then headed south to join the pursuit.[37]

The Santa Fe holdup at Belén had been a rare success, and its unfortunate aftermath had resulted in the death of three of the pursuers. Although Walters and Johnson had not touched the mail car, they had impeded its movement and thereby committed a federal crime. On June 6, U.S. Marshal Foraker telegraphed U.S. Attorney General John Griggs, informed him of the Belén robbery and the deaths of the three men, and then secured permission to put Chief Deputy Horace W. Loomis on the hunt. With the addition of this federal deputy to the ranks of county deputies and Wells, Fargo agents on the chase, the net around Walters, Johnson, and Pipkin tightened.[38]

CHAPTER 8

Chase and Capture

"I had rather be killed than taken alive."

Bronco Bill Walters

Remounted, Bronco Bill and Kid Johnson continued west after their encounter with Ray Morley. Evans Coleman ran into them at the end of May near Walter Baird's W Slash Ranch, northeast of St. Johns. They rode "two Mexican ponies worth about six bits apiece," and they were "the worse sight you ever saw," Coleman recalled. "Well, it looks like you fellows must have jumped the United States Army," the cowboy judged.

"We jumped something worse than the United States army," one of them replied. "Been in the damnest scrap your ever saw." The fight had been a terrible affair in their estimation. "They brooded on that killing and would have given all the money back they got if it hadn't have happened." They knew they were wrong, and Walters insisted, "I don't want to kill any man, and if I can possibly get away from an officer without killing him I will. Yes, they may get me some time, I guess they will alright, sure. But I had rather be killed than taken alive."[1]

Walters and Johnson rode on to the W Slash spread, where they sought out V. A. Word, the cowboy who had previously tended to Ed Colter. Word dressed their wounds and they paid him for two good grain-fed horses before they set out for the Double Circle horse camp on Black River. When questioned later, Word understandably insisted that they had taken the horses by force.[2]

Within days, the *Arizona Bulletin* reported that "they were last heard from Bluesome [*sic*] in New Mexico and in all probability are now located in the Black River country where it is believed such characters are harbored." More emphatic, the *St. Johns Herald* insisted they were already in the Black River country and informed its readers that "well known parties have had long interviews with them. They showed one person over $7,000, the proceeds of their recent raid." The account continued: "Both men are wounded. 'Broncho' is shot thought the left thigh, while Johnson 'got it in the neck.'" The *Bulletin* later confirmed the accuracy of the *Herald*'s report and complained, "This gang of outlaws and murderers have a rendezvous in the Black River country, and they are harbored there, fed and furnished, by friends who are no less detrimental to a law-abiding country than is 'Broncho Bill' himself." The *Bulletin* had little more regard for the agents of the express and railroad companies, "dress parade detectives, who are noted most for their gallantry and efficiency through the columns of the newspaper." The paper begged the legislature to establish a company of Arizona Rangers to "make the country too hot for 'Broncho Bill' and his kind and drive them to death or to seek other field of operation." While the *Bulletin* ranted, Walters and Johnson arrived at the Double Circle Ranch. They were in bad shape.[3]

George Felshaw, the ranch's horse wrangler, liked both of them, even though they had rustled Double Circle horses. Born on November 9, 1875, the native of Panqiutch, Utah, had immigrated to Graham County with his parents in 1887. In addition to horse wrangling, Felshaw also ran the dairy, but it was neither horses nor milk that Walters and Johnson needed. On their account, the wrangler rode the twenty-five miles to Fort Apache to seek the advice of a doctor. He explained to Captain Edward Everts, the fort's physician, "Two of the boys got in a little scrape and got shot up a bit." Everts gave Felshaw some medicine and told him how to tend the wounds with a silk handkerchief. Felshaw "would put it on like he was doctoring a sick kid," Evans Coleman told western historian J. Evetts Haley. Running the handkerchief through the wounds to clean them, Felshaw tested the boys' toughness and found that "you couldn't kill them." Over the next couple of weeks, Bronco Bill and Kid Johnson recovered enough to ride and disappeared for several days. When they came back, they showed the stunned wrangler the loot. "I never saw so much money in my life—silver and greenbacks and anything else that was legal tender. They sure had the money," later described by the *St. Johns Herald* as a roll of $1,000 bills "as large as a man's arm." But would they have the opportunity to spend it with Deputy Loomis on their trail?[4]

Horace W. "Will" Loomis, the brother-in-law and chief deputy of former U.S. Marshal Edward Hall of New Mexico, had single-handedly thwarted the High Five gang's robbery of the Atlantic and Pacific train at Rio Puerco (on October 2, 1896) and killed gang member Code Young. At the onset of his marshalcy in 1897, the Republican Creighton Foraker's decision to retain Democrat Loomis as an office deputy was a testament to the high regard in which the deputy was held, and W. B. Childers, the U.S. attorney for New Mexico, echoed Foraker's assessment. On June 11, Loomis appeared in Santa Fe before John P. Victory, the U.S. commissioner for the First Judicial District, and swore that Walters, Johnson, Pipkin, Colter, and Burnett had robbed the train at Grants on March 29, 1898. Moreover, in violation of section 5473 of the Revised Statutes of the United States, they had attempted to rob the U.S. mail by assaulting R. A. Wilson, the mail clerk, "and threatening him with dangerous weapons."[5]

With a warrant stuffed in his pocket, Loomis headed from Santa Fe to Springerville and began an undercover investigation. To insure that Loomis's effort was not exposed, which would "almost certainly render his trip a failure, if not render his return alive also doubtful," Marshal Foraker sought permission from the U.S. attorney general to forgo the usual requirement of collecting receipts. He requested that Loomis "render his expense account on oath without vouchers, not exceeding $2.00 per day in addition to his necessary R. R. fare and horse hire. I can see no hope of success on any other terms." General Griggs granted the request on June 20.[6]

On June 27, Loomis updated the marshal:

> No change in situation here, the wounded men I hear are able to ride. Reported that some of them took the Mexican money and went south to get it exchanged, better call the attention of the marshal of Arizona to the matter, Bisbee is the point likely to be reached—I doubt they have left yet—I am going tomorrow toward Black River with a fishing party and hope in a few days to be asked to go to the River with another crowd, thus will I gradually work in; am unidentified—so far—and can go in safely, I think. The people here think that Broncho Bill is an escaped man with a life sentence, so, possibly the "Bill" they know is another man, aside from our "Bill" of New Mexico, but I am positive that he is the same.[7]

Loomis was correct—it was the right Bill.

Walters and Johnson, meanwhile, headed south to "the vicinity of Old Baldy Peak, near the headwaters of the Little Colorado, the Black, and the White Rivers." Later, Foraker wrongly attributed their flight to Loomis's presence in Springerville. In fact, the outlaws had reached the Black River country well before Loomis's arrival.[8]

In another letter to Foraker, posted the same day. Loomis advised, "The boys are planning another raid in New Mexico, so all the cowboys talk to one another." He wrote that St.

George Creaghe, the Apache County sheriff and friend of Kid Johnson's, had resigned his office because of the gang, and the deputy further wrote that "Johnson's neck and Bill's shoulder and leg are on the mend." He also relayed the rumor that "trouble is brewing somewhere eastward" and cautioned the Wells, Fargo officials to "be on watch for a while," particularly "in and about La Joya for strange and suspicious characters." Experienced at thwarting train robbers, Loomis urged that shotgun-toting guards be stationed on the trains amid the passengers and not in the express cars. Unable to turn up further leads, Deputy Loomis left Springerville on June 30, and was back in Santa Fe on July 3.[9]

Foraker, meanwhile, wrote to J. H. Hurley, the superintendent of the Santa Fe Railway at Las Vegas, New Mexico, on July 1 requesting a pass for Deputy J. J. Sheridan to go "to the vicinity of Clifton, Solomonville, Bisbee and north to Cienega, Luna, and thereabouts on a 'still hunt' for evidence and matters pertaining to the parties who have recently been holding up trains." Sheridan, a native of California, had immigrated to Silver City in 1892, where he served as a Wells, Fargo messenger between that place and El Paso. He was appointed undersheriff of Grant County in 1894 and accepted the position as chief deputy to Marshal Foraker in 1898, just in time to go on a hunt for Walters and Johnson. Three days after Foraker's request for Sheridan's pass—on Independence Day—Walters and Johnson announced their presence—not at La Joya, New Mexico, as Loomis suspected, nor in the still-hunt range followed by Sheridan, but at Geronimo, Arizona.[10]

Located on the site of old Camp Thomas, Geronimo served as a station on the Southern Pacific's Gila Valley, Globe and Northern railway line from Bowie Station to Globe. On the evening of July 4, Geronimo's locals gathered at the schoolhouse to celebrate the holiday and dance away the evening. Walters, whose love for music and dancing had previously led to an arrest, possibly coerced Johnson to join him. The two first stopped at James Newton Porter's mercantile in quest of new clothes. Porter, a Grayson County, Texas, native who drove his cattle herd to Graham County in 1888, had his hand in a number of enterprises. In addition to his Geronimo store and a second store at nearby Fort Thomas, he ran the Geronimo, San Carlos, and Globe stage line, stopped previously by Walters and Johnson. He also oversaw a large ranch near the San Carlos Apache Reservation. Porter readily met Walters and Johnson's needs—five new suits—in exchange for something over three hundred dollars. According to the *Bulletin*, they "also bought every cartridge in town that would fit their guns." They packed their purchases and rode some distance from town before they reined in. Walters dismounted, donned new pants, and tossed away the old pair. The two then returned to town to make another purchase. When they arrived back in Geronimo, Bill reached for the money in his pocket; it was gone. He had to race back to retrieve the discarded pants and their money-filled pockets. With their shopping spree finished, the two fugitives headed to the schoolhouse for a Fourth of July shindig.[11]

"'Broncho' Bill does most of the dancing while Johnson stands watch around the door," the *Bulletin* reported. "Bill got too much liquor on board at the dance and because a girl refused to dance with him he pulled his sixshooter and cleared the hall." The *Bulletin*'s competitor, the *Graham Guardian*, agreed that the self-proclaimed temperate outlaw got drunk, and, labeling Walters a two-gun man, asserted that he drew a brace of pistols, which he proceeded to fire into the floor.[12]

Deputy Jeff Milton, about to give chase, soon gathered even more of the details:

> Bill walked down the line of young women who were sitting at the side of their helpless escorts along the wall in front of the windows.

> "May I have the honor of this dance?" Bill said politely to the first girl.
>
> Quietly she replied, "I beg to be excused."
>
> The next girl received the request and gave the same answer. This was continued until Bill reached the last girl, redheaded Tilly Windsor. When she refused Bill exclaimed, "Damned if you don't dance," pulled out his six-shooter and began firing at the floor near her feet while his companions [Milton believed that Pipkin as well as Johnson attended the dance] began shooting out the lights. Through the open windows behind them, tumbled the young folks whose party had come to such an unexpected end.[13]

A local variation of the story has it that Jimmy Hinton and fourteen-year-old Addie Cornett, his future wife, were at a dance in Globe in April 1898 when Bronco Bill Walters, Red Pipkin, and Kid Johnson rode in. In this version, it was Addie who was asked to dance by Walters after he got the permission of Jimmy Hinton. Held at the wrong place and at the wrong time, this tradition has its problems, but Addie surely might have been one of the young ladies who denied Bill's favor at Geronimo.[14]

About a week following the dance, Walters was seen in the vicinity of Eden, a small Gila Valley settlement. On July 14, M. C. Allen, who had been in the valley for a couple of months seeking to get into the cattle business, also reached Eden and John D. Halladay's nearby hot springs. That night, he was robbed and killed by two men. First reports linked Bronco Bill to the crime. Later information revealed that the owner's son, David Halladay, along with his partner, George Wright, had murdered the ill-fated cattleman. Walters and Johnson, meanwhile, had fled back into the Black River country, where Red Pipkin rejoined them. During the last week in July, William O. Gibbons, a St. Johns teamster, encountered all three of the gang.[15]

Out looking for some horses, Gibbons became disoriented in the mountains near Springerville. He wandered about for some time before he stumbled onto a cabin in the midst of a large pasture. He saw no sign of life, save for three grazing horses. Drawing closer, he could see that they still carried saddles. Convinced that the cabin must be occupied, he approached and knocked. There was no answer to his banging, but the door stood partially ajar. He stepped inside to find three men sound asleep. The slumbering men wore holstered revolvers; their Winchesters were leaned up against the bed. He knocked again and suddenly found himself staring at six-shooters in the hands of the aroused men. As Gibbons carried no arms, the outlaws holstered theirs and, putting on their best smiles, they asked his business. He related that he had lost his way and was only there to seek directions. The helpful bandits pointed out the way, and an undoubtedly relieved Gibbons headed toward St. Johns. The boldness of the twenty-seven-year-old stockman increased in direct proportion to the distance that he put between himself and the three outlaws. By the time he reached St Johns, he insisted to the locals that had he known that he would walk in on three train robbers "he would have conquered them all by killing one or two while they were asleep." In turn, the *St. Johns Herald* cautioned, "It would not be safe for one man to try and take all them alive as they are known to be bad men and would not give up alive." The *Herald*'s admonition was sound, and a move was afoot to capture or kill them—and it involved more than one man.[16]

In June, Jeff Milton received news that Walters, Johnson, and Pipkin had returned to Arizona. He later claimed that a cowboy from the Black River area reached Nogales with a challenge from Walters. "I got a message for you I don't like to deliver," said the cowboy. "It is from Bronco Bill." He went on to say that Walters was in the Blanco (White) Mountains and was in need of some good horses and plenty of blankets. Bill hoped that Milton would bring some of both into the area so that he could take them away from the lawman.

"You tell the son of a bitch I will be up there after him one of these days," replied Milton, "with some good horses and blankets!"[17]

Whatever the source of the information, and Milton's story is inconsistent with the subsequent unfolding of events, he and George Scarborough turned bounty hunters. "We knew we had desperate men to encounter and went to work in a careful manner," Scarborough later reflected. "We were undertaking this job on our own hook and we couldn't afford to make any mistakes. We are not in the employ of Wells Fargo or anyone else, but made up our minds to make a trail for the reward that had been offered for Broncho Bill and his partner Johnson."[18]

Scarborough and Milton outfitted themselves at Tucson through the generosity of Epes Randolph. Following a railroading career in the South and Midwest, Randolph had reached Arizona in 1895 and served as president of the Arizona Eastern Railroad, the Ferrocarril Sud-Pacífico de Mexico (Southern Pacific Railroad Company of Mexico), and as division superintendent of the Southern Pacific in Arizona and New Mexico. He offered horses, equipment, and money. Most importantly, he offered special trains.[19]

Scarborough and Milton headed north, but not directly into the Black River country. They had been tipped that the gang would attempt a holdup near Holbrook (in northeastern Arizona's high plateau country), so they gathered the equipment and horses and headed east on a Southern Pacific train to Deming, where they boarded the northbound Santa Fe. They unloaded at Albuquerque and set up camp near the recently founded University of New Mexico. It was a temporary stop; they soon traveled south to the junction with the Santa Fe Pacific at Isleta and boarded a westbound train to Holbrook.

Jefferson Davis Milton (1861–1947) and George Adolphus Scarborough (1859–1900) in El Paso. Courtesy Haley Memorial Library and History Center. Midland, Texas.

They lingered about Holbrook for several weeks, but their informant proved unreliable. Then they received news by telegram of the outlaws' July 4 appearance at the dance in Geronimo, on the other side of the White Mountains.[20]

They reboarded their stock and equipment and returned south. At Deming, they picked up Bill Martin and Eugene Thacker. Martin, the cowboy at the Diamond A Ranch who had recovered stock rustled by Walters, could identify the outlaw. Thacker, the twenty-one-year-old son of the veteran Wells, Fargo detective, was out to gain experience. On July 13, the foursome continued on to Bowie Station, where an engineer with his engine awaited their orders. He coupled on to their cars, and they headed up the Gila Valley, Globe and Northern line to Buttermilk Point, about fifteen miles from Geronimo, where they unloaded their equipment and stock. They sent word to San Carlos for some Apache scouts—to be used only for the first few days—and then set out to capture or kill some outlaws.[21]

Aware that desperadoes and their sympathizers abounded in Arizona's White Mountains, Milton and his posse chose to avoid established trails, to track their quarry at night, and to bypass all cowboy encampments. (Later, Scarborough would instruct a roving reporter: "Don't you ever go trailing along behind an outfit like that. They can lay behind a rock and pick you off too easy.") Skirting the Gila River, they reached San Carlos the first night, then headed across the Natanes Plateau for Fort Apache, on the east fork of the White River, over fifty miles away.[22]

The four arrived at the fort—established as an army post twenty-eight years earlier—but did not linger. They rode along the White River toward its headwaters in the White Mountains, some twenty-eight miles northeast. Days passed and discouragement grew as they crisscrossed their way through the mountains. The search moved into the third week. Suddenly, something caught their attention. Milton's wife, Mildred, later dramatized

The Southern Pacific's Gila Valley, Globe and Northern depot at Geronimo, Arizona. Courtesy Graham County Historical Society.

the discovery: "Four horsemen, struggling to the summit of Old Baldy [11,403 feet above sea level] . . . paid scant attention to the distant view. Death might be lurking near. Their keen eyes scanned their immediate surroundings. Almost at once a cairn of stones on Baldy's bare pate demanded investigation. In it was a beef can marked with a Diamond A brand. 'Bill's work, or I'll eat my sombrero,' drawled Martin, for Bill had once worked for the Diamond A's." Martin should have started chewing: the Diamond A was registered to nearby Alpine rancher Prime T. Coleman, and the cairn was most likely the work of a local cowhand. In any case, the discovery erased their discouragement.[23]

From the top of Baldy, they gazed out on Springerville, about twenty miles away. They descended and rode toward the headwaters of the west fork of the Little Colorado River, then descended into Lee Valley and continued southeast toward the

Wells, Fargo special guard Eugene Thacker, ca. 1900. Courtesy of John Boessenecker.

east fork of the Black River. They struck the river and followed it southwest beyond the confluence with the west fork, then likely veered west through dangerous country to approach Burnt Corral, a pen frequently used by the Double Circle. It was Thursday, July 28. They had heard that Walters hung out in the area and approached cautiously, set up camp, and staked out the corral. The next day, John C. "Johnnie" Gibson, a Double Circle's cowpuncher, rode up during Milton's watch. From his hiding place in the brush, the lawman could see that

The Double Circle's horse camp on Black River. Rufus "Climax Jim" Nephew second from left. Original photograph in the collection of the authors.

this was not one of the men he sought. Gibson, in turn, glanced through the brush and spotted Milton's eyes looking back; the cowboy said nothing. Exposed and fearful that Gibson might broadcast their presence, Milton stood up and took the cowboy into custody. Gibson agreed to guide the party to the Double Circle's horse camp at McBride Crossing, about four miles south southeast on Black River.[24]

As night descended, they cautiously approached a glade on the west bank of the river where Hampson's hands had set up a rope corral and erected a large old tent along the trail between Solomonville and Fort Apache. Almost immediately, they stumbled on wrangler George Felshaw. Fearful that he would expose them, they seized the part-time outlaw nurse and then warily crept toward the tent. Suddenly, they threw back the tent flap and drew down on the cowboys concealed inside. J. E. Howard, Tom Bennett, Henry A. Banta, Rufus Nephew (alias "Climax Jim"), and an unnamed bear hunter quickly found themselves disarmed. They joined Gibson and Felshaw under guard. With little else to do, the lawmen, cowboys, and bear hunter turned in for the night. Scarborough afterwards detailed their plan for the next evening. "We had heard nothing of the outlaws, but had made up our minds to raid some of the adjacent cow camps Saturday night and see what we could find."[25]

Early Saturday morning, July 30, Scarborough awakened Milton, who decided to catch some fish for breakfast. About eight o'clock, he and Tom Bennett headed for the river and a fishing spot about one hundred yards from camp. Martin set off to round up the horses, while Thacker and Scarborough stood watch over the Double Circle's hands. About nine o'clock, three horsemen started down the steep trail off of the mesa on the east side of the river, three to four hundred yards away. The lead rider zigzagged his horse down through some large rocks that bordered the trail, reached the ford, and spurred his mount across the icy water that flowed about three feet deep. As he drew near the camp, his two companions, still up the slope, began to shoot at a rattlesnake, coiled under one of the large rocks. Already holding a half-dozen cowboys, Scarborough set out to add these three to his collection.[26]

The shots aimed at the snake rang out above the two anglers. Bennett started to run. Milton pulled his six-shooter and yelled, "Don't you run, don't run yet!"

"By god, somebody is going to be killed here today!" Bennett cried back.

"If you don't be quiet, somebody will be killed!" Milton scolded. "They are not shooting at us." Milton later explained that he heard no bullets going by and "would have run myself if I had." He stuck his fishing pole in the bank, turned to Bennett, and ordered, "Come on. Let's walk to camp. Let's walk

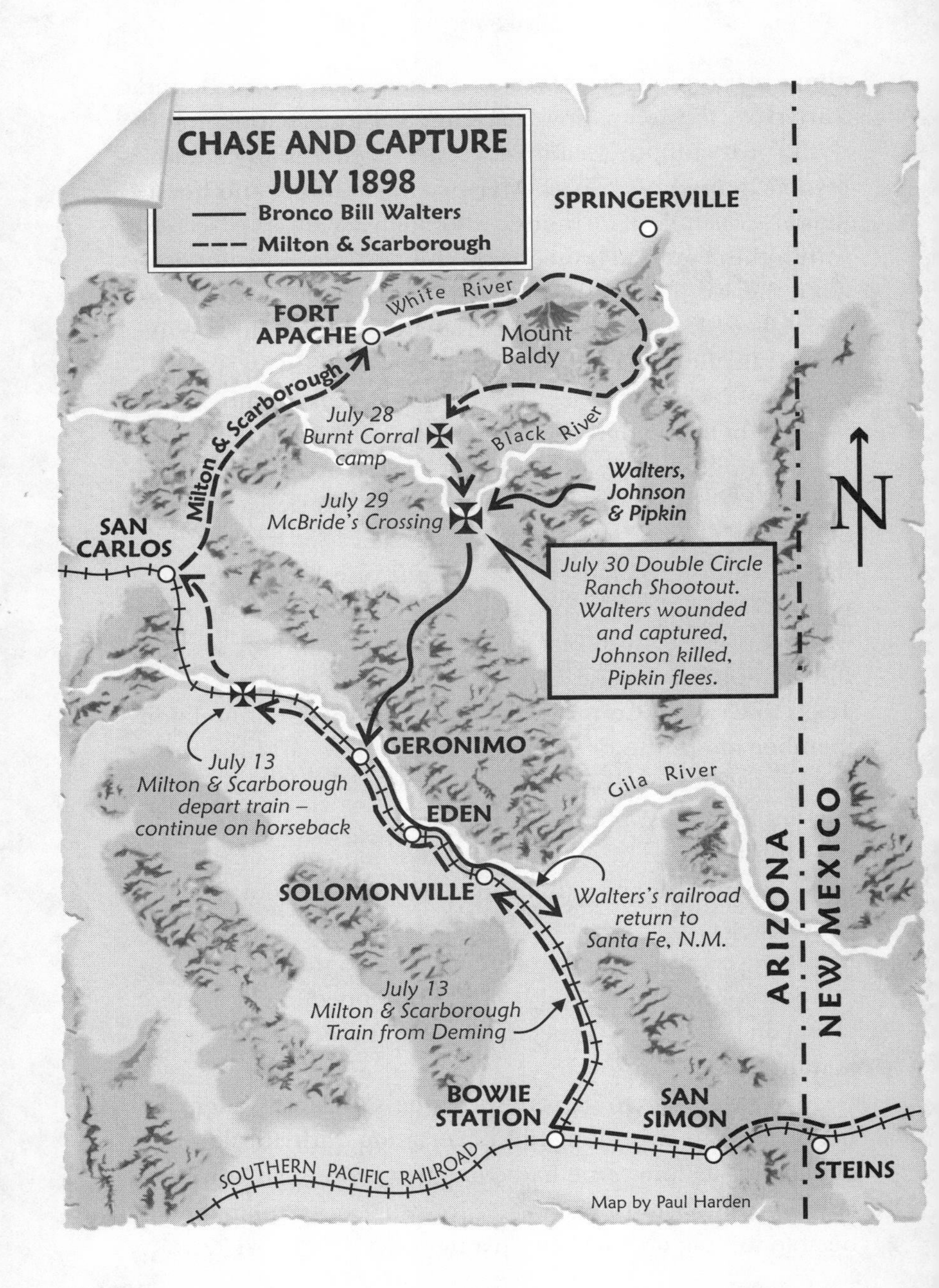

CHASE AND CAPTURE
JULY 1898
Bronco Bill Walters
Milton & Scarborough
SPRINGERVILLE
White River
FORT APACHE
Mount Baldy
Milton & Scarborough
July 28
Burnt Corral camp
Black River
July 29
McBride's Crossing
Walters, Johnson & Pipkin
SAN CARLOS
July 30 Double Circle Ranch Shootout. Walters wounded and captured, Johnson killed, Pipkin flees.
N
GERONIMO
July 13
Milton & Scarborough depart train – continue on horseback
Gila River
EDEN
SOLOMONVILLE
Walters's railroad return to Santa Fe, N.M.
ARIZONA
NEW MEXICO
July 13
Milton & Scarborough Train from Deming
BOWIE STATION
SAN SIMON
SOUTHERN PACIFIC RAILROAD
STEINS
Map by Paul Harden

along like nothing had happened." As Milton and Bennett started for the camp, however, something was happening.[27]

Bronco Bill, the lead rider, had reached the camp and reined in his horse. With Martin away tending the horses, Milton off wetting a line, and Scarborough and Thacker secreted within the tent, no lawmen were visible. Walters swung down from the saddle and called out to Howard and Banta to ask about some horses. Bill was "ahaw-hawin' and jokin' and like-athat." Inside the tent, Scarborough turned to one of the cowboys. Excited, he asked, "Who is it, who is it, who is it?"[28]

One of them pointed to Walters and whispered, "Hinton."[29]

It is doubtful that Walters used Hinton as an alias. Fifteen months earlier, Scott White, a U.S. deputy marshal and sheriff of Cochise County, had wrongly identified "Black Jack" Christian as Henry Jackson Hinton. Might one luckless cowboy named Hinton have enjoyed the dubious distinction of being wrongly confused with Black Jack at one time and with Bronco Bill at another? Several Hinton families had emigrated from Texas to Graham County, Arizona, about 1890, but no family member meets the description of an outlaw, and the moniker Henry Jackson Hinton remains a mystery.[30] Whatever his current handle, Walters remained wary.

Outside the tent, aware that Scarborough could hear every word, Howard winked at Bill and told him to ride out. The outlaw's instincts stirred—a trap. "I guess I don't want to stop here," he answered and started to climb back into the saddle.[31]

Scarborough grabbed his rifle and stepped out of the tent. "Hold on there Cap," the veteran outlaw hunter calmly ordered, "I want to speak to you."[32]

The jaws of the trap were springing shut, and Walters had no interest in a prolonged conversation with the lawman. He knew that "the game had come to a showdown," and that although he would not escape, Johnson and Pipkin "might be able to drag it" if he put up a fight.[33]

"In a second Bill had his sixshooter spittin' fire," Scarborough recounted later to journalists. "As soon as I could bring my Winchester into play I opened up."[34]

As Walters and Scarborough brought their guns into action, Milton arrived and joined the fray. Thacker also came running and "took a hand in the little game" as the Double Circle's cowboys dove for any available cover. Scarborough and Milton continued to fire at Walters as the outlaw raced across the glade toward the river. The fourth shot tore into Bill and smashed the bones in his shoulder and upper arm. He fell to the ground unconscious about seventy-five yards from the camp.[35]

Scarborough and Milton had no time to celebrate. "A bullet rung by [Scarborough's] ear and tore up the earth a short distance behind." Milton yelled, "George, did that bullet go through you?"[36]

"No, but, goddam, I heard it," Scarborough hollered back.[37]

Up the trail that descended from the mesa, Johnson and Pipkin took refuge behind the large rock that previously had sheltered the snake. About eight feet high and eight to ten feet across, the boulder offered a protected position from which they, too, joined in the melee. "I could just see their hat brims," Scarborough later explained. "We commenced a bombardment of the rock and made it so hot for them that they ran. As they came from behind the rock we shot both horses when Johnson took refuge behind a large Juniper tree close by and returned the fire." Suddenly, a bullet from one of their rifles struck the tree, right below Johnson's nose; instinctively, he stepped backward and a second bullet plowed through his hips.[38]

The *Western Liberal* reported, "Milton all this time was shooting, but it is thought that it was Scarborough's bullets that got both men." The *Liberal* got it right. "All I could see was his hips," Scarborough said. "I took a dead rest and fired and Johnson fell over and commenced to yell like a panther. I knew that he was bad hit." Even so, years after Scarborough's death, Milton inserted himself into his partner's role and took the credit for having shot Johnson. He even claimed to have uttered a variation of those fateful words, "Cap, let me speak to you a minute." Evans Coleman immediately called Milton's hand: "Now I don't want to start any controversy with Mr. Milton. But say, Mr. Milton, lets just get this capture straight. Some times we get our wires crossed and get things mixed up and forget to give the captured and the participants their due share of the credit."[39]

Any dispute over who fired the fatal shot was of little matter to Johnson, who agonizingly cried out to Pipkin, "I'm done for, you get away."[40]

Pipkin crawled to the top of the hill, looked down, and saw Scarborough "standin' spraddle-legged right out on the flat alookin." Pipkin thought, "Well dad gum, I'll just take one pop at him more." He fired his .30-30 rifle at Scarborough; the bullet struck between Scarborough's legs and kicked up the dust. Pipkin edged his way back to Johnson and unbuckled the dying man's money belt, which held some six thousand dollars. Red later claimed to have turned the belt and money over to Johnson's sister, though no surviving reports suggest that Alice Johnson ever received any of the Belén money.[41]

Scarborough continued his fire as Pipkin again crawled away. According to Socorro County native Henry Graham, one round grazed the outlaw across the fleshy part of the hip; more likely, the bullet struck him across the right knee. Regardless, Red disappeared into the heavy undergrowth that covered the mesa and was able to flee on foot. "We never saw him again," Scarborough bemoaned, but Graham saw him shortly after the shoot-out. Red rode up straddling a pillow, testifying, he believed, to a wounded hip. Graham probably inferred that the pillow protected a hip when, in fact, subsequent records mention no such scar but, rather, note a gunshot wound to Red's right knee. The pillow kept Red from banging his wounded knee against the saddle's jockey.[42]

Some distance away, the Double Circle's hands made a stretcher out of poles and canvas with horseshoe nails and carried Kid Johnson across the river and into camp. Scarborough's bullet had busted through the Kid's hipbones and sliced through his liver and kidneys. Milton strolled out to where Walters had fallen. He assumed that the outlaw was dead. He reached down, grabbed the heels of Bronco's boots, and started to drag the outlaw back to camp. The abruptness of the jerk forced the blood out of Walters's mouth. He regained consciousness, gasped for breath, and cleared the blood that had clogged his lungs. Milton's action saved the outlaw's life. Bronco was laid out next to Johnson. "Both men made an awful fuss," according to Milton. "So much noise finally got on our nerves so I said at last, 'Bill, they tell me that you laughed at a man you shot and called him a coward because he made a howl. Why don't you brace up and be a man.'"

"'Oh,' he said, 'You don't know how it hurts, you don't know how it hurts.'"[43]

Milton sent a rider to Clifton to inform authorities. He then ripped a page out of the memorandum book that he carried in his vest pocket and pinned a note reporting that two men were badly hurt and needed a doctor. Frank M. King, the self-styled "Cowhand Author," sent out a story to the Associated Press claiming that the note read, "Send one coffin and a Doctor, Milton." Milton later denied King's story. "I just wired in that two men were injured and were needing a doctor." At a later date, Mildred Milton, Jeff's wife, denied the story directly to King. Disregarding the input of those who should have known, both King and J. Evetts Haley inserted the message into their respective works.[44]

Milton detailed Climax Jim to ride to Fort Apache, twenty-five miles to the northwest, for the post doctor. The twenty-one-year-old cowboy had already established a dubious reputation and would spend much of the next few years as a guest of the Graham and Apache County jails. Nevertheless, Climax

Rufus "Climax Jim" Nephew (1876–1921). Original photograph in the collection of the authors.

did as Milton ordered. When he reached Fort Apache, however, Doctor Everts, who previously had supplied George Felshaw with medical supplies for the same two men, wanted no part in the affair. The commanding officer, Lieutenant Colonel J. W. Powell, had to order Everts to accompany Climax.[45]

While riders carried word of the battle to nearby settlements, Red Pipkin, still afoot, fled east. He struck Freezeout Creek and followed it toward the headwaters, where he came upon Johnny Brown, a ranch hand tending a small herd of cattle. He helped himself to the cowboy's horse and rode to Allen Chitty's ranch later in the day. Chitty, along with Monte Slaughter, James B. Hinton. Jr., and Jesse Cox, was himself a cattle rustling suspect and known by lawmen to be friendly with the gang. According to Milton, Chitty listened to Pipkin's account, then raced to Fort Apache and claimed, "There was a bunch of men out there killing everybody in the country." More probable, at least as reported by the *St. Johns Herald*, Chitty learned of Pipkin's fear that Scarborough and Milton would "kill Johnson before they took him to New Mexico." By this version, Chitty rode to Solomonville only to find that Sheriff Billy Birchfield was out of town, and Deputy Ben Olney was unwilling to interfere with deputy marshals. Pipkin, meanwhile, continued east to Jim Owens's ranch at Malay Gap.[46]

That night, Dr. Everts arrived from Fort Apache. There was little he could do for the wounded men in the field. Curiously, he judged that Bronco Bill would not survive and that Kid Johnson would; he was wrong on both counts. Fearful that he was about to be trapped in the midst of a range war, he would not stay but provided Milton with morphine to ease the outlaws' pain. Kid Johnson died at the horse camp later that night. "Before his death his yells could be heard for two miles. 'Tell father,' he said, 'not to grieve for me. I brought it all on myself. Tell him to hold no one responsible for my death.' Here he was seized with a paroxysm of pain. His features were convulsed and his cries made a man's blood turn cold. With a last effort he continued, 'Just tell him, boys, that Bill said Good Bye.'"[47]

The next morning, Milton, who, in the opinion of cowboy J. E. Howard, was the only lawman there "with a hart [*sic*]," carved Johnson's initials into a rock that he placed over the grave. Howard had little use for Scarborough, "a mean old overbearing son of a bitch after he had us disarmed & we had no guns." But he felt "pretty sorry for Bill Johnson—there wa'n't no use being sorry for these fellows—but couldn't help being sorry for him." A few days later, bears reportedly dug up Johnson's remains. What remains survived the depredation were later removed to the Double Circle Ranch cemetery.[48]

Chitty's distorted description of Saturday's events also brought an unnamed deputy and a posse of heavily armed men to the Double Circle's horse camp. "Let me talk to you," said Milton, who knew the deputy.

"If those fellows should see me here talking to you . . ." the deputy said, referring to the locals who had gathered. Milton angrily cut him short.

"Goddamn you," Milton yelled, "What are you doing here if you ain't friends! If you ain't our friends you get out of this camp and get out right now, because we don't need any such deputy sheriffs in this neighborhood!" The deputy took him at his word; the posse pulled out and rode away. On Sunday, the day following the shoot-out, Ben Clark, a Graham County deputy, also visited the camp from Clifton, as did Deputy Simpson from Geronimo.[49]

On Monday morning, August 1, Milton and Scarborough prepared to ride out. They tied an improvised a cradle-bed on a packhorse, then gently laid Walters, his arm splinted and tied across his chest, into the bed and started for Geronimo, fifty miles to the south. Bronco's pain eventually became unbearable. Quietly, he said, "Boys, just throw this pack outfit over the hill and saddle me a horse, and I'll lead the way into town." They got him onto the horse, and, in what Scarborough considered a fine display of nerve, Bill rode to the front of the procession. "Although suffering great pain every step, he laughed and joked with the posse, telling of numerous little scrapes in which he had played a part. Whistling and laughing, and shot through and through, he went to meet his fate as if it was a picnic excursion."[50]

The party reached Geronimo two days later, and Walters was taken before Louis Reashau, the U.S. commissioner for the Second Judicial District. Bill waived all legal rights to a requisition hearing. Reashau ordered that the wounded outlaw be delivered into the custody of the U.S. marshal for the Territory of New Mexico and instructed Deputy Milton to carry out the transfer. Three weeks after they had stepped off the train, Milton and Scarborough again boarded the Gila Valley, Globe and Northern, once more bound for New Mexico, this time with Bronco Bill Walters in custody.[51]

CHAPTER 9

Bad Days for Bad Men

"I opened the ball, boys."

Bronco Bill Walters

The Gila Valley, Globe and Northern train that carried Bronco Bill and his captors chugged down the line from Geronimo toward Bowie Station and the junction with the eastbound Southern Pacific. "Instead of the big, bully, wild and ferocious looking desperado I had expected," wrote a journalist who rode along, "before me lay a boy with features like a girl; his once clear blue eyes had been dulled by pain, but no complaint was uttered by those thin lips that remained shut tight, as in death." Making the best of a bad situation, Walters occasionally sipped whiskey, ate peaches, and smoked a cigar. When the train pulled into Solomonville, the county seat of Graham County was filed with people straining to catch a glimpse of the notorious outlaw. Some on the platform pushed close enough to peer into the car where Walters lay on a cot. "Bill," Milton whispered, "do you suppose if I raised up your head you could raise up and say 'Boo!' to these fellows?"[1]

"I will try to say it to the sons of bitches," Walters agreed. "He raised up and said 'B-o-o!!' and those fellows run over each other and some fell clear of the platform." Laughter so overcame Bill that "it nearly killed him."[2]

Bowie residents, every bit as curious as the folks at Solomonville, also turned out to see Walters when the train reached the junction. The lawmen hustled him off the train and into a hotel, away from the gaze of the curious onlookers. After a light supper, Bill spoke with a handful of reporters. "I have been a cowboy for the past twelve years and have traveled over a great part of Arizona, Texas, New Mexico, and Old Mexico. I have had some pretty scary times in those twelve years," he said as he stared directly into the eyes of the attentive journalists. "There is no man that can say I ever murdered anybody. These marks on my neck and shoulder will show that. When I rode into that horse camp last Saturday morning I knew the game had come to a showdown. I knew there was no escape left for me but I thought if I made the fight the other boys might be able to drag it. I opened the ball, boys, and you know the rest."

"Mr. Walters, do you deny these charges that are made against you?" questioned a correspondent for the *Los Angeles Daily Times.*

"Well, by God young feller," Walters coyly glanced in his direction and drawled, "if you'll please tell Bill what he is charged with, he might answer that question for you."[3]

After a restful night, Walters was able to sit up the next morning. He ate breakfast in the hotel's dining room before being escorted back to the depot. Although wobbly, he strolled back and forth along the platform as he and his captors awaited the arrival of the eastbound Southern Pacific. His large black hat hid his eyes from those of the spectators.[4]

The train pulled in from the west, and he was ushered on board. Seated in the day coach, he smiled and waved his hand to the small crowd of onlookers that had turned out. The train carrying Walters and the deputies continued east into New Mexico. When they reached Deming, Bill protested that the lawmen were out to kill him when they put him in room thirteen at the local hotel. He survived the experience, but when he and his escort reached Socorro, they found a mob in a violent mood.[5]

"You go to this door," Milton cried out to Scarborough, "and if any one comes in this door, I will kill him." He turned to the Sheriff Holm Bursum and cautioned, "You keep your people away from this car, we won't stand for any foolishness!" Although the situation remained tense, they were able to continue on to Santa Fe without interference. By the time they reached New Mexico's capital, on Saturday, August 6, agent John Thacker and Walters's longtime nemesis, Cipriano Baca, now a deputy U.S. marshal, had joined them. They handed Bill over to the custody of Marshal Creighton Foraker, and Milton and Scarborough took the return train to Socorro. The Thackers evidently provided the *Daily New Mexican* with an account of the shoot-out that attributed Walters's arrest to young Eugene Thacker. "This claim is about what the Liberal prophesied would be made," editor Don H. Kedzie of the *Western Liberal* gloated, "but it came quicker than the Liberal expected it would." Marshal Foraker, meanwhile, had escorted Walters to the hospital ward at the New Mexico Territorial Penitentiary.[6]

The penitentiary had expanded considerably since Bill's last imprisonment. Most noticeably, a new cellblock wing had been added to the south end of the main building; the wall had been extended proportionately in the same direction. It is doubtful that Walters, still critically wounded, paid much attention to the changes. He had some energy left, however. From his hospital bed, Bill received a reporter from the local newspaper. "Propped up in bed with pillow and fanned by a convict was William Walters, cowboy and bad man from the woolly west, pale, wounded and defiant in appearance," the journalist noted before he posed the first of a series of supercilious questions:

"Are you in pain?" Walters said that he was not, although "it was plainly to be seen that the effort to frame the word hurt him."

"Did you rob the train?"

"There have been many train robberies," Bill replied, "which do you mean?"

"At Belén?"

"No."

"Where were you born?"

"I lived fifteen years in Arizona," he replied, taking pains to falsify his answer.

"Who started the fight at the time of your arrest?"

"I reckon we did."

"Are you guilty?"

"Did you come here to get my confession?"

"No."

"Well, my lawyers will look out for me," the outlaw responded as he handed the reporter the business card of a Solomonville attorney.

"Well, if you were innocent why did you attack the posse?"

After his string of equally supercilious answers, Walters frowned and excused the reporter: "Say, get out of here, leave me alone. I don't want to talk to you." The dismissed journalist left, having learned next to nothing.[7]

Medically, Walters was in a bad way. Medical problems temporarily outweighed his legal difficulties. His surgeons found that his wound was much more severe than first imagined; Scarborough's bullet had smashed the bones in Bill's upper arm and shoulder and left the ligaments badly torn. They removed all of the broken bones and expected, when their patient regained some strength, to amputate his arm above the elbow. Although no artery had been cut, the doctors offered him little hope of survival. They did report that he "endured the suffering when being operated on with a great deal of nerve," and they concurred in the opinion that "the only thing that will pull him through is his meanness." Whether it was their skill or his cussedness that prevailed is uncertain, but within a couple of weeks it was apparent that the arm was mending. Walters would survive, the arm would not be amputated, and he would be able to stand trial. He would also be able to resume operations: "[I] will need the arm to handle the bridle, while [I] work [my] pistol with [my] left."[8]

While Walters recovered from surgery and held court for foolish correspondents, Red Pipkin, still on the lam, recruited men for a new venture. Almost two weeks after the shooting on Black River, Henry Graham encountered Pipkin and a fellow called Sam Dills in New Mexico Territory near the V Cross T headquarters on the Plains of San Agustin. Graham, who spent his life on the Arizona–New Mexico border, had finished gathering horses for the outfit when the two approached on a couple of jaded steeds. The pillow that Red straddled indicated that he still suffered from the wound he received at Black River. Graham inferred that the bullet had grazed Red's hip. More probably, it protected Pipkin's right knee from banging against the saddle's jockey. The two joined the hands for dinner, after which Pipkin announced, "Well, I want to tell you boys we don't want to hurt nobody, but we want some horses and we're gonna take 'em."

"I'll tell you fellers," replied the cowboy running the horse wagon, "These boys is all just got small bunches of horses and cattle. The V Cross T outfit down there, the Red River Cattle Company about four miles down here has got two fellas there afeedin' twelve head of horses. Why don't you fellers go down there and get the grain horses instead of takin' our grass horses?"

Pipkin and Dills took the suggestion to heart and rode on to the V Cross T. When they arrived, they ambled up to a couple of hands about to feed their two horses. "Now boys, we 're gonna take a couple of horses," Pipkin explained. "We don't want to hurt you boys but just keep still and don't go to the house until we get gone."

"We're working for wages," replied one of the hands, "and we can't let these horses go."

"Yes, you can," the redhead fired back, "You can just tell 'em that there's two men come and taken 'em." With that, Pipkin and Dills saddled the two horses and rode off.[9]

Climax Jim, who had witnessed the capture of Walters and ridden for medical assistance, was another probable recruit to Pipkin's cause. Born Rufus Nephew on November 17, 1877, to French Canadians Octave and Celia (née Daneau) Nephew, this District of Columbia native was on the verge of becoming something of a legend. He had abandoned the East Coast for eastern Arizona in the early 1890s with little but a rustler's running iron and had entered the Territorial Penitentiary at Yuma when only seventeen years old. Three years after Pipkin recruited his gang, Climax made offhand allusions to prior train robbery and explained, "Once hunted, a man has to rob a train or steal cattle to buy grub," then promised, "I reckon I've been about as bad as any of them, but after this you'll never hear of me robbing a train or burning out brands." Nephew's statement prompted George Smalley (publisher and editor of the *Tucson Post*) to record in his notebook, "Climax Jim who was not identified *at the time* [authors' emphasis] as a member of [Bronco Bill's] outlaw band, rode alone after that and engaged in cattle rustling."[10]

Evans Coleman reinforced Smalley's belief that Climax had aided Bronco Bill's gang and told historian J. Evetts Haley that Jim had tipped the train robbers that the Santa Fe would be carrying substantial money on its way south from Belén on the day of that holdup. "Piecing together and tieing [*sic*] in little incidents that kind of built up a trail of circumstantial evidence" convinced Coleman "that Climax knew a lot more [about the gang's robberies] than he would tell." Jim, "as we found out later took a very active part in some of those holdups," Coleman wrote on still another occasion. "Yet [Jim] was never suspected, or even suspicioned, and how we found out was [by] connecting up a few brand-burning incidents in which Climax was mixed up."[11]

As Pipkin gathered recruits Sam Dills and Climax Jim, Creighton Foraker reported Bill's arrest and Kid Johnson's death to Attorney General John Griggs with "pleasure." The marshal's delight proved short-lived. During the early hours of the morning of August 14, Red Pipkin led yet another assault on the Santa Fe Pacific train at Grants.[12]

Westbound passenger train no. 1 had pulled out of Albuquerque at five minutes past nine o'clock on the evening of August 13 and chugged west to Grants without incident. Nothing seemed amiss when it pulled out of Grants station three-quarters of an hour past midnight the next morning. However, unseen by those on the platform, three men who had boarded the engine held guns trained on young Mark Bocklett, the engineer, along with his fireman.[13]

Intimidated by the cocked revolver held to his head, the engineer pulled no. 1 forward. The locomotive had barely picked up steam when, about three-quarters of a mile down the road, Bocklett was ordered to stop it. The bandits then herded the engineer and fireman back along the tracks past the mail and express cars, where they were forced to uncouple the passenger coaches. The group returned to the engine as conductor W. H. Barney, concerned about the stop, started forward. A voice from within the express car called out for him to get back with his lantern "quicker than ——." Barney was a veteran conductor and not a fool. He readily complied. Meanwhile, Bocklett pulled on the throttle and moved the shortened train forward.[14]

The locomotive traveled barely two lengths when the owner of the voice in the express car applied the air brakes. Then the air "released and the train was allowed to go forward, only to be stopped again. This was repeated until the desperadoes made the engineer uncouple the air hoses at the engine," a reporter later learned. Bocklett ran the train west another mile until one of the outlaws ordered a final stop. Two of the bandits walked to the express car, fired into the air, and demanded entry. Inside, the omnipresent Charles Fowler waited with guard A. C. Mott and messengers Charles J. Goodman and Elbert H. Comfort. They answered with a volley of their own. The foursome "put up such a hot fight that [the bandits] did not get into the express car, and gave it up for a bad job and left." The terse Wells, Fargo account understated the action. Unable to shoot directly at the outlaws for fear that a bullet might strike the engineer or fireman, the defenders of the express car were disadvantaged. The bandits faced no such restriction, but fared little better. They exchanged thirty to forty shots with Fowler and company before withdrawing with nothing to show for their efforts. "Strange to say," a reporter with the *Los Angeles Daily Times* opined, "no one was shot, although the firing was at short range."[15]

After the bandits' flight, the Wells, Fargo people conducted a search and turned up Bocklett and his fireman hidden under the embankment, where they had been ordered to remain by the fleeing outlaws. The hunt soon also "disclosed a sack containing four giant powder cartridges, primed, fused, and sewed up in pieces of gunny sack, ten pieces of Hercules No. 2 powder, a coil of fuse, a package of caps, and two empty paper shells for a ten-gauge shotgun." Significantly, the dynamite was found in almost the same place that it had been secreted following the March 29 holdup. Although the find suggested that the same gang did the work, it also posed a puzzle that the *Rocky Mountains News* was quick to point out: "'Broncho Bill' is in the penitentiary, 'Kid' Johnson has been killed once, and 'Black Jack' [Christian] about six times since the successful robbery at Grants[;] it is hard to say who will be credited with the job."[16]

Fowler telegraphed Deputy Newcomer in Albuquerque, but no Bernalillo County posses formed without assurance from the Santa Fe that expenses would be covered. John and

Eugene Thacker, joined by Valencia County deputy Boleslo Romero, reached Albuquerque on the evening of August 15 and continued west to Grants to organize a pursuit. The senior Thacker believed four men, led by Red Pipkin, had tried to rob the train.[17]

Pipkin and his band briefly returned to the Eagle Creek region. One day during the first week in September, three of them rode into the headquarters of Joe Hampson's Double Circle Ranch. As they approached, Pipkin dismounted and confronted Joel A. "Joe" Terrell, the range foreman, and a couple of his stock drivers, Jackson "Jack" Cornett and Henry A. Banta. "We want some fresh horses, have you any in the corral here?"

"No, the horses are all in the pasture," Terrell responded.

Pipkin and one of the ranch hands rode to the pasture, while his two companions stayed to guard the house. Red helped himself to three horses and returned. The outlaws saddled up; Pipkin exchanged his old saddle for Terrell's new one, then turned to the foreman and threatened, "Both of us cannot live in the country together and we will give you three days to get out." The three outlaws then rode off in no particular hurry.[18]

Tucson's George Smalley later wrote, "Bad men all stand together as a rule." He maintained that Terrell and van Armin "were going to testify against 'Climax Jim' and others at the next term of the court, but the men refused to be frightened." Smalley's assertion was only partially accurate. Although Pipkin might well have attempted to dissuade testimony against Climax Jim, and Terrell and van Armin later did testify later in a case brought against the affable rustler, there were no outstanding indictments against Nephew in mid-September 1898 and there was no need for their testimony. "Both men refused to be frightened," Smalley continued. "They stayed in the country."[19]

Kedzie, the colorful *Western Liberal* editor, was quick to add: "The Liberal is not informed as to what these gentlemen intend to do, but from what it knows of them it does not think they intend to desert the ranch. They are not the kind of men to be scared out. It is very likely they will return to their ranch, properly prepared for Mr. Pipkin, and when they get through with him he will be in a condition to enable them to receive the reward offered for his useless carcass."[20]

Kedzie's observation proved correct. Joe Terrell did not get out. In fact, he went on to become the Double Circle's general manager. Pipkin, on the other hand, did get out—and soon. Prepared for any encounter with the redheaded outlaw and his companions, a posse composed of George, Ben, and Dan Olney, joined by John Epley, Frank Dysert, Joe T. McKinney, E. A. Van Arnim, and Joe Terrell left Solomonville for the Hampson ranch. "Pipkin has undoubtedly flown to parts unknown for the present," the *Western Liberal* opined. "But," in the newspaper's opinion, "these men will make it known to friends of Pipkins [*sic*] in that section that if any harm comes to E. A. Van Arnim or Joe Terrell in the discharge of their duties, that this county will not be large enough to hold them. It will undoubtedly have a good effect and we hope it will forever quiet the disturbance that has been brewing in that isolated section of the country for the last few months."[21]

In that live-and-let-live region of the Southwest, Pipkin had violated the cardinal rule; he rustled local stock and no longer deserved the sanctuary characteristically offered by the Black River country and its people. Cowhands that "rode for the brand," in this case the Double Circle's mark, were prepared to surrender him to authorities if the opportunity arose. To forestall any future disturbance, Double Circle's owner Joe Hampson hired George Scarborough and a posse to "guard the ranch and his interests" until the end of the late fall round up. With the delivery of the cattle to Geronimo at the onset of November, Hampson discharged Scarborough. Yet, reports that Pipkin and a partner remained in the Black River country prompted Scarborough, his son Ed, and several others to return to that region. On November 25, they overtook a suspect armed with a Winchester and "riding a splendid horse." When called upon to halt, the man seized his Winchester and started sending bullets toward the makeshift posse. A running fight followed. A bullet fired by George Scarborough struck the fellow in the shoulder and dropped him from his horse. He was taken to Fort Apache for treatment where, although he used the name Johnny Williams, he was identified as one of the Woods brothers who worked cattle for Graham County merchant James N. Porter.[22]

Meanwhile, Marshal Foraker, also anxious to round up the remnants of the Bronco Bill gang, telegraphed the attorney general to finance Cipriano Baca "at five dollars per day not to exceed thirty days to go with posse hired by Wells Fargo Express Co."[23]

While lawmen searched Arizona and New Mexico for Pipkin, the conjecture of the *Western Liberal* proved accurate; Red had fled the region and had ridden to Moab, Utah. Local tradition indicates that Moab's citizens were in the midst of organizing a posse to run down a gang of rustlers. Red joined the posse, but when they overtook the rustlers, "they were met by an unanticipatedly hot reception." The pursuers became the pursued, but Pipkin slipped into a thicket and, as the rustlers rode past, he shot two of them with his rifle. Stunned, the outlaws turned and rode back toward their stolen stock; Red shot two more, and the fifth rustler fled.[24]

Failing to find Pipkin in western New Mexico, Cipriano Baca returned to Santa Fe. Walters had recovered sufficiently from his wound by the onset of December, and Baca escorted him to Socorro for trial. On December 6, a Socorro County grand jury returned three murder indictments against Bronco Bill. That same day in Santa Fe, at the request of Deputy Will Loomis, Commissioner John P. Victory issued an alias warrant to apprehend Bronco Bill, William Johnson, Jim Burnett,

Dan Pipkin, and Ed Colter for an unlawful attempt to rob the U.S. mail and for an assault on R. A. Wilson, the mail clerk, during the March 29 robbery at Grants.[25]

Judge Humphrey B. Hamilton of Socorro had sentenced Walters to a thirty-day jail term only one year previously. Now he accepted the role of Bronco Bill's defense counsel. His client was arraigned on the murder charges on December 12 in the courtroom of Charles A. Leland, judge of the Fifth Judicial District Court. Bill entered a not guilty plea. The next day, he added the colorful and controversial Elfego Baca to his defense team. Historian Larry D. Ball has pointed out the irony that accompanied Baca's selection. An Hispanic whose notoriety depended in large part on his renowned shoot-out with Anglo cowboys, Baca would now rise to defend an Anglo cowboy for killing two Hispanos and a Navajo Indian.[26]

Twenty-four hours after joining the defense team, Baca argued before Judge Leland that public prejudice against the defendant would prevent the impaneling of a fair and impartial jury in Socorro County and entered a motion for a change of venue to Chaves County, predominantly Anglo. Leland granted the motion and set a trial date of March 15, 1899. Walters was returned to the penitentiary in Santa Fe to be held in the hospital to await trial.

As the March date approached, the prosecution sought to subpoena witnesses on behalf of the territory. On February 20, Judge Leland had issued subpoenas for fifteen witnesses. Eight days later, however, "because of a lack of funds with which to prosecute said cause[s] at the March 1899 term of [the Chaves County District] Court," Leland was forced to issue an order to recall the witnesses. Lack of funds delayed Bill's fair and speedy trial.[27]

While Walters languished in prison, the search for Red Pipkin intensified. San Juan County officials soon learned that the local hero was a fugitive, and Willard George William "Dick"

Butt, the county sheriff, took Pipkin into custody at Moab on March 7, 1899. Wells, Fargo agent John Thacker sped to Moab, took custody of Pipkin, and hauled him to Winnemucca, Nevada, on March 12, and, by coincidence, temporarily jailed him with Leslie Bowie and James Shaw, two good-for-nothings wrongly accused of complicity in the Southern Pacific holdup at Humboldt on July 14, 1898. Meanwhile, after having been notified of Pipkin's capture, Marshal Foraker wrote to Eugene Thacker on March 9 and informed him, "Red is well and saucy, is grumbling about the heat. Broncho is in bad shape, I fear that he will hardly last until he is tried."[28]

Back in Graham County, Arizona, where Red's rustling had occurred, the *Guardian* represented Pipkin's capture as "a sure indication that the days of the outlaw are passing." The redhead "has had every advantage on his side for making good his escape, yet the officers have followed him for months through a country almost impossible to penetrate and captured him within 1000 miles of where the first fight occurred." Although the *Guardian* overstated its case, the capture was a sure indication that Wells, Fargo and, more especially, John Thacker had not lost any doggedness. On March 15 Eugene Thacker reached Winnemucca from Tucson with the federal warrant. Pipkin acknowledged his identity and chose not to fight extradition; young Thacker escorted him back to New Mexico Territory.[29]

Thacker and Pipkin reached Albuquerque, and the agent handed his prisoner over to Marshal Foraker on March 18. Two days later, Red waived examination before United States commissioner H. R. Whiting and was bound over to the United States grand jury on the charge of obstructing the mail. Indicted gang member Jim Burnett had almost certainly been killed by his cohorts; William "Kid" Johnson was certainly dead; young Ed Colter had long since been sent out of the area by his family; Bill Walters remained incarcerated in the

Wiley E. Jones, Graham County, Arizona's district attorney, ca. 1898. Courtesy Graham County Historical Society.

New Mexico Territorial Penitentiary and awaited trial; and Daniel "Red" Pipkin was now jailed in Albuquerque. The Bronco Bill gang would ride no more.[30]

Red faced the certainty of a federal charge of attempted robbery of the U.S. mail, the probability of New Mexico charges of train robbery, and the possibility of a murder charge—the latter two both capital offenses. Additionally, Wiley E. Jones, the Graham County district attorney, had obtained an Arizona indictment on the charge of grand larceny for the rustled Double Circle horses and stolen saddle. The Arizona court issued a bench warrant for Pipkin's arrest, and Jones petitioned Charles Henry Akers, secretary of the territory and Arizona's acting governor, to request a requisition for the outlaw from New Mexico's governor, Miguel Otero.[31]

As Pipkin's legal quagmire thickened, Bronco Bill's was barely less murky. On September 2, lead attorney Hamilton entered a motion to return the venue from Chaves County to Socorro County as "the grounds set forth and contained within the original motion for a change of venue have been removed, and [Walters] believes that the County of Socorro is free from exceptions and he believes he can have a fair and impartial trial therein." Mindful of Chaves County's fiscal problems, Judge Leland promptly granted the motion and set a trial date of November 23, 1899.[32]

Almost four weeks after Hamilton's motion, the grand jury in Albuquerque heard the testimony of Charles Fowler and the father-and-son team of Thacker and Thacker on September 28. Their testimony resulted in the indictment of Pipkin, Bronco Bill, and the others on charges of attempted robbery of the U.S. mail and felonious assault on the mail's custodian, R. A. Wilson, during the first Grants attempt. The court set a trial date for the March 1900 term. In lieu of a $2,500 bond, ninety-three-year-old Aser Pipkin put up his farm as security, as did other family members and friends.

The court freed Red on October 9, but his release did him little good. With the arrival of a requisition from Arizona, Sheriff Thomas S. Hubbell arrested Red on the new charge. But, in the opinion of Edward Bartlett, the territory's solicitor general, Hubbell held Pipkin "without any authority of law."[33]

On November 23, with Pipkin jailed in Albuquerque, the Socorro courthouse filled with spectators for the trial of William "Bronco Bill" Walters. If they expected a show, Walters disappointed them. To avoid a protracted trial, and to avoid the hangman, Walters changed his plea to guilty of second-degree murder in the killing of Daniel Bustamante (case no. 1691). Judge Leland dismissed the charges in the remaining two cases (nos. 1692 and 1693) and pronounced a sentence of confinement within the penitentiary "at hard labor for and during the full term of the natural life of the said William Walters."[34]

William "Bronco Bill" Walters at the time of his December 14, 1899, admission to the New Mexico Territorial Penitentiary. New Mexico Department of Corrections Glass Negative Collection, New Mexico State Records Center and Archives, Santa Fe.

Almost three weeks later, on December 14, Charles F. Blackington, the Socorro County sheriff, returned veteran inmate Walters to the New Mexico Territorial Penitentiary. Bill joined an assortment of particularly violent prisoners. About 27.5 percent of New Mexico's prison population had been convicted of violent crimes, and one-half of those convictions had resulted from the crime of murder in various degrees. Entered on the records as prisoner number 1282, Walters fit right in. His sentence dictated that the red brick structure at Santa Fe would be his home for the remainder of his days.[35]

Walters's future, though not pleasant to anticipate, was assured. Pipkin's, on the other hand, remained uncertain.

CHAPTER 10

Stars and Bars

"I'm a peace officer now, and a damned good one."

Daniel "Red" Pipkin

With Bronco Bill sentenced to spend the rest of his life in the New Mexico penitentiary, and Ed Colter, Red Burnett, and Kid Johnson out of commission for one reason or another, only Red Pipkin faced an Albuquerque courtroom appearance for the attempted robbery of the United States mail. A conviction carried with it a sentence of imprisonment at hard labor for not less than two or more than ten years. The Territory of Arizona also sought his presence to answer a grand larceny indictment. Threatened by these and possibly other legal entanglements, Pipkin hired the services of a high-powered Albuquerque attorney, Bernard Shandon Rodey.

A native of County Mayo, Ireland, Rodey had immigrated with his parents to Quebec, Canada, in 1862. He studied law in Boston and arrived in Albuquerque in 1881 as the private secretary to the general manager of the Atlantic and Pacific Railroad, later the Santa Fe Pacific. Admitted to the New Mexico bar in 1883, Rodey opened a practice in Albuquerque and served as city attorney in 1887 and 1888. He won a seat in the territorial senate in 1889, and soon authored the statute that created the University of New Mexico and fixed its Albuquerque location.

Attorney Rodey's first task was to dissuade New Mexico governor Miguel Otero from granting Arizona Territory's requisition for Pipkin. Otero was already resisting Arizona's effort to extradite notorious train robber Tom Ketchum, who had been captured and held in New Mexico following a failed effort to hold up the Colorado and Southern Railroad at Folsom, New Mexico, on August 16, 1899. Ketchum was also Arizona's principal suspect in the July 2, 1899, murders of R. M. "Mack" Rogers and Clinton D. Wingfield, co-owners of the old sutler's store at Camp Verde, an abandoned military fort in Yavapai County. Authorities there had a rope awaiting his return. Otero, however, was determined to stop train robbery within New Mexico, to hang the convicted train robber as an object lesson, and rejected the Ketchum requisition on November 14, 1899. He assured Arizona governor Nathan O. Murphy that New Mexico's courts and juries would uphold the territorial statute of 1887, as well as the sentence that mandated convicted train robbers "shall suffer the punishment of death."[1]

The next day, New Mexico's solicitor general, Edward Bartlett, judged the Arizona Territory requisition for Pipkin to be "fatally defective." It lacked assurances that the extradition of Pipkin would meet the ends of Arizona justice; it failed to stipulate that there was sufficient evidence to convict him; and it neglected to affirm that the named agent, Ben Clark (sheriff of Graham County), was the proper authority and had no private interest in the case.[2]

The day after Otero received Bartlett's opinion in the Pipkin case, lawyer Rodey made a move to keep Pipkin within federal jurisdiction and out of the hands of both Arizona and New Mexico territories. He presented Otero with new arguments: the United States had not waived its right to Pipkin; the rights of the United States trumped those of a territory; and under the common law, the United States held Red to answer a charge graver than the Arizona allegation of horse stealing. Rodey also quoted Otero's own statement concerning Tom Ketchum from the previous Saturday's *New Mexican*: "It is against public policy to turn over to another Territory a person charged with a crime in New Mexico." As that was the governor's stated position with respect to Ketchum, surely it must also apply to Pipkin, Rodey argued.[3]

Arizona prosecutor Wiley Jones swiftly complied with Bartlett's demands. All the same, Bartlett labored overtime and again advised Otero that the requisition remained irregular. Charles Akers had signed it without any title, yet the stationery had styled Akers as "Acting Governor." As it happened, he was the secretary of the territory, but it was Harry R. Tritle, the assistant secretary of the territory, who attested to the requisition. Therefore, the requisition was not "signed by the Governor, by the Secretary of the Territory acting as Governor, nor by the Secretary of the Territory" as required. Moreover, the pedantic solicitor general, also in receipt of Rodey's arguments, concluded that Otero lacked authority to hand Pipkin over to any other jurisdiction without the consent of the U.S. attorney.[4]

U.S. Attorney William Burr Childers soon forwarded his own carefully crafted equivocation: "I do not feel that I am called upon to consent to the removal of 'Red' Pipkin to Arizona," and suggested, "Instructions might be had from the Attorney General of the United States." Bartlett forwarded Childers' letter to Otero, showing that the U.S. attorney "distinctly refuses to give his consent." On November 30, Governor Otero finally decided that, since Arizona sought to try Pipkin on a lesser charge, he would not surrender the redhead until the disposal of the attempted robbery case then pending in federal jurisdiction.[5]

From his Wells, Fargo office in San Francisco, John N. Thacker wrote to Marshal Foraker on March 6, 1900, to learn if Walters would testify against Pipkin. Foraker replied that he would consult with Childers about getting Bronco to testify. That same day, Childers sought subpoenas for the prosecution's witnesses in Pipkin's forthcoming trial, set for March 20. Considering that the government charged Pipkin with attempted mail robbery at Grants on March 29, 1898, the list was curious at best. In spite of Thacker's interest, Walters's name was curiously absent from the list. Eugene Thacker, who had been present at the Black River shoot-out and had returned Pipkin for trial, had no firsthand knowledge of the attempted robbery but was subpoenaed. Double Circle cowboys Henry Banta and J. E. Howard were also present at the Black River shoot-out, and Joe Terrell had suffered the loss of three horses, but, again, they had no first-hand knowledge of the train robbery. Nonetheless, Childers wanted them to testify. Monte Slaughter and Claire Peery, known to be close friends of Pipkin's, could have hardly improved the government's case. Pete Slaughter's oldest son, Monterey "Monte" Slaughter, had worked hard honing his quarrelsome reputation, while Peery, Pipkin's onetime mentor, could generally be found in Slaughter's company. Yet, the prosecutor wanted their testimony as well. What evidence the prosecution hoped to obtain from T. W. Jones, John Brown, and a "Mexican at San Rafael" remains unknown.[6]

Only one of the subpoenaed witnesses could offer any testimony directly relevant to the attempted robbery—Charles Fowler. Surviving documents, moreover, indicate that Marshal Foraker served subpoenas only on Thacker, Fowler, Banta, and Terrell. This may go some distance toward explaining why Judge Jonathan W. Crumpacker deemed the evidence insufficient to secure a conviction and dismissed the case.[7]

Pipkin still faced probable territorial charges of train robbery and possible second-degree murder indictments for the Vigil, Bustamante, and Wuerro killings. Conviction of the former promised a broken neck or strangulation. Conviction of the latter demanded a sentence that could range from seven years to life imprisonment. No longer under federal control, Red readily waived extradition and voluntarily accompanied Graham County undersheriff Ben Olney, to Arizona, free of New Mexico's jurisdiction and the possibility of sharing Ketchum's fate. Tom Ketchum would be hanged on April 26, 1901.[8]

Jailed in the Solomonville *calabozo,* which was conveniently attached to the courthouse, Pipkin shared a reunion with Climax Jim, also a guest of Graham County. On April 4, 1900, Sheriff Clark marched the two to the courtroom of Fletcher Morris Doan, judge of the Second Judicial District from 1897 to statehood in 1912. Known for his strict and sometimes tyrannical manner on the bench, Doan required that spectators, as well as defendants, jurors, witnesses, and attorneys wear coats within his courtroom, even on the hottest summer day. Climax Jim heard Doan order his continued incarceration to await delivery to the sheriff of Apache County to face further rustling charges. Then it was Pipkin's turn to stand before the judge.[9]

Arraigned on a grand larceny charge, Pipkin entered a plea of not guilty, and his attorneys entered a motion for a continuance to allow time to gather witnesses. The court returned Red to the custody of Sheriff Clark, who hauled the redhead back to Graham County's jail to rejoin Climax. Sometime during the day, the two probably learned that only the day before, outlaws had ambushed George Scarborough at Triangle Springs, less than fifty miles south of Springerville in the Chiricahua Mountains. He died from his wounds on April 5. Red could hardly have been expected to mourn Scarborough's passing, but at least Graham County's guest had an airtight alibi.[10]

When the trial date of April 13 arrived, so, too, did attorney Rodey to assist Solomonville's Childress Ellis Moorman, a former Graham County's district attorney. The court continued the case to the October term. Monte Slaughter, Claire Peery, and Albert H. Pratt of Springerville stood Pipkin's bond. They supplied a letter from the Apache County treasurer, who

Graham County Courthouse, Solomonville, Arizona, 1900. The jail and yard is on the far right side. A. N. Segal, *Souvenir of Graham County, Arizona: A Collection of 138 Graham County Views* (ca. 1905). Courtesy of the Bev and Kevin Mulkins Collection, Tucson.

attested to their net worth. Twice the court ruled the instrument flawed, however. Each time, Red's attorney's returned it to Apache County for correction. The third effort proved successful; the court freed Pipkin on one thousand dollars' bail on July 16.[11]

Pipkin and Moorman were in the Second Judicial District Court on October 11 to hear Judge Doan set a trial date of October 15. Rodey, a Republican and the attorney of record, had, in the meantime, thrown his hat into the ring in quest of the New Mexico delegate seat in Congress. His ultimately successful campaign was in its final days, and he had to withdraw from the case. On October 15, Pipkin arrived in the company of Albuquerque attorney Thomas N. Wilkinson. The newly hired Wilkinson requested a further continuance, but an impatient Judge Doan denied the motion. Wilkinson then moved for a change of venue. Again, Judge Doan ruled against the defense. Prosecutor Wiley Jones announced his readiness, and Wilkinson could do little but allow that "he was as near ready as he could be at this term of court."[12]

During jury selection, Wilkinson challenged every juror for cause. An irritated Judge Doan accepted seven challenges, overruled twenty-four, and seated a jury. Wiley Jones first called Joe Terrell to the stand. Following the range foreman's testimony and that of Double Circle hands Henry Banta and Jack Cornett, Doan ordered the court in recess until later that evening. When the trial reconvened, Jones recalled Cornett and then rested.[13]

The defense opened its case by calling Graham County rancher and outlaw confederate Allen Chitty to the witness box. Double Circle cowboy George Tankersley and Morenci resident William G. Eusor, a Texas-born stock raiser, followed him. Pipkin also testified on his own behalf, but there was little that he or his attorney could do to impeach the testimony of three eyewitnesses. Judge Doan then instructed the jury, and the jurors retired to deliberate.[14]

The jury returned the next morning and asked to hear the instructions repeated. Judge Doan recited them, and the jury again retired. Later in the day, the jury members returned to the courtroom, and foreman Harry L. Castle read their verdict—guilty. A polling of the members followed; then Judge Doan ordered Pipkin into the custody of Sheriff Clark to await his sentence.[15]

Pipkin returned to the courtroom on October 25. His attorney entered a motion for a new trial. Judge Doan denied the motion and then asked Red, "Have you anything to say or legal cause to show why the judgment of this court should not now be pronounced against you?"

Pipkin replied, "I have nothing to say."

Doan delivered a stern lecture and then handed down a stiff sentence—ten years imprisonment in the Arizona Territorial Prison at Yuma. Pipkin entered through the prison's sally port on October 30. Prisoner number 1695 posed before the camera, had his hair shorn, took a bath, put on the prison uniform of horizontal black and yellow stripes, and was again photographed. Admission documents reveal that the redheaded, hazel-eyed, self-described cattleman stood five feet, seven and a half inches tall and weighed 155 pounds. He acknowledged that he drank and smoked but avoided opium. Rather than an Arkansas nativity and a New Mexico education, he curiously claimed a Texas birth and schooling. Red kept his record clean, and, with time off for good behavior, he walked out seven years later on April 24, 1907.[16]

Pipkin traveled to Fort Apache on Arizona's San Carlos Reservation, where he got a job with Bob Merrill, who ran the slaughterhouse. Red helped to kill and dress the beef for delivery to the cavalry, and, although he ate with the Merrill family, years of incarceration or fear of entrapment gave him a yearning for open spaces—he slept in a bedroll in the brush near the Merrill home. Some nights he regaled Merrill's children with fanciful tales about stage robberies in California,

Arizona Territorial Penitentiary at Yuma, seen from the west bank of the Colorado River. Original photograph in the collection of the authors.

Daniel M. "Red" Pipkin on his arrival at the Arizona Territorial Prison, Yuma, October 30, 1900. Courtesy Yuma Territorial Prison State Historic Park.

and about how he and his partner "would start at San Francisco and rob four express companies heading south. [We] would go into Mexico, sell [our] horses, and catch a ship for Hawaii. [We] would live like kings for a while. [We] would save enough

Pipkin after processing at the territorial prison. Courtesy Yuma Territorial Prison State Historic Park.

money to get back to San Francisco, get new horses and saddles, then hit the four express companies again."[17]

About 1909, Pipkin moved to Farmington, New Mexico, where he lived a year with his brother Polk before he traveled on to Gallup to work at a variety of jobs. He also married around 1911, but his wife, Katy, died a few years later. Horace Earl Pipkin remembered that his uncle "was a guard for a saw mill Co. near Thoreau New Mex. And while there a fellow stole a saddle and a horse from the Co. Red followed him and overtook him the next day. Red retrieved the horse and saddle, gave the thief $5.00 and sent him on his way afoot."[18]

Red eventually settled in the mining community of Allison, a couple of miles west of Gallup. Founded as a company town by the Victor American Coal Company and named for official Fletcher J Allison, the town was sold to the Diamond Coal Company in 1917. In an ironic turnabout, Pipkin became a guntoter, for Diamond Coal, the McKinley County undersheriff to Sheriff Robert L. "Bob" Roberts, and a stalwart of McKinley County's Republican Party.[19]

One day Prime Coleman, an old Apache County acquaintance, encountered Pipkin, sporting a star and wearing a six-shooter on the streets of Gallup. "Why, hello, Red. What the hell are you doin' here?"

"I'm a peace officer now, and a damned good one," replied Pipkin. "Come on, let's have a drink. I'll tell you about it."[20]

As Pipkin settled in New Mexico and pinned on a shield, several people heard from their old comrade, Bronco Bill. On September 24, 1909, Walters wrote from prison to his former boss, Henry Brock:

> Dear old friend. My friends are going to try to get me out of this and I don't know but you can help me too. You will remember that the talk was made by the officers before my arrest that they would kill me and make the arrest after they was shore [*sic*] that I was dead.

And if you know such to be the case you can do me all the good in the world by writing Mr. J. W. Raynolds, the superintendent. What we are trying to do is to show that the men who were after me had no intention of arresting me but to shoot me down wherever found. My friends are going to take my case up to the board of parole October 9 and there is not much time to spare. The officials here are doing all they can for me but they advise me to write someone that knew the case and have him write to the super and I learned your address and thought it possible that you had herd [*sic*] this talk and [would] write the people for me.
Yours in haste,
W. Walters
/s/ Bronco Bill[21]

Walters claimed that "officers before my arrest [had said] that they would kill me and make the arrest after they was shore that I was dead." Brock wrote to superintendent James Wallace Raynolds and agreed that Bill's assertion "was the general opinion." It is certain that Brock was not the only individual from whom Walters sought help, as some powerful personalities pressed for Bronco's release. Little more than a month after Bill wrote to Brock, Governor George Curry received an appeal from U.S. Senator Joseph W. Bailey (D-Tex.). Although apologetic for repeatedly bothering Curry, Bailey stressed, "When my friends are in trouble I must do my utmost to help them," and informed the governor that Walters was "related to some of the best people in Texas, who are my warm friends." Those relations sought Walters's release. By New Mexico's standards, his imprisonment had been unusually lengthy.[22]

Between the opening of the New Mexico Territorial Penitentiary in 1884 and New Mexico's statehood in 1912, seven years and nine months was the average length of confinement for a life sentence. After nearly ten years behind bars, Walters had already served more time than most lifers. His good conduct, moreover, had earned him an appointment as a hospital steward the previous March 15, 1909. Perhaps Bronco Bill deserved a pardon. To reach a determination, the governor contacted Frank W. Clancy, New Mexico's attorney general, in quest of information that might allow him to honor Bailey's appeal. Clancy, in turn, contacted Superintendent Raynolds, who professed to know nothing of the details of Walters's crime. Clancy also wrote Harry M. Dougherty, the Socorro lawyer who had previously served as Socorro County's district attorney. Dougherty had been aboard the Santa Fe train at the time of the Belén robbery. Wells, Fargo had also employed him to assist in Walters's prosecution. Yet he provided the attorney general with little more than a vague outline of Bronco Bill's career. John E. Griffith, Dougherty's partner and the current district attorney, did little better. He supplied Clancy with meager details concerning Walters's 1896 larceny case and a few specifics about the 1899 murder charges. The attorney general also received a brief communication from Bronco's old nemesis, Holm Olaf Bursum, who had served a spell (1899–1906) as penitentiary superintendent and Bronco Bill's keeper. Bursum's reply, summarized by Clancy, stressed that "Bronco Bill never had a good reputation, and that his career in New Mexico never was creditable, and expressing his belief that his residence would be more satisfactory, either inside of the penitentiary or outside of the territory." Based on the sparse information gathered, clemency didn't seem to be in order. Attorney General Clancy explained to the governor, "[I] would much prefer to recommend the pardon of this prisoner if I could do so, but from the investigation I have made, I cannot discover that he is a proper subject for executive clemency."[23]

Governor Curry wanted to oblige Senator Bailey. He could turn to nothing in Clancy's report, however, that offered justification. On January 10, 1910, Curry wrote Bailey that he found it "impossible to extend executive clemency to [Walters] at this time," but hinted that Bill had been a "good prisoner in recent years, and it may be possible to have him paroled later." The governor's rejection of Walters's petition for parole closed one avenue for release; the dejected inmate turned to another. The *Santa Fe New Mexican* broke the news on April 17, 1911.[24]

"Bronco Bill is at large! That noted murderer, train robber, crack shot, former cow boy of Grant County and desperado, with a more thrilling history than Diamond Dick or some other heroes of the novel library, and whose face has the half amused smile 'that won't come off,' made his escape from the penitentiary sometime last night and in a thoroughly thrilling manner worthy of the man and his career." Kinch Mullins, convicted for the murder of Tony Stauffacher and serving a ninety-nine-year sentence from Chaves County (no. 1726), had escaped with Bill.[25]

Walters later explained the reason for his action. He had "heard a few days ago there was nothing doing on the pardon."

> It was spring; what little sunlight leaked down there into the prison yard seemed to get into my bones; the birds were singing around the place and I saw some sparrows puttin' up a nest way up on a drain pipe. It was too much for Bronco. I says to myself, "Bronco, let's see what we can do for ourselves; let's climb over the wall and see if we can beat 'em to Mexico.
>
> I took another prisoner who wanted to go, got a ladder and stuck it up against the wall. It was Sunday night, a trifle cloudy and I kept in the shade.
>
> There was a guard on the wall and I thought he saw me several times. He walked into one of the houses on top of the wall and I started away. I kept myself between him and another cupola that was on the wall. Once on the wall I tied a rope and slid down outside.

> The other man came down too. I had only one good arm and the rope cut into my wrist almost to the bone. It made me wince but I kept sliding until I struck the ground outside and then I ran. The other man sprained his ankle and decided to return and gave up. I let him go.[26]

Mullins's decision to join in the flight did Walters no favor; only when Kinch came back did the penitentiary's inattentive guards learn of the escape. An official announcement soon followed: "No. 1282, William Walters, alias 'Bronco Bill,' escaped from the New Mexico penitentiary, the night of the 16th of April 1911. Age about 43 or 44 years old, brown hair, blue eyes, face very much seamed. Right arm from the shoulder down absolutely useless from gun shot wounds."[27]

With an eclectic assortment of items—forty dollars, some letters, a few photographs of his niece, and a selection of surgical tools—Walters headed southwest toward Cerrillos, where he intended to catch a train bound toward Mexico. After a walk of close to twenty miles, he struck the Santa Fe line near Waldo early the next morning (April 17). Rethinking his escape route, he walked nearly fifty miles farther along the tracks past Santo Domingo Pueblo, Algodones, and Bernalillo to reach Albuquerque on Wednesday night, April 19. He hoped to enjoy anonymity. "I only knew two people here who would likely recognize me," Walters later told a reporter. "One was Ben Williams of the Santa Fe (Railway); I was afraid of meeting up with Ben. I had $40 in cash and knew I could get through all right." Walters did not mention just how he had come to know Williams.[28]

French-born Ben Williams had settled in Las Cruces, New Mexico, at the onset of the 1890s and worked variously as a deputy U.S. marshal, constable, Doña Ana County deputy sheriff, New Mexico Cattle Association inspector, and collector for the Singer Sewing Machine Company. He also enjoyed the dubious distinction of having once been shot by Albert Fall, the future New Mexico senator and principal in the Teapot Dome scandal. In the late 1890s, Williams took a position as special agent for the Santa Fe Railway at La Junta, Colorado, and transferred to Albuquerque about 1910. He later operated the Ben Williams Detective Agency in El Paso. Williams and Walters must have encountered each other in or near Las Cruces before Bronco Bill's capture and imprisonment.[29]

The night he reached Albuquerque, Walters ate supper at the Mint Restaurant on Second Street and later took a room at a rooming house on South First Street. "I was worn out from the long walk. I lay in bed a long time wondering what I had best do."[30]

> I'll admit the old temptation was strong in me to go back to the old life. I knew none of the old boys were left, but I kept feeling like I ought to go out and buy me a couple of good guns and make a run for it. I used to do it that way, and until they plugged me in this shoulder, I usually made good.
>
> I thought it over for maybe an hour, and then I says to myself, "No bronco, you've been mixed up in the killing game long enough. No more guns for you. If you get away you win. If they get the drop on you, it's back to the penitentiary.
>
> I rolled over and went to sleep, and it was late when I woke up. I got a snack to eat, but I didn't parade around any, and I kept my lame arm from swinging all I could.[31]

That Thursday morning, April 20, Walters again headed south. A fourteen-mile stroll brought him to Isleta and the Santa Fe Pacific junction depot. Isleta was also the home of Charles Mainz, the Santa Fe's special officer. In recent years, the depredations of hoboes on the Rio Grande Division of the Santa Fe had necessitated that the company take precautions to protect employees and passengers. Isleta was, in the words of the *Topeka State Journal,* "the grand rendezvous of the great unwashed," and Mainz was "the special officer who leads the strenuous life along the junction [and] keeps them moving pretty fast through that point." The officer spied Walters. It was evident that the well-dressed, well-mannered, and soft-spoken Walters was not one of the knights of the road. Mainz nevertheless thought it his duty to strike up a conversation with the stranger. Bill, who gave the appearance of a cattleman, said his name was Woods and explained that he and a partner intended take up land in the Rio Grande Valley. Something about the story tweaked a suspicious nerve ending. Mainz asked Walters to walk to his cabin near Isleta Pueblo, only a couple of blocks east of the depot. Walters, who was doubtless walked out, could do little but accept the invitation. When they arrived, Mainz told Bill to remove his coat and sit down. As Walters did so, his useless right arm became obvious. The officer's swift search revealed that "Woods" carried a Plaza National Bank (Santa Fe) deposit book in the name of William Walters.[32]

"I saw the game was up, and admitted who I was," Bill later told a reporter. "Just for a minute I wished for a gun. I'm glad I didn't have one; I don't want to kill. I won't try it again. There isn't any use to running from an officer without a gun, and I've quit using 'em. I will never use another gun as long as I live. I have killed enough in my time, and I will never kill another man. I could have fought my way out of New Mexico, but I've quit the bad game for good."[33]

With Walters arrested and shackled, Mainz and his prisoner later boarded the northbound number 8 and quietly slipped into Albuquerque shortly after seven thirty o'clock that evening. They walked several blocks from the Santa Fe depot to Ruppe's drug store at 807 South Fourth Street in the Barelas neighborhood, where Mainz telephoned Deputy Fred B. Heyn to alert him to their arrival. He then escorted Walters to a cell in the Bernalillo County jail. The next morning, April 21, authorities returned Bill to his familiar cell in Santa Fe to resume serving his sentence. When asked if he feared retribution, the cheerful convict replied, "No I don't reckon they'll hold it against me when I get back in prison. I always treated the officers right and I don't see that they can get mad now, just because I took a notion to leave."[34]

Walters's assumption proved correct, even though Bronco had been the only prisoner to successfully escape since Governor William Mills's appointment of Cleofus Romero as warden. His capture especially pleased officialdom, but Bill did not share their joy. Forty-two-years-old and in his twelfth year of imprisonment, Bronco Bill faced a bleak future.[35]

CHAPTER 11

Last Gasps

"And one of those whirlwinds came up and spun the wheel right around and around."

Henry Brock

As Bronco Bill Walters readjusted to prison life following his short-lived freedom, international events were building toward the August 1914 outbreak of war in Europe. After two and a half years of neutrality, America's relations with Germany reached the breaking point in 1917. When a German submarine sank the USS *Housatonic* on February 3, President Woodrow Wilson announced the severance of diplomatic ties. That same day, Walters agreed to the terms of a conditional parole agreement offered by the Board of Parole of the State of New Mexico. In addition to the standard condition that he "abstain from crime and lead an upright, frugal, and industrious life," he also accepted the requirement that, upon parole, he would "proceed at once" to Colorado City, Texas, and remain there at least twelve months.[1]

Throughout the month of March, German submarine attacks against American merchant ships confirmed the ineffectiveness of armed neutrality; war was imminent. So, too, was freedom for Walters. On recommendation of former governor

William C. McDonald, Captain Fred Fornoff of the New Mexico Mounted Police, and prison superintendent Thomas Hughes, the Board of Penitentiary Commissioners gathered on March 29 to discuss Walters's confinement. They concluded their session with the resolution "that the said William Walter [*sic*], Register No. 1282, be pardoned, as recognition and reward for the service rendered the State in the Institution Hospital."[2]

The United States declared war on April 6, 1917. Six days later, William J. Barker, a Santa Fe attorney and prison commissioner, informed newly elected Governor Washington E. Lindsey of the board's decision. Lindsey approved the once notorious outlaw's parole agreement, which stipulated that he be employed outside of New Mexico for at least twelve months and warned, "If he does right he need have no fear of being re-arrested. If he does wrong he must expect the inevitable penalties." A job offer from cattleman Earl Clay Morrison (1878-1969) a lifetime resident of Mitchell County, Texas, met the board's conditions. How Morrison and Walters made contact is unrecorded—there is no evidence they were related. Bill, who had spent seventeen years and four months behind bars, immediately left for Texas; he arrived on April 20, 1917, when western Texas was amid a major drought.[3]

Lawyer and author Max Coleman, whose tales of Bronco Bill are largely apocryphal, claimed Walters had studied chemistry in prison and was paroled to go to France during World War I. In fact, Bill worked in the prison hospital and was paroled to go to Texas. Salty John Cox went a step beyond Coleman and sent Bronco to France during the war as a Red Cross ambulance driver. Although the surgeon general of the army mustered 4,760 men, organized and trained by the American Red Cross, into the U.S. Army Ambulance Corps on August 30, 1917, there was no interest in forty-eight-year-old cowhands with disabled right arms. Even so, hardly three weeks after he reached Texas, Bill, too old for the draft, wrote to the Board of Penitentiary Commissioners on May 10 from Dodge (Walker

County, Texas) and indicated his desire to enlist and go to France. Walters's presence in Dodge, barely nine miles east of Huntsville at the junction of the Trinity Valley Southern and International Great Northern railroads, prompts unanswerable questions. Most likely, he was not consorting with inmates at the Texas State Penitentiary; that would be a clear violation of his parole agreement. Considering his probable east Texas origins, visits to relatives may explain his presence.[4]

On October 1, Walters again wrote to the Board of Penitentiary Commissioners; the content of this letter is unrecorded. It is apparent, however, that he remained in Texas until the terms of his parole expired in April 1918—but not much longer. He soon resurfaced in New Mexico using the alias Walter Brown and went to work for Socorro County rancher Fred Martin.[5]

Located near the Alamo River, the Martin ranch offered Bill the opportunity to search for the coins buried following the Belén robbery. He and Fred Martin became good friends who spent quite a bit of time unsuccessfully seeking the money. A couple of years later and certainly disappointed by his failure to recover any of the secreted Belén plunder, Walters returned to his familiar haunts in New Mexico's boot heel and adopted the alias William C. Brown. Though his disabled arm prevented the resumption of his cowboy life, he again signed on at the Diamond A. Henry Brock, the one-time superintendent, related that Bronco was put to work as a windmiller on the old Lang spread that made up the southernmost portion of the Diamond A range.[6]

Windmillers made continuous rounds maintaining the mills, and ranches typically furnished them with a personal chuck or covered wagon. They rarely showed up at ranch headquarters. Although Aermotor Company of Chicago, the world's dominant manufacturer of windmills, introduced an auto-oiled model in 1915 that theoretically required only annual oiling, problems with the oiling system necessitated replacement by an improved version (model 602) the next year. Regardless, it was a number of years before large ranches completed the changeover to the newer models, and the older windmills required regular oiling. Back at the ranch where he had hired on twenty-five years before, Walters must have felt quite at home as he made his rounds oiling and repairing the mills.[7]

Bill soon became acquainted with young Jethro Sparkman Vaught, Jr., from nearby Deming. In a 1956 interview with New Mexico journalist-historian Howard Bryan, Vaught, then an Albuquerque attorney and federal bankruptcy judge, reflected on his 1919 meeting with the former outlaw. Vaught had joined his parents on a trek to the headquarters of the Hatchet Ranch, owned by a syndicate headed by Mahlon T. Everhart and nestled in the Hatchet Gap between the Big and Little Hatchet mountains. They stayed the first night with Lee Caldwell, a deputy in the town of Hachita. "We went into the kitchen and were introduced to an old cowpuncher [Walters was then fifty years old] who was warming himself by the fire," Vaught recalled. "The man was introduced to us as Bill Brown, but we learned later that he was Bronco Bill Walters." Later that night, Vaught shared a room with Bill. Walters removed his outer clothing to expose striped prison underclothes. "I was scared to death and ran screaming to my parents. My parents eased my fears, and Bronco was very upset that he had scared me. We slept in the same room that night."[8]

The next morning, Walters joined the Vaughts on the trip to the Hatchet Ranch. Over a period of time, he became particularly fond of Jethro. During the next two years, he taught the youngster to ride and shoot. "Bronco Bill was the finest shot I ever saw," Vaught asserted. "He would shoot running jackrabbits with his six-shooter from a fast moving Model T Ford, and would shoot the heads off ducks with a rifle." Bill also advised Jethro to "mind my parents, to keep out of trouble, and to work hard in school so that I wouldn't grow up to be an old cowpuncher like he was." One thing that Bill never discussed, however, was his life as an outlaw. When Jethro asked him about hidden money, Bill only donned his crooked grin and said, "Those cowpunchers have been talking to you."[9]

While Walters adapted to life out of prison and stayed out of trouble, his old cohort, Red Pipkin, moved inexorably toward new difficulties. So, too, did America. The nation's entry into World War I increased the need for copper and coal and forced up the price. Simultaneously, emergent industrial unions sought recognition, better and safer working conditions, and higher pay. As patriotic fervor swept the nation, the Industrial Workers of the World (Wobblies)—socialist, radical, and suspected of being pro-German—worked to expand its membership among the migratory workers, or bindle stiffs, in the western mining and lumber camps. During the last week of June 1917, Senator Charles S. Thomas (R-Colo.) charged that IWW leaders cooperated with German agents to stir up strikes among Germans and Austrians with the goal of crippling smelters and industries throughout the West. Arizona's governor, Thomas Campbell, also supposed a "sinister German character" behind the activities of these agitators. "Whether or not there is German influence behind these strikes," the governor insisted, "these strikes are directly aiding the enemy of the United States." Rhetoric of this sort encouraged a swift response.[10]

On the morning of July 10, over two hundred armed men swarmed over the Wobblies and their sympathizers at Jerome, Arizona. The mob herded the workers into cattle cars and transported them to Kingman, where they were freed with orders not to return. Two days later, a *New York Times* editorial described the IWW as "a nucleus of disorder and sedition," and insisted that "its proceedings, whether inspired by Germany or by inveterate devilry, are noxious beyond wont." That same day, in response to a rumor that the IWW had been infiltrated by pro-Germans, Cochise County's sheriff, Harry Cornwall Wheeler, one-time captain of the Arizona Rangers (1907–1909), enlisted a force of 1,200 deputies. Assisted by this "Citizens Protection League," Wheeler and his gang rounded up over 2,000 IWW members and sympathizers then striking against three of Bisbee's mining companies. That afternoon, the *posse comitatus* shoved 1,186 of the strikers into cattle cars and deported the miners to Columbus, New Mexico. Strikes within Arizona's Globe-Miami district threatened a similar response from Gila County's sheriff, Tom Armer. Outside of Arizona, the IWW was suspected of destroying a flour mill and poisoning stock on nearby ranches at Klamath Falls, Oregon. At Butte, Montana, the Metal Mine Workers' chapter, formed by alleged IWW leaders, attempted, but failed, to launch an effective strike; in Gallup, New Mexico, intensified anti-IWW sentiment offered the Gallup American Coal Company an opportunity to repudiate labor agreements.[11]

The Colorado-based Victor Fuel Company had a contract with the United Mine Workers of America (UMW). When Victor Fuel sold its Gallup mines to Gallup American, "the miners were given to understand that the contracts would be lived up to for such a period as they were written." The miners were naive. In the words of Worthington Risdon, the state mine inspector, Gallup American soon "imported a lot of gun men from other parts of the state and from Texas and Colorado. These men were commissioned as McKinley County deputy sheriffs and [the company] immediately strapped a big gun on each of them. Several of these men are ex convicts and others under indictment for highway robbery." Red Pipkin, McKinley County's undersheriff, supervised the unsavory bunch; he was in familiar company. With their force in place, Gallup American repudiated the contract with the UMW local and announced that the "only way the workers could continue at work would be under such conditions as the mine owners saw fit to extend them." The UMW went out on a July 1 strike; a month-long labor dispute followed.[12]

On July 30, the McKinley County Council of Defense, organized under an act of Congress and the legislature of New Mexico, proclaimed its patriotic intention to keep the mines "running at full blast for the purpose of insuring no suspension of the transportation of munitions and military equipment, and the necessary food for our armies." Hardly impartial, local businessman and leading Republican stalwart Gregory Page chaired the committee, which numbered Sheriff Bob Roberts, along with mine superintendents Sharp Hanson (Southwestern) and Peter Westwater (Allison), among its members. Thomas E. Purdy (the Santa Fe Railroad's agent at Gallup) and Judge John Robert McFie, an attorney for the Gallup American Fuel Company, joined them. Not only did McFie enjoy the distinction of having sat on the New Mexico Supreme Court longer than any man in the history of the territory (1889–93 and 1897–1912), but he had also sent Bronco Bill off to his first term in prison twenty-six years earlier.[13]

The next day, in an effort to thwart the strike's extension, Sheriff Bob Roberts went into action. McKinley County was amid an era when either "big-nosed, hard-fisted Bob" or his older brother, D. W. "Dee" Roberts, would serve as sheriff. The brothers shared the belief that "enough force would solve all difficulties," the New Mexico journalist and author Erna Fergusson opined, and the Roberts brothers believed that this was the time for force. Bob Roberts ordered the arrest of thirty-four citizen-agitators, "said to be Industrial Workers of the World." William H. Hanns, U.S. commissioner and editor-publisher of the *Gallup Independent*, whose editorials had encouraged the IWW, was among those arrested. Brought before the Council of Defense, he promised not to support future IWW activities and was released.[14]

Roberts held the men at the courthouse all day; some condemned the sheriff's refusal to bring his prisoners before a judge for arraignment, but the day's events had not concluded. That night, Undersheriff Pipkin and mining company thugs mounted horses and herded the agitators (including Frank Hefferly, the UMW's district president, and his brother, Rudolph Hefferly) from the courthouse to the railroad station.

Loaded on to the Santa Fe's special train number 22, the strikers were deported by the Council of Defense to Belén. The vociferously pro-Democrat Hanns sardonically allowed that the Republican Pipkin "had probably served his usefulness" as a herder. The deportation, however, did not forestall an extension of the strike. On August 1, the District 15 officers of the UMW expanded the walkout to include the Diamond Coal Company and the Gallup Southwestern Coal Company.[15]

Frank Hefferly soon telegraphed George R. Craig, the district attorney, and insisted that the deportees were "law-abiding and in no way connected with the I.W.W." Craig, in response, traveled to Belén to interview the men and determined that Hefferly's assertion was true; two-thirds of the men belonged to the UMW and fully a third were not even miners. Among the latter was a farmer who had driven his team into Gallup to buy a pump, only to find himself on the train to Belén; his team and wagon still stood behind the hardware store where he had left them.

Craig returned to Gallup on August 3 and launched an investigation of the deportation. Mine inspector Risdon also traveled to Gallup and reported to Governor Lindsay that local citizens were infuriated by the "boisterous and offensive manner" in which gunmen representing the interests of Gallup American and Diamond coal companies paraded "up and down the streets and side walks of the town." No friend of the UMA or the IWW, Risdon informed the governor that many believed the deportations were "without provocation," and a "disgrace to the community." Gunmen prevented a doctor and the telegraph operator from going to their offices, and yet "another ordered Chas. Chris[t]man the town marshal off the street. Others rode horses into the crowd of women and children and used foul language," Risdon reported.[16]

These investigations brought rapid condemnation from Governor Lindsey: "The deportation of individuals from one county to another or from the state of New Mexico to another jurisdiction as a possible escape from the burden of local law enforcement has at no time met with my approval." The governor immediately sent Fred Fornoff, the former captain of the New Mexico Mounted Police, to Gallup to advise the County Council of Defense. They certainly needed advice. The editor of the *Carbon City News* harangued against their "absolute despotic authority, [which] has been condemned in no doubtful terms by 98 per cent of the people of Gallup."[17]

On August 3, Fornoff reported to the governor that there would be no further deportations, that the miners would return to work, that the "usefulness of the County Council of Defense [was] impaired to such an extent that they are no help," and that "there are too many gun men here." The next day, he informed Lindsey that he had advised "Sheriff Roberts to protect all returning men deported." Albuquerque attorney Pierce Rodey, the son of Pipkin's former defense attorney, also arrived to induce men to go to work and to instruct Roberts "to protect and keep from molestation all returning deported." Lindsey, in turn, directed Sheriff Roberts "to protect men deported from your County, July thirty-first ultimo, upon their return so long as they act within the provisions of the law," and Roberts agreed to comply. Fornoff next advised that the men at Belén, including Frank Hefferly, should not return in a body and that "the gun men have disappeared from Gallup." On August 4, ten of the deported men returned to Gallup. Three days later, the miners at the Allison and Southwestern mines returned to work, and shortly the miners also returned to the Gallup American mines.[18]

Critical of Pipkin's "usefulness" in the 1917 deportations, editor Hanns was even less forgiving when, little more than a year later, Red shot Pat Lucero, the night marshal, on the streets of Gallup. According to the *Independent*, on Monday evening, September 2, 1918, Deputy Pipkin had attempted to assault Mrs. William C. Mattox, "with whom he is believed to have become infatuated. Pipkin met the woman on the street as she was accompanied by a neighbor boy and girl." He "grabbed her by the arm and tried to force her into an auto which he had gotten out of," the report continued. Labeled a Republican "gang leader" and "henchman of the gang of outlaw republicans" by the *Independent,* Pipkin allegedly fired two shots at her as she escaped. Sam James, another gunman employed by the Diamond Coal Company, moved to constrain Pipkin. A fight broke out between the two.[19]

Night marshal Lucero arrived on the scene and attempted to intervene in the new brawl. Witnesses related that James turned on Lucero, struck him in the face, then pulled his gun and fired a shot that missed the marshal. Lucero, in kind, yanked his revolver and fired two shots at James. His marksmanship was no better. Lucero then turned and ran. Pipkin pulled a gun and fired at the fleeing lawman. His aim proved more accurate. A soft-nosed bullet plowed through Lucero, just below the hip, and shattered a leg bone. He fell to the ground but still managed to fire three more wayward shots in James's direction. The wounded marshal reached St. Mary's Hospital in "very dangerous condition." City marshal Christman, a Democrat, arrested Pipkin and James and hauled them off to the Gallup jail; Sheriff Roberts, a Republican, then appeared and took his two minions into county custody.[20]

Not surprisingly, the shooting of Pat Lucero divided the town along party lines. Some Gallup residents believed that the entire affair was a put-up job to disparage the local Hispanic population, predominantly Democratic. Had Lucero been killed rather than wounded, McKinley County's Republican officials could have concocted almost any story. Certainly, this was the opinion of the *Independent* when it editorialized, "The republican gang are attempting to bring as much pressure as possible to bear on the town Democratic administration, and are using the ignorant criminals to do the dirty work for them."[21]

The next day, Dora Mattox filed a complaint against Red before Justice Joseph Schauer, charging that Pipkin had fired a gun at her. Republican party boss Gregory Page, no stranger to violence, also appeared and presented the judge with an affidavit that questioned Pipkin's ability to get a fair hearing in Schauer's court. Schauer transferred the case to the court of another justice of the peace, who was, in the opinion of the *Independent*, favorable to the interests of the Diamond Coal Company. The justice ordered Red to appear before the McKinley County grand jury, and Page posted Pipkin's $500 bond.[22]

While Pipkin awaited action by the grand jury, tension mounted between the Republicans in the McKinley County Sheriff's Department and the Democrats of the Gallup Police Department. If the not unbiased account in the *Independent* can be believed, Sheriff Roberts, Pipkin, and several other deputies, accosted Marshal Christman and "invited him to a shooting scrape, and called abusive names and threatened to annihilate the town peace officers and some of the town officials." Pipkin, the report continued, "Stood behind [Roberts] as he was doing his little tirade and patted the sheriff on the back and told him to stay with it." As Christman was off duty at the time, he "did not have any shooting irons on his person, which is perhaps a lucky thing for someone." One result of the confrontation was the convening of a town meeting. Gallup mayor Arthur T. Hannett, a future governor of New Mexico, chaired the gathering, and a committee of ten was organized to present resolutions to the owners of the Diamond Coal Mine, the McKinley County commissioners, the district court, and state officials demanding that Pipkin and James be discharged as deputies.[23]

Editor Hanns also opposed Pipkin's deputy sheriff commission. "The peculiar thing about this deputy commission is that it was the same commission that the official Republican distorter of truth [the *Carbon City News and McKinley County Republican*] said had been taken away from him last year," the editor railed. "By the way, we would like to know why an exconvict ever had a commission in McKinley County[;] if the republican administration was not plotting against organized government, what did they need him for?" It was a rhetorical question, given Hann's partisan reputation. He could not resist providing an answer, however. "The Town administration knew full well that the republican gang would protect the outlaws, so that they might help him [presumably Gregory Page] later in some blackmail deal or some election fraud."[24]

State officials listened to the concerns and sent Captain Herbert J. McGrath, of New Mexico's Mounted Police, to Gallup. The one-time Grant County sheriff and longtime Republican interviewed Pipkin, whose party ties served him no good purpose this time. McGrath relieved Red of his commission as deputy sheriff. Nonetheless, the *Independent*'s editor remained unsatisfied. He grumbled, sardonically, "It does [no] great deal of good to remove this scrap of paper officially declaring Pipkin a deputy sheriff, when he is allowed to carry a deadly weapon at all times, and endanger the lives of some innocent woman or boy with whom he might come in contact."[25]

On November 23, the grand jury indicted Red on two counts of assault with intent to kill and one charge of assault while armed. He entered a plea of not guilty three days later. On November 29 his attorneys, Ernest A. Martin and B. D. Richards, filed motions to change the venue in the three cases. The next day, the judge ordered the trial moved to Bernalillo County. Red posted $3,500 bail and was released.[26]

The case brought by the State of New Mexico against Dan Pipkin opened on Wednesday, April 9, 1919, in the Albuquerque courtroom of Judge Mayo E. Hickey. A bevy of Gallup dignitaries were on hand, including Sheriff Bob Roberts and Gregory Page for the Republicans, and Marshal Christman, his son, and various other Democrats. The defense concluded its case the next morning. Because the evidence established that it was a wild shot of Pipkin's that wounded Lucero, the jury convicted Red of a lesser offense of assault with a deadly weapon. Pipkin's attorneys entered a motion for a new trial

Red Pipkin (1919), inmate no. 4368. Courtesy New Mexico Department of Corrections Glass Negative Collection no. 4368, New Mexico State Records Center and Archives, Santa Fe.

on April 27. Red, meanwhile, remained free on bail. He returned to Albuquerque on April 29 to hear the motion overruled. Judge Hickey promptly entered judgment and sentenced Red to one to two years in New Mexico's state penitentiary. He also granted an appeal to the state supreme court that Pipkin remain free on bail. On May 23, Red abandoned the appeal, and the judge immediately ordered his commitment to the state prison.[27]

Pipkin entered the New Mexico State Penitentiary the next day, little more than two years after Bronco Bill's release. He inaccurately gave his place of birth as Amarillo, Texas, indicated that his wife, Katy, was then in Prescott, Arizona, and, in spite of the twelve years of his life spent in a Mormon communal environment, claimed to have had no religious instruction.

Red kept his record clean and, with good behavior, was released with a full pardon on November 23, 1920.[28]

Pipkin returned to New Mexico, settling about three miles north of Gallup at Gamerco, the company town of Gallup American Coal. He hired on as a guard and watchman at the company's mine. Henry Brock, Bronco Bill's old boss at the Diamond A, was also a resident of Gamerco. The former ranch superintendent had moved to Gallup in 1912 and had served as McKinley County's undersheriff until 1916 before becoming a guard for Gallup American. Pipkin and Brock spent at least some time reflecting on the old days; it was from Pipkin that Brock garnered some of his tales regarding Bronco Bill.[29]

On June 16, 1921, little more than six months after Pipkin's release, Bronco Bill tended a windmill near Hachita that had been thrown out of gear. He climbed up to begin his repairs, but evidently neglected to tie down the wheel. Henry Brock explained what happened next: "One of those whirlwinds came up and spun the wheel right around and around you know, just turned it around and around like it did when they have these whirlwinds that shoot up a streak that looks like dust for hundreds of feet and not bigger than a stove pipe." The blades of the spinning wheel knocked him from his perch; he tumbled to the ground.[30]

Cowboys hauled the badly injured old cowboy into Hachita, and, according to old-timer Jack Stockbridge, Bill wanted them to get in touch with Hammer Livingston, another Diamond A cowboy who also owned a little ranch on the west side of the Little Hatchets, some thirty miles away. Bronco wanted to tell Hammer where the money was buried but died before Hammer reached him. Another story, by Jethro Vaught, related that when placed on the bed, Bill gasped, "Go bring the boy to me." A cowboy assumed that Bill intended to reveal the location of the money to Vaught. He jumped into a Model A, raced to get young Jethro at the Hatchet ranch, and aroused the sleeping youngster. "I got dressed, jumped into the car

Bronco Bill's headstone, Hachita Cemetery, Hachita, New Mexico. Photograph by the authors.

with the cowboy, and we raced to Hachita," Vaught later told Howard Bryan. "When we entered the house, we were told that Bronco Bill was dead." In a few terse words, the *Lordsburg Liberal* announced the passing of the former desperado, "Word comes from Hachita that William Brown, aged 48 [52], known to old-timers as 'Broncho Bill,' a native of Texas, but a resident of this state for many years, an employe [*sic*] of the Victoria Land and Cattle company, fell from the tower of a wind mill at old Hachita, and died four hours later." His friends buried the fifty-two-year-old Walters on the northern edge of the little Hachita cemetery, just south of town.[31]

Not surprisingly, the passage of time had modified and amplified the Walters saga. The *Silver City Independent* correctly informed its readers of his recent employment with the Victoria Land and Cattle Company and of the circumstances of his accident, but wrongly enlisted him into the High Five (Black Jack) gang. Compounding its errors, the *Independent* even attributed the November 24, 1883, robbery of the Southern

Pacific at Gage, New Mexico, to the colorful cowboy. Almost predictably, the account failed to mention any of his actual crimes save for the killing of Deputy Frank Vigil. Death had claimed Jim Burnett, Kid Johnson, and now Bronco Bill. Ed Colter's status or whereabouts remained a mystery. Only one former gang member stayed active; Red Pipkin continued as watchman, guard, strikebreaker, and all-around head-pounder for the Gallup American Coal Company.[32]

President Franklin D. Roosevelt had barely launched his plans for national economic recovery when the National Miners Union (NMU), a more militant alternative to the United Mine Workers Union and thought by many to be an affiliate of the American Communist Party, won recognition. On the night of August 28, 1933, members of Gallup's NMU local 4025 voted to strike for higher wages against Gallup's coal companies the next day. On August 29, some nine hundred miners walked off their jobs. Although the civil administrations, law enforcement personnel, and courts of Gallup and McKinley County continued to function, Governor Arthur Seligman (1931–33), induced as much by John L. Lewis and the UMW as he was by the mine owners, declared martial law and ordered out the National Guard. General Osborne C. Wood headed to Gallup with two troops of cavalry and a machine-gun unit. As the force surrounded the town, a curfew, checkpoints, and an ordinance against mass gatherings became part of Gallup's routine. With passing weeks, "organizers are being sentenced by court-martial and held in jail under appalling conditions," Dorothy Day, writing for *The Catholic Worker*, reported. "Picketing is forbidden, armed strikebreakers are being deputized to attack strikers." Red Pipkin, a coal company guard and still a crony of McKinley County law enforcers, was certainly among the strikebreakers.[33]

Some of the mines began to reopen as the UMW signed up those miners who would cross the NMU picket lines. Other out-of-work miners were promised jobs with emergent New

Deal agencies. Martial law was lifted on January 31, 1934, and the strike seemed close to a settlement. Yet a number of miners remained out of work, especially those most active in the NMU, many of whom had been brought up to Gallup from Mexico to break the 1917 strike. In the aftermath of that earlier strike and the deportations, quite a few of those imported miners built shacks on a 110-acre tract of land just west of Gallup—land called Chihuahuaita and owned by Gallup American.

For reasons never disclosed, Gallup American sold Chihuahuaita in 1935 to Clarence F. Vogel, a New Mexico state senator. Vogel, in turn, offered to sell lots to the tenants. Out-of-work strikers and blacklisted leaders of the NMU had no means to make payments. The choices seemed clear—go back to work or face eviction.[34]

Events moved swiftly. Senator Vogel appeared before Judge William J. "Bail-less" Bickel, the local justice of the peace and sought a writ of eviction against one Victor Campos. Bickel granted the writ and Gallup American guards, appointed as special deputies, served the writ on Campos, emptied his little adobe of his belongings and furniture, and boarded up the door. Pipkin, as a Gallup American guard, almost certainly had some involvement. Later, protected by darkness, Campos and friends broke through the boards and hauled the furniture back in. Deputies soon arrested them. On April 4, 1935, an angry crowd gathered outside the Southerland Building where Bail-less Bickel held court. Campos and NMU agitator Eziquel Navarro were arraigned on charges of breaking and entry.

With angry shouts coming from the growing crowd gathered outside on Coal Avenue, Sheriff M. R. "Mack" Carmichael decided to escort Navarro back to jail first and then return for Campos. It also seemed wise to take Navarro out the rear door and into the alley that led to Second Street and the jail. Carmichael, Undersheriff Dee Roberts, and two deputies, Edison L. "Bearcat" Wilson and Hoy Burgess, entered the alley with Navarro. The first of perhaps twenty shots rang out moments later. Before the sound of the final blast ceased reverberating through the narrow alley, Carmichael lay dead, Wilson was shot in the right side, and Burgess was clubbed and stabbed with an ice pick. Unscathed, Dee Roberts shot and killed rioter Ignacio Velarde and mortally wounded Solomon Esquibel. Other rioters suffered from gunshot wounds, and Pipkin and other Gallup American guards joined with sheriff deputies to conduct house-to-house searches for additional mob members. The roundup, which resulted in widespread arrests but only three second-degree murder convictions, was Red's last association with violence and mayhem.[35]

The year after the Gallup riot, fifty-nine-year-old Red Pipkin, the last of the Bronco Bill gang, fell victim to one of his own bad habits. A heavy smoker, he had contracted mouth cancer. On August 3, 1937, his illness forced him to give up his job with Gallup American. About half past eight on the morning of July 6, 1938, two residents of his boardinghouse heard what they afterward described as a sound like a firecracker. Later in the day, when Pipkin failed to put in an appearance, the boarders went to investigate. They found him lying on the floor with a bullet wound in his right temple. By his side rested a pearl-handled pistol and a note that "expressed suicidal intentions." He insisted "that no one else be blamed for my deed," and requested that the pistol be given to a friend "who is signed on a note of mine at the bank."[36]

Officials ruled Pipkin's death a suicide. Otherwise, the Gallup press wasted few words in reporting the death of Red Pipkin, "a colorful character in this section of the southwest" and one of the last of the nineteenth-century outlaws. Final rites awaited the arrival of Red's two surviving brothers, Polk from Redwood City, California, and Richard from Springerville, Arizona. On July 10, 1938, with Rollie Mortuary officiating, Pipkin was laid to rest at Gallup's Hillcrest Cemetery.[37]

Daniel "Red" Pipkin's headstone, Hillcrest Cemetery, Gallup, New Mexico. Photograph by the authors.

With the death of Bill Walters in 1921 and the suicide of Red Pipkin in 1938, Bronco Bill's infamous gang finally passed from the scene to survive only in history and in a myriad of legends and anecdotes.

Afterword

Violence in the Southwest

"Bronco Bill" is a catchy handle occasionally subjected to the alternative spelling "Broncho" in late-nineteenth-century news accounts. Indeed, author Eugene Manlove Rhodes, who counted a number of outlaws and gunmen as friends, once wrote that "spelling bronco correctly" was first on his list of hobbies. And one of his characters remarked, "I've been trying to break folks of spelling bronco that-a-way for years, writing letters, and arguing, and it does no good. Folks seem to think a bronco is a horse afflicted with bronchitis, or consumption, or puny some way. B-r-o-n-c-o—is a Spanish word signifyin' wild. The *c* had the sound of *k*—always."[1]

Spelling notwithstanding, one can dine at Bronco Bill's in Alabama and Oregon, dance to country sounds at Bronco Bill's in Florida, Texas, and Pennsylvania, or bet a bankroll at Bronco Bill's Colorado casino. The nickname inspired a comic strip (*Broncho Bill*) and a song ("Bronco Bill's Lament"). Gilbert M. "Broncho Billy" Anderson starred in one of America's first motion pictures (*The Great Train Robbery*), and almost three-quarters of a century later, Hollywood icon Clint Eastwood starred in another—*Bronco Billy*. What is more, Bill Walters was not even the first to wear the moniker. Thomas "Bronco Bill" Skeen rode Oregon's Owl Hoot Trail a few years before

Walters gained notoriety. An erroneous report of Skeen's death in Grant County, Oregon, prompted the local press to protest, "There has not been a man by that name in Grant County since our recollection. Because every third man you meet in Harney county is sailing under the cognomen of 'Buccaroo Jim,' 'Scarface Charley,' 'One-Fingered Tabby,' 'Wild Bill' etc., it is no reason that the residents of Grant county should be falsely accused of carrying unlawful names."[2]

Bronco Bill was a beguiling nickname, and Bill Walters was a captivating personality. He reached the Black River country of Arizona, where he seemingly mesmerized three young cowhands—little more than overgrown juvenile delinquents—as well as a deserter from the United States Navy. Soon, the Bronco Bill Gang had a name synonymous with the lawlessness and murder that plagued the Southwest in the 1890s. The character and extent of that violence has undergone continual reassessment since the 1968 publication of Robert R. Dykstra's seminal *The Cattle Towns: A Social History of the Kansas Cattle Trading Centers* and his contention that the level of violence in the American West had been overstated by nineteenth-century sensationalists. Embellishment aside, a review of the newspapers, court records, and penitentiary records of the American Southwest in the 1890s indicates widespread crime and bloodshed, particularly in New Mexico, where the gang was active.

An 1896 analysis of crimes and criminals by the United States Census Office produced thought-provoking findings. At the onset of the decade, 21 percent of America's inmate population had been incarcerated for violent crimes (against the person). The country's Western Division (Arizona, California, Colorado, Idaho, Montana, Nevada, New Mexico, Oregon, Utah, Washington, and Wyoming) at 22 percent approximated the national average, but individually, New Mexico's violence considerably surpassed that norm. Forty-six percent of the 115 inmates confined in the territory's penitentiary had been convicted of violent crimes. New Mexico's jails held eighty additional prisoners. Some were nonviolent, but many were not—especially those awaiting trial for violent offenses. New Mexico Territory's 1890 collection of violent criminals exceeded the national average by a significant margin and likely exceeded the almost 30 percent average found in America's most violent section, the South Central Division (Alabama, Arkansas, Kentucky, Louisiana, Mississippi, Tennessee, and Texas). By the end of the 1890s, the penitentiary's inmate population had doubled; those convicted of violent crimes accounted for slightly more than half of the prison population. More than one-third of the felons served sentences for various degrees of murder. New Mexico Territory of the 1890s was a violent place, and the late-nineteenth-century cowboys who turned to outlawry casually accepted the violence that accompanied the ill-fated decision to ride the Owl Hoot Trail. But mere acceptance of violence was not a guaranteed fast lane to success. Ineptitude was also a hallmark of most gangs of the decade—not remarkable, considering that a cowhand's range education failed to include classes on how to heist a train.[3]

Bronco Bill's cowboys forsook herding in favor of train robbery. Their lamentable choice resulted in an almost comical effort to ride off with the contents of the Wells, Fargo express car at Grants, New Mexico. As they became somewhat more accomplished, their determination also resulted in the tragic deaths of two New Mexico deputies and a Navajo tracker, as well as two of their own. The other three gang members suffered gunshot wounds—a permanently disabling injury in Bronco Bill's case. Pipkin and Walters also served prison terms—unusually long ones for that era.

Arizona's territorial legislature recognized that juries were historically hesitant to convict rustlers due to the harshness of the penalties—as many as ten years for stealing a two-dollar calf—and reduced many forms of stock stealing from felony to misdemeanor status at the turn of the century. Even so, only five months earlier, Red Pipkin failed to engender any sympathy from the jury of his peers that readily convicted him of a rustling offense carrying a ten-year sentence. Allowing time off for good behavior, the territory released him seven years later.[4]

Bronco Bill fared even worse. During the twenty-eight years that passed from the opening of the New Mexico Territorial Penitentiary in 1884 to the advent of New Mexico's statehood, various factors—gubernatorial pardons, commutations to fixed sentences (with good-time service usually reducing the latter), and an occasional death—fixed the average length of confinement for a life sentence at seven years and nine months. Walters, who maintained a good-conduct record and had earned a position as steward in the penitentiary's hospital, had served nearly a decade when Senator Bailey from Texas sought executive clemency for the lifer. Governor Curry nevertheless rejected the senator's plea. When Governor Lindsey finally granted Bronco a conditional parole, he had served eighteen and one-half years as a guest of the territory and later the state of New Mexico—an imprisonment record that few of that era would match.

Individually, the members of the Bronco Bill gang were not the stuff of legend. Collectively, their lawlessness assured them a measure of outlaw immortality, their tales sprinkled with fact and fable. "Outlaw tales are most suited to this [mythologizing] process," wrote historian Frank Richard Prassel, "since the lives of fugitives abound with gaps and confusion. Imaginative contributions or bits taken from other stories may then complete the desired picture. Contradictions and even easily detected errors can coexist with a few leading facts." Although a lot of fiction was woven into the yarns told of the band, a fact remained constant—those who rode with the Bronco Bill Gang were deadly.[5]

APPENDIX

Who Was Bronco Bill Walters?

"One of life's less rewarding pursuits is attempting to trace the career of William H. 'Broncho Bill' Walters."

Philip Rasch

Author and illustrator Ross Santee wrote about the Old West: "Names don't mean nothin' in this country, for no one ever asks any questions around a cow outfit, at least not personal questions. It's not considered polite, in the first place, and in most cases it's not apt to be healthy." Anonymity sheltered runaway husbands, debtors on the lam, fallen scions, and the like. It also protected riders of the owl hoot trail. This tradition of privacy and secrecy, at least in part, also explains the frequent lack of letters and diaries capable of providing insight into an outlaw's personality or an explanation or rationalization of his actions. In the unlikely event that William "Bronco Bill" Walters left a written record, it remains well concealed. Without such resources, frustrated biographers must turn to recollections of others in an effort to unearth details of their subject's formative years and of the events that might offer motive for their subject's conduct. Again, the particulars of Bronco Bill's early years evidently remained unknown to his contemporaries, who identified him not only as William Walters, but also as William Raper, "Kid" Swingle, William Brown, Bill Williams, Ed Nixon, Ed McIntosh, and Bill Andrews. Without comprehensive information, but hard-pressed to recount the story of a colorful bandit, early writers freely substituted lively fiction for undiscovered fact and further impeded the quest for relevant material. This obfuscation later prompted western historian-author Philip Rasch to grumble, "One of life's less rewarding pursuits is attempting to trace the career of William H. 'Broncho Bill' Walters. Most of what has been written about [Walters] is historically worthless, to be kind about it." Any effort to reconstruct Walters's story must begin with a repudiation of that "historically worthless" material.[1]

Creighton M. Foraker, Grant County rancher and New Mexico's U.S. marshal, dubbed him William Raper when he reported Walters's 1898 capture to U.S. Attorney General John Griggs. The U.S. District Court, Second District of New Mexico, continued the misidentification and charged the said William Raper with attempted robbery of the U.S. mail. Yet William "Bill" Raper, the third-born son of Thomas and Susan Warfield Raper, existed in his own right and had shared considerable notoriety with his mother and brother in the mid-1880s.[2]

Sue Warfield, born about 1844 in Australia or England, depending on what she had a mind to tell the census enumerators, immigrated to America with her family and grew up the darling of a Nevada mining camp, where she developed into a "daring horsewoman and a deadly shot." By the age of fifteen, she had resettled in Forest City, California, where she was shortly wooed and won by Indiana native Tom Raper. She married the miner in Forest City, California, on March 6, 1860, and son Joseph W. was born the following year.[3]

Shortly after Joseph's birth the Rapers abandoned California and settled in Paradise Valley, Nevada, where sons Robert (born 1863) and William (born 1865) joined the family. One tradition argues that husband Tom soon suffered a gunshot wound at the hands of hostile Indians; it is certain that Sue's brother, Joseph Warfield, was killed on June 2, 1865, during an attack launched by Paiute, Bannock, and Shoshone Indians intent on driving settlers out of Paradise Valley. Another tradition argues that Raper accidentally shot himself when he attempted to seize his weapon from the wagon as the Indians attacked. In either case, the incident left him crippled, and he and Sue shortly separated. Sometimes linked to Robert Payne, formerly captain of Company E, First Regiment of Nevada Volunteer Cavalry, Sue shifted her baggage to Pine Valley, near Carlin, and launched her felonious career rustling cattle and heisting jewelry. She soon picked up the handle "Bronco Sue" and solidified her reputation as "the worse [*sic*] rustler that ever anybody was down here," according to one who knew her when she was a young girl in Nevada.[4]

Outstanding grand larceny indictments eventually forced Sue to flee Nevada. She soon appeared in Pueblo, Colorado, as Susan Stone, but shortly headed south, settled in Alamosa, and acquired the stage line that plied the seven-mile route between Conejos and San Antonio on the Colorado line. By 1882, Sue had reached Espanola, New Mexico, north of Santa Fe, with yet another husband Jacob, "Jake" Youncker. Born in Missouri, this son of a French father and a German mother reportedly had immigrated to Colorado from Independence, Arkansas. The newlyweds set up housekeeping in Rio Arriba County and later ran a saloon at Wallace (present-day Domingo), then a bustling railroad town northeast of Albuquerque. In 1883, the pair abandoned Wallace in favor of White Oaks in Lincoln County, reportedly to reunite with Sue's sons, but Youncker unexpectedly died from smallpox. Sue dug a grave, buried her late husband, and took up with a Scotsman, Robert Black.[5]

Widow Youncker and Black headed to Socorro, where Sue opened a boardinghouse and he operated a saloon. Although accounts vary as to details, the two evidently had a falling out over the proceeds from the sale of two cattle ranches, and Black went on a binge. Sue had the city marshal arrest her drunken lover and threatened Black's life if he came back. Late in the afternoon of August 6, 1884, Black placed life and limb in jeopardy and returned. They quarreled, and he fell victim to a bullet from a smoking .44-caliber revolver in the hand of Bronco Sue. The Socorro County grand jury initially entered a finding of self-defense and ordered her discharged from custody.[6]

Sue moved to nearby Doña Ana County, where she met and married Charles Dawson. In common with others who took up with Bronco Sue, Charlie found his remaining days few in number. John H. Good, a Doña Ana County cowman who allegedly had an affair with Sue, was the central figure of a bitter range rights feud with southeastern New Mexico cattleman Oliver Lee. Good shot and killed Dawson on December 8, 1885, at La Luz, nine miles from Tularosa. Western historian C. L. "Doc" Sonnichsen described the situation: "Dawson had quarreled with Good about cow business and they parted with a 'shoot-on-sight' understanding. The meeting happened on the streets of La Luz . . . and there was a hot little gunfight." Dawson had left his house with his stepson, William Raper, and another fellow. Bronco Sue followed behind, toting a rifle, evidently to protect her son rather than her husband. "Dawson's formidable wife, came in at the end with a Winchester," Sonnichsen continued, "but her husband had already stopped a bullet."[7]

William Raper filed a complaint that resulted in Good's arrest, but Raper, in turn, was arrested on a cross complaint of assault with intent to kill; he eventually was acquitted. Bronco Sue appeared as a prosecution witness at Good's hearing, but the neighboring Socorro County court soon ordered her arrest as well. Good offered the standard frontier plea of self-defense—he had legitimately repelled force with force—and Justice of the Peace Humphrey Hill ordered his release following a hearing. Sue, on the other hand, again faced the charge that she had murdered Robert Black.[8]

The murder trial of Bronco Sue took place on a change of venue in Grant County in mid-December 1886. Colonel Albert J. Fountain, the region's Republican kingpin, served as her lead counsel. As the trial progressed, her sons provided most of the evidence against her. Most damaging, Bill testified that his mother had killed Black to prevent him from sending her to jail for rustling, and that she planted an axe by his body to support her claim of self-defense. Notwithstanding the boys' testimony, the jury found her not guilty; there appeared to be more local concern about her sons giving evidence against her than there was about her guilt or innocence.[9]

New Mexicans quickly forgot Sue and the Raper family intrigues. Yet, the colorful nickname that Bronco Bill shared with Bronco Sue evidently convinced Marshal Foraker that train robber Bill Walters must be the son of Sue Raper. On December 8, 1898, when John P. Victory, the U.S. commissioner for the First Judicial District of New Mexico, issued a warrant to apprehend William Raper, alias "Bronco Bill," the misnomer gained official recognition. These legal proceedings aside, Bronco Bill Walters was *not* Nevada-born William Raper; neither was he "Kid" Swingle.[10]

The confusion between Bronco Bill and Swingle began two days following the May 24, 1898, robbery of the southbound Santa Fe near Belén, New Mexico, when Thomas Hubbell, the Bernalillo County sheriff, opined that the two robbers were "Kid" Johnson and Kid Swingle. Hubbell correctly identified Johnson but wrongly named Swingle.[11]

Grant S. Swingle (Kid Swingle), born July 19, 1863, and the native of Polk County, Missouri, first turned up in Apache and Graham counties, Arizona, about 1886. Swingle family sources disclose that he settled at Ab Johnson's ranch in Luna Valley, just across the line in New Mexico. Swingle's nephew later revealed that his uncle considered the Texas-born Johnson a good friend and "thought that Ab was one man who could always be trusted."[12]

The *Clifton Clarion* reported in August 1887 that Swingle, "a well known rustler and horse thief, who has been operating in Graham and Apache counties," had been lynched on the trail between Black's ranch and Gold Gulch. Nevertheless, lawmen shortly discovered that he remained sufficiently animate to participate in the September 16, 1887, holdup of the Atlantic and Pacific eastbound train near Navajo Springs and the seizure of $13,210.20. Two days later, Snowflake residents Osmer D. Flake and Joe Herschie joined Deputy Joe T. McKinney's Apache County posse and followed the trail of three riders west to foothills of the Mogollon Rim, where they found an occupied dugout. The lone camper shared his food and "chatted until quite late," but Flake suspected that the man was no innocent cowhand. He recognized their host as one of the robbers—Kid Swingle—"whom I afterwards knew as Moore." McKinney thought Flake was mistaken; he changed his mind the next morning, however, when the posse reached the Holbrook-Heber road, where the outlaws' tracks reappeared—but only those of two horses, not the three the posse had trailed west.[13]

The next month, a *Silver City Enterprise* report accused Swingle of the October 4 holdup of the Holbrook and Fort Apache Express coach about twenty miles east of the post. In addition to snatching the registered mail, the lone desperado also liberated a draft on the Bank of California, payable to the San Francisco postmaster, William J. Bryon, and seized $140 from the sole passenger, a recently discharged soldier. Later that month, on the night of October 31, reports credited Swingle with stopping Udall, LeSueur & Co's Navajo-to–St. Johns buckboard. After he rifled the registered mail and grabbed eighty dollars belonging to Wells, Fargo, he insisted that the driver (coincidently named Joseph W. Walters) run that rig toward St. Johns. On the Kid's command, Walters halted the wagon after they had traveled about five miles, and the two awaited the appearance of the buckboard from St. Johns to Navajo. Four hours later, the Kid's prey arrived. Again, he ransacked the registered mail. Commodore Perry Owens, Apache County's flamboyant sheriff, rode in pursuit of the lone highwayman, confident that he would capture the "valiant knight of the road." Some days later, however, unable to strike Swingle's trail, he returned empty-handed. "The redoubtable gentleman will hold up no more buckboards in the vale of tears," the *St. Johns Herald* nevertheless predicted.[14]

The *Herald* proved correct; Swingle had fled Apache County and resurfaced at the family home near Humansville, Missouri. Authorities notified T. W. Johnson, the Apache County district attorney, and Sheriff Owens traveled to Missouri to learn that the elusive outlaw had moved on to Morgan (Bosque County), Texas. A cable to Texas secured the Kid's arrest. Owens traveled to Morgan and took custody, only to let Swingle slip away near Toyah, Texas. The escape evidently marked the end of his brief career in Arizona; Swingle family sources believe he later settled in California, used the alias Frank Williams, was imprisoned, and was killed in a prison break.[15]

Was Grant Swingle the Frank Williams who was killed on the afternoon of June 27, 1893, along with George Conant (aka George Sontag), Anthony Dalton, "Buckshot" Smith, Charles Abbott, and Hiram Wilson, during an attempted a breakout from the Folsom prison quarry? Although there are intriguing coincidences in the tales of the two men, present evidence neither supports nor refutes this Swingle family belief. Moreover, Joseph T. McKinney, the Apache County, Arizona, undersheriff, believed that Swingle was killed at Pine Cienaga, New Mexico, over a poker game. The fate of Kid Swingle remains a mystery.[16]

Two circumstances may have accounted for Sheriff Hubbell's erroneous identification of Swingle as one of the Belén robbers. Hubbell was probably aware of Swingle's association with Ab and Emeline Johnson of Luna, the parents of Kid Johnson.

That Bronco and driver Walters shared their surname likely added to Hubbell's confusion. Even so, Kid Swingle was not Bronco Bill, but other aliases remained.

Following Walters's August 1898 capture, a reporter for the *Los Angeles Daily Times* wrote that Bronco used the names Ed Nixon and Ed McIntosh, handles that have not been encountered in other accounts. Bill evidently did adopt the alias Bill Andrews during his sojourn in Apache and Graham counties, Arizona. It was as Andrews that local cattlemen Prime T. Coleman and his younger brother Evans Coleman came to know Bronco Bill in the Territory's Black River country. Whether Bronco ever used the alias Bill Williams is, however, questionable.[17]

In a 1945 interview with western writer and historian J. Evetts Haley, former JAL Ranch manager Bob Beverly, "one of the real characters of cowboy history," related that "Bronco Bill Williams" was from east Texas and came out to West Texas and worked for the Bar B Ranch for some time. During the summer of 1890, Beverly cowboyed for the 69 Ranch in Knox County, Texas. He recalled that Bronco Bill, along with Fred Higgins (later the sheriff of Chaves County, New Mexico) and Will Rainbolt (later a Chaves County deputy), had driven a herd of Spanish cow ponies up from Mexico, avoided the duty, and brought them to the ranch of former Lincoln County deputy Buck Guyse on the Hondo River west of Roswell, New Mexico. Later that summer, Beverly claimed to have joined the three at Seymour, Texas, a town just starting to boom in anticipation of the Wichita Valley Railroad's arrival from Wichita Falls (finished September 11, 1890). They had driven those same ponies from Guyse's ranch to Texas in search of a market. At Seymour, Walters, Beverly, Higgins, and Rainbolt promoted a six-hundred-yard horse race between the local favorite, Coyote, and the Guyse-owned Pickpocket. On race day, even with Bronco Bill aboard Pickpocket, Coyote raced to victory.[18]

Penniless, Bronco Bill returned with Beverly to the 69 Ranch and its twenty-five-dollar monthly pay. He stayed on through the fall and made quite a bit of money playing poker before he and Beverly headed for the horse races in Dallas. "Bronco Bill Williams was with me at the Dallas Fair in 1890," Beverly told Haley. "We decided to go to the fair and win or lose on the races there. The last time I saw Bronco Bill was in the St. George Hotel there in Dallas. I loaned him about half the money I had . . . just gave it to him and I never saw him anymore." Beverly accurately described Bill as "pretty much of a scrapper, but was a nice fellow . . . one of the nicest you ever saw," later learned from Higgins that Bronco had left for Arizona, "throwed in with [George] Musgrove [*sic*] and that bunch [the High Five gang]," and had gone "plumb to hell."[19]

Beverly's claim that he and Bronco Bill attended the 1890 state fair in Dallas is problematic. Governor David R. Francis opened the 1890 Texas State Fair and Dallas Exposition on October 18. Only two days later, Bronco Bill was certainly at Separ, New Mexico, over seven hundred and fifty miles away—and he had been in nearby Hachita before he had reached Separ. Despite the details he provided, Beverly's identification of Bronco Bill as Bill Williams is dubious at best.[20]

In "Life of a Desperado" (*Southwest Review*), which appeared ten years after Walters's death, Marion Maxwell "Max" Coleman revealed another alias and laid the cornerstone for most of the apocryphal Bronco Bill stories. A native of Hood County, Texas, Coleman enjoyed his first encounter with western New Mexico when he reached the Circle Ranch (owned by Nation's Land and Cattle Company) at Quemado in 1903 and began to hear tales told of Bronco Bill. Coleman later moved back to Texas and started a law practice in Lubbock. Unaware of Walters's true name, he used Bronco's post-prison handle, W. C. Brown. Coleman also revealed his lack of knowledge about Bronco's past when he claimed that Bill, while still in his early twenties, was "initiated to powder smoke in the Horrell fight around Lampasas, then started rustling and headed northwest." Walters, almost certainly born in 1869, would have been only seven or eight years old at the time of the Horrell brothers' 1876–77 feud with Pink Higgins.[21]

So who was Bronco Bill Walters? After his 1898 apprehension, and with little reason to deceive a reporter about his name and age, Bill revealed, "My true name is William Walters and I will be twenty-nine years old next October." He made a similar admission to New Mexico penitentiary authorities in 1891 when he acknowledged that he was twenty-two years old and born in Austin. In 1899, he again told authorities that he was a native of Austin, and was thirty years old. Eleven years later (1910), prison officials reported to the census enumerator that Walters was forty-one years old, although at the time of his 1911 escape, they issued a bulletin that described him as forty-three or forty-four. Walters provided prison officials with several other clues about his past—his parents had been Roman Catholics, they were deceased prior to 1891, and Bill had been on his own since the age of eleven—meager details that lead to few revelations.[22]

The sacramental records of St. Mary's Church (now Cathedral) in Austin contain no records, baptismal or otherwise, for a William Walters or a Walters family. The 1880 Texas census, however, does enumerate a William Walters of the appropriate age, a resident within the household of Louisiana natives William R. and Mary Small in Harris County just east of Houston. His possible appearance in the Small's household is consistent with his assertion to penitentiary officials that he had been on his own since the age of eleven, and a Harris County nativity for Walters conforms to Bob Beverly's recollection of his east Texas origin. Ten years earlier, the 1870 Texas census intriguingly had enumerated five young Walters children, six to fifteen years of age, living with the Jonathan and Mary Jane Busley family of Lynchburg, also in the Harris County. Mary Jane Walters had married Jonathan Busley only months before the census enumeration. The presence of five Walters children in the household suggests that she was likely a widow at the time of the wedding. Although no William is listed, possibly a breakup in the Walters family resulted from the death of a father and a mother's remarriage, and he was placed with another relative. No other evidence supports this hypothesis, however, and no child of the Walters surname was baptized within either of Harris County's two Catholic churches between 1868 and 1871. Little more has been ascertained about Bill's Texas background, though evidence suggests that Bronco Bill had family ties to some prominent Texans.[23]

U.S. Senator Joseph Weldon Bailey (D-Tex.) wrote New Mexico Governor George Curry in 1909 to inform that Walters was "related to some of the best people in Texas, who are my warm friends." The senator regrettably did not name these relatives, and Bailey's papers, now held by the Dallas Historical Society, are very incomplete for the 1907–12 era. No letter or memo survives to indicate who contacted the senator on Walters's behalf. Apache County, Arizona, cattleman Evans Coleman added credence to Bailey's assertion, however, when he told Texas historian J. Evetts Haley, "I met a fellow a few years ago that said Bronco was from a fine family, was a good family, and that it cost his family a lot of money to get him out of jail." The *Silver City Enterprise* also implied noteworthy connections when, after Walters's jail break on February 16, 1891, it reported, "There are strong suspicions that members of a very respectable Silver City family are implicated in the rescue of the criminals."[24]

Surviving records and recollections also establish that Walters had attended common school, and that he matured into a slender young man who stood about five feet, nine inches and weighed roughly 135 pounds. New Mexico Senator Holm "Olaf" Bursum (1867–1953), the one-time sheriff of Socorro County who had chased him and, as superintendent of the New Mexico Territorial Penitentiary, later confined him, recalled

Walters as "a good natured fellow. Kind of hatchet-faced, always smiling, dark complected, brown-eyed—slender." Similarly, Bill's one-time employer, Walter Birchfield, remembered Bronco as "dark complected, had kind of a set iron jaw, soft-spoken, dark eyed, and wouldn't have been taken for an outlaw; but he was a dead hard hombre, and had been an outlaw all of his life."[25]

If Walters's assertion that he left home about 1880 is true, his activities during the rest of that decade remain as vague as those of his childhood years. Without attribution, Tucson author and retired policeman Lorenzo Walters (no known relation) wrote that following "several train holdups," Bronco Bill fled the "Land of Nobody Knows Where," only to drift into Albuquerque, where he hired on with the Santa Fe Railway's paint gang. He further claimed that Bill had stolen a pocket book and watch from the Santa Fe–operated Alvarado Hotel in Albuquerque. Although he wrote only seven years after the death of Bronco Bill, much of Lorenzo Walters's information is unreliable—western bibliographer Ramon F. Adams devoted over six pages exposing Lorenzo Walters's errors of fact. Regardless, at the time of his 1911 escape, Bill Walters demonstrated considerable familiarity with the Duke City, and the *Albuquerque Evening Herald* reported, "He has been in the county jail in Old Albuquerque on several occasions before and remarked last night [April 19, 1911], that it had been a long time since he had visited Old Albuquerque." At the time of his escape, Bill "then started down through the Santa Fe (Railway) yards, and it was sure a surprise to see the size of them. Fourteen years ago [1897] there was only one track down there, and it wasn't very long." Although Bronco also expressed particular concern about encountering Santa Fe's special officer Ben Williams, who could identify him, it is evident that he knew Williams from Las Cruces, not Albuquerque.[26]

Old-time southwest cowboy Ben Kemp related yet another New Mexico anecdote. One afternoon in the spring of 1888, a boy in his late teens rode a jaded horse to Henry M. Porter's V+T (V cross T) Ranch at Ciénaga. On a range that extended from north of Datil, south to the top of the Black Range, and west across the Plains of San Agustin to the Gila River, V+T stock drifted from the Rio Grande to the Arizona line. The vast spread employed about sixty men, two wagon bosses, and occasionally hired itinerant cowboys. The young fellow, who answered to the name of Bill, asked Charley Woodley (wagon boss for the Gila division) if there was a need for another hand. Woodley told him no, but said he could hang about for a few days until he and his horse were fit to leave.[27]

One morning, Kemp's tale continued, some of the hands decided to have a bit of fun at the newcomer's expense. They conspired to mount Bill on the most unmanageable horse in the ranch's remuda and gleefully anticipated his flying dismount. When Kemp spotted the boy jerk a hank of hair from the horse's mane, and use it to wrap around his spur rowels, he knew the schemers would be in for the surprise. "As the boy swung into the saddle, the outlaw horse went high in the air and used every trick he knew to dislodge his rider, but the boy kept his seat without pulling leather, and when the horse finally gave up and quit, he was scratched [by the rowels] from neck to rump as though two bobcats had caught him." The astonished V+T hands bestowed the handle "Bronco Bill" on the young fellow, and Woodley offered him work busting broncos for the ranch. Bronco readily accepted the job. Over the next seven months, he demonstrated that "he was an expert rider and enjoyed working with broncos."[28]

Beyond Bronco's ability to sit a horse, there was another surprise in store for Kemp—at least that was his story. That spring, shortly before Bill's arrival at the V+T, Kemp claimed that a lone robber had held up the bank at San Marcial, about 150 miles away. A posse had followed the bandit's trail to a spring at the eastern base of the San Mateo Mountains. The trail mysteriously disappeared amid the prints left by watering cattle, and no horse tracks led away from the spring. One morning, soon after Bill's arrival, Kemp claimed to have noticed that Bronco's saddle had fallen from the top rail of the pole horse corral. Upon striking the ground, the saddlebags had sprung open to reveal four bull hoofs, trimmed to be fitted to a horse's hoofs. Kemp kept the information to himself, and, a few months later, when it was time to trail the steers to Magdalena, Bill asked for his time. He had never revealed his true name.[29]

It remains uncertain that Kemp's "Bronco Bill" was, in fact, William Walters. In the late 1880s, Bill could not have cowboyed for the Bar B and later the 69 Ranch in West Texas as Bob Beverly asserted, and simultaneously have been breaking broncs for the V+T in New Mexico. Also, the only recorded holdup of a bank at San Marcial was the November 23, 1892, robbery of Jasper Newton Broyles's grocery (which served as the local bank) by Newt Harold (alias Jim Taylor, alias Morgan) of Missouri. Several factors, however, argue in Kemp's favor.[30]

Nineteen years old in the spring of 1888, Bill was the proper age, and the V+T's range was a locale with which he later had familiarity. The young fellow's expertise in the saddle also strengthens the case for Walters, as do the recollections of Cole Railston.

A native of Doniphan, Missouri, Railston had immigrated to Engle, New Mexico, about 1885 by way of Indian Territory and Wyoming. After a brief stint cowboying for the Double Circle outfit north of Clifton, Arizona, he reached Magdalena, New Mexico, in 1887, and later rode for the Bar H Bar, the J Half-Circle, the Bar N Cross, and worked for the Livestock Sanitary Board before he hired on with Porter's V+T as general manager of the Gila division. He, too, remembered the hatchet-faced outlaw, although his recollection was less than flattering. "Broncho Bill as to looks, you couldn't compare him to anything unless it was some ridiculous pictures. Would guess he was about five [feet], six or seven [inches], and bony, no flesh and an awful crooked bony ugly face." There is no mistake that Railston captured the essence of the thin, iron-jawed desperado, and must have crossed trails with Walters somewhere east of the Rio Grande on the Jornada del Muerto or west of Socorro on the Plains of San Agustin. If Bill left the V+T in the fall of 1888, he headed south, for he soon appeared in New Mexico's "Boot Heel" region.[31]

Prospectors had discovered copper a few miles east of Silver City at the onset of the nineteenth century. A settlement christened Santa Rita del Cobre quickly emerged. Convict labor from New Spain mined the ore; mule trains carried the copper down the Janos Trail into Chihuahua and Sonora in northern Mexico. In late 1880, with the arrival of the Southern Pacific Railroad, Separ emerged as a cattle-loading station for the valley ranches. Obstreperous cowboys from the vast Diamond A Ranch, thirsty miners from the Eureka mining district in the nearby Little Hatchet Mountains, and boisterous railroad workers, mixed together in the small but eclectic community. It was just the kind of place that would attract Bronco Bill.[32]

Some years later, a *Santa Fe Daily New Mexican* report placed Bill in Separ as early as 1889, when one M. P. Moore sought "Walters and his pal for horse stealing." Moore, the story continued, "found them asleep, but he had scarcely entered the house before Walters was up with a six shooter in each hand; but the fearless Moore had the muzzle of a double barreled shot gun on his chest and Walters dropped his weapons." Walters unquestionably possessed "great nerve," Moore judged, but the *New Mexican*'s account of the encounter is an amalgam based on a later event.[33] Even so, as early as 1890, Harvey Whitehill, the Grant County sheriff, labeled Walters an "old time rustler and horse thief who had a record here several years ago." Yet no evidence of that record exists in either the Grant County Docket Books or the "Register of Prisoners Confined in the County Jail 1877–1895."[33]

These pieces of the Bronco Bill puzzle leave us with precious little. William Walters was probably born in Texas in 1869, possibly near Austin or Houston, to a family that enjoyed some prominence. A family tragedy or other incident may have caused him to head off on his own hook at an early age, but he kept up at least some family contact, as evidenced by a few photographs of an unnamed niece that he carried at the time of his 1911 capture. He perfected his talent as a horse wrangler and cowboy—possibly in West Texas—before he headed to New Mexico while still in his late teens. He may have gained at least some familiarity with Albuquerque and the V+T range on the Plains of San Agustin before he surfaced in the southwest corner of the territory—New Mexico's boot heel—as a veteran cowhand. In the fall of 1890, Walters, by his reckoning, approached his twenty-first birthday. Only then did his life and story cease to be anecdotal.[34]

Notes

Abbreviations

AHS	Arizona Historical Society
ASL	Arizona State Library, Archives and Public Records
KSHS	Kansas State Historical Society
LBBT	Louis Bradley Blachly Transcripts, University of New Mexico
NAB	National Archives Building, Washington, D.C.
NACP	National Archives at College Park, Maryland
NARA (PRLN)	National Archives—Pacific Region (Laguna Niguel, Calif.)
NARA (RMR)	National Archives—Rocky Mountain Region (Denver)
NMSRCA	New Mexico State Records Center and Archives
NSH	Nita Stewart Haley Memorial Library and J. Evetts Haley History Center
TANM	Territorial Archives of New Mexico
UNM	University of New Mexico
WFB	Wells Fargo Bank, Historical Services, San Francisco, California

Introduction

1. Some wrongly attribute the first railroad heist to John and Simeon Reno and their October 6, 1866, assault on the Ohio and Mississippi passenger train near Seymour, Indiana. The North Bend holdup predated

the Seymour robbery by more than one year. See Eden, "America's First Train Robbery."

2. *Cincinnati Daily Times*, May 6, 1865.

3. Ibid., May 7, 1865.

4. Hume and Thacker, *Report*, 3; *New York Times*, May 12, 1889, September 22, 1892, April 28, 1897.

5. *New York Times*, January 11, 1898; Harlow, *Old Waybills*, 437; Pinkerton, *Train Robberies*, 30–43.

6. Pinkerton, *Train Robberies*, 4–5; Pinkerton, "Highwaymen," 537.

7. Act of June 8, 1872, ch. 335, 1-327, 17 Stat. 320, "Notice of Reward," Post Office Department, Office of the Postmaster Inspector, Washington, D.C., September 27, 1897.

8. *Annual Reports of the Post-Office Department . . . 1897*, 800.

9. Pinkerton, "Highwaymen," 537; *St. Louis Globe-Democrat*, reprinted in the *New York Times*, April 8, 1896.

10. Territory of New Mexico, Statutes of 1887, ch. 9, p. 44 (cited in *Albuquerque Daily Citizen*, November 9, 1897).

11. Territory of Arizona, Statutes, House Bill no. 2, "An Act defining certain offenses Against the Public Peace," February 28, 1889; *Arizona Weekly Journal-Miner*, July 31, 1889; Third Judicial District Court, Yavapai County, *Territory of Arizona v. Harvick, Halford, Stiren, and Smith*, case no. 36; Harvick, "Canyon Diablo Train Robbery," 8–11, 48–51.

12. Second Judicial District Court, Pinal County, *Territory of Arizona v. Frans Oscar Torén*, case file no. 132; Benjamin J. Franklin, Proclamation of Commutation of Sentence, September 2, 1896, Records, Secretary of State (Arizona); *Arizona Daily Gazette*, September 5, 1896; *Tombstone Prospector*, September 15, 1896. See also Tanner and Tanner, *"Up Goes Your Hands!"*

13. White, "Bad Man's Nemesis," 24–25. See also Tanner and Tanner, "Scott White."

14. First Judicial District Court, Cochise County, Minutes, vol. 9, 291, *Territory of Arizona v. William Downing*, case no. 745A; *Bisbee Review*, reprinted in the *Arizona Daily Citizen*, December 24, 1900; Tanner and Tanner, "'Quarrelsome' Bill Downing."

15. Burton, *Deadliest Outlaws* and *Dynamite and Six-shooter*, "An Act for the Suppression of Train Robbery in the Territories of the United States" (Act July 1, 1902, c. 1370, §§1, 32 Stat. 727); Tanner and Tanner, "Rewards and Justice."

16. Hampton, "Brigandage on our Railroads," 665–66, 668.

17. Knight, "How to Repel Train Robbers," 254–55.
18. "Modern Dick Turpin," 63; *New York Times*, December 26, 1896.
19. *New York Times*, January 30, 1897.

Chapter 1. Open Spaces, Tight Places

1. *Southwest Sentinel*, October 21, 1890; *Silver City Enterprise*, February 20, 1891; Grant County, Register of Prisoners Confined in the County Jail 1877–1895, 139, NMSRCA, cited hereafter as Grant County, Register of Prisoners; Grant County, Third Judicial District Court of New Mexico, *Territory v. Miles McGinnis*, case no. 3417, NMSRCA. See Appendix for an essay on Bronco Bill Walters's origins.

2. *Silver City Enterprise*, October 24, 1890.

3. Ibid., December 27, 1889, October 17, 1890; *Southwest Sentinel*, October 21, 1890; John T. "Salty John" Cox, Albuquerque, N. Mex., interview by Louis Blachly, June 7, 1952, LBBT.

4. Annie A. Parker served as postmistress from March 17, 1888, to April 16, 1895 (U.S. Post Office Department, Records of the Division of Postmasters, Post Office Appointments, New Mexico, vol. 74, ca. 1891–96, p. 257—Separ).

5. Alexander, *Sheriff Harvey Whitehill*, 9, 25n.2, 283, 286–87n.55; *Silver City Enterprise*, October 24, 1890, and July 8, 1910.

6. Ollie Whitehill Belle, interview by Blachly, October 24, 1953, LBBT.

7. *Silver City Enterprise*, October 24, 1890, February 21, 1898, and March 4, 1902; *Southwest Sentinel*, October 21, 1890; Grant County, Register of Prisoners, p. 139.

8. *Silver City Enterprise*, February 20, and March 13, 1891.

9. Ibid., February 20, 1891; Grant County, Register of Prisoners, 139. The date of escape was recorded as February 17, 1891.

10. Wayne Wilson, Silver City, N. Mex., interview with Blachly, January 16, 1956, LBBT.

11. *Silver City Enterprise*, February 20, 1891.

12. Ibid., March 13, and February 27, 1891.

13. Ibid., March 13, 1891.

14. *Southwest Sentinel*, March 10, 1891.

15. Hornung, "Cipriano Baca," 42; *Silver City Enterprise*, March 13, 1891.

16. *Silver City Enterprise*, March 13, 1891.

17. Ibid.

18. Cox, interview by Blachly, June 7, 1952, LBBT.

19. Sonnichsen, *Tularosa*, 50; Meadows, *Pat Garrett and Billy the Kid*, 105; Cox, interview by Blachly, June 7, 1952, LBBT.

20. *Silver City Enterprise*, March 13, 1891; Grant County, Register of Prisoners, p. 139.

21. Grant County, Third Judicial District Court of New Mexico, Criminal Docket Book G, pp. 227–28; Journal L, pp. 554–55, Journal M, pp. 26–27; *Silver City Enterprise*, May 29, 1891.

22. Grant County, Register of Prisoners, p. 139; N.M. Territorial Penitentiary, Admission Records, William Walters, no. 485, NMSRCA; *Santa Fe Daily New Mexican*, August 7, 18, 1885; Governor Edmund G. Ross Journal, August 21, 1885, pp. 274–75, NMSRCA.

23. Territory of New Mexico, Legislative Assembly Papers, Report of the Special Standing Committee of the Council on Penitentiary, February 23. 1887, pp. 5, 7, 12, NMSRCA.

24. N.M. Territorial Penitentiary, Admission Records, William Walters, no. 485.

25. *Silver City Independent*, May 1, 22, 29, 1891, May 19, 1908; 1880 U.S. Census, Silver City, N. Mex.; *Southwest Sentinel*, June 2, 1891. Drew Hunter later turned to raising goats on the Gila River. He moved to Lordsburg in 1906 where he died of tuberculosis on May 22, 1908 (*Silver City Enterprise*, May 22, 1908).

26. Cox, interview by Blachly, June 7, 1952, LBBT; *Western Liberal*, June 19, 1896; *Deming Headlight*, June 19, 1896.

27. Brock and Cox, interview by Blachly, April 11, 1953, LBBT.

28. Birchfield to Haley, November 2, 1939, NSH; *Globe-Democrat*, September 3, 1896; *Silver City Enterprise*, September 4, 1896; *Tombstone Prospector*, September 10, 1896; Edward L. Hall, U.S. marshal, Santa Fe, N. Mex., letter to Judson Harmon, U.S. attorney general, Washington, D.C., September 2, 1896, United States Department of Justice file 13.065, NACP (cited hereafter as Justice file 13.065).

29. Bryan, *True Tales*, 87; Brock and Cox, interview by Blachly, April 11, 1953, LBBT; Walter Birchfield, El Paso, Tex., letter to Haley, November 2, 1939, NSH.

30. Brock and Cox, interview by Blachly, April 11, 1953, LBBT; Bryan, *True Tales*, 87; Birchfield to Haley, November 2, 1939, NSH.

31. Birchfield to Haley, November 2, 1939, NSH.

32. Grant County, Register of Prisoners, p. 25, NMSRCA.

33. *Silver City Enterprise*, February 21, 1896.

34. Ibid. Harry M. Dougherty, the Socorro County district attorney, later confused both the date and the site of the burglary when he filed information that the burglary occurred on February 14, 1895 (Socorro County, Fifth Judicial District Court of New Mexico, *Territory v. William Walters*, case no. 1571, NMSRCA).

35. *Socorro Chieftain,* February 21, 1894.

36. Ibid., March 6, 1894; *Albuquerque Morning Democrat,* February 29, 1896; *Silver City Eagle,* March 4, 1896; *Socorro Chieftain* March 6, 1894; Governor William Thornton, penal papers, requisitions, NMSRCA.

Chapter 2. Bronco's Luck

1. Cox, interview by Blachly, June 7, 1952. LBBT; Jeff Milton, Tombstone, Ariz., interview by J. Evetts Haley, March 4, 1948, NSH; *Deming Headlight,* April 3, 1896. Burrell Quimby Musgrave, a first cousin of High Five outlaw George Musgrave's father, arrived in Deming about 1895. He was twice arrested for violating Sunday law in May 1895. Almost immediately after the Walters shooting incident, Musgrave moved to Las Cruces (Grant County, Third Judicial District Court of New Mexico, *Territory v. B. Q. Musgrave,* case nos. 39810 and 4002, Docket Book G, 511 and 522; *Western Liberal,* September 4, 1896; Tanner and Tanner, *Last of the Old-Time Outlaws,* 19, 53, 145, 168, 284–85n.42).

2. *Silver City Enterprise,* April 8, 1896; Cox, interview by Blachly, June 7, 1952, LBBT.

3. *Deming Headlight,* April 3, 1896.

4. *Silver City Enterprise,* April 8, 1896.

5. *Deming Headlight,* April 3, 1896; *Santa Fe Daily New Mexican,* April 3, 1896; Milton, interview by Haley, December 2, 1942, NSH.

6. *Silver City Enterprise,* April 8, 1896.

7. Cox, interview by Blachly, June 7, 1952, LBBT; *Silver City Enterprise,* November 29, 1895.

8. *El Paso Daily Times,* June 2, 1896.

9. Ibid., June 2, 1896; *Western Liberal,* April 10, 1896; *Silver City Enterprise,* April 10, 1896.

10. *Western Liberal,* April 24, 1896; *Silver City Enterprise,* April 24, 1896; *El Paso Herald,* reprinted in the *Silver City Enterprise,* April 24, 1896; *Deming Headlight,* April 10, 1896.

11. Cox, interview by Blachly, June 7, 1952, LBBT.

12. Ibid.; Cox, "Salty John Cox and Bronco Bill," 24.

13. Cox, interview by Blachly, June 7, 1952, LBBT

14. Ibid.

15. *Western Liberal*, May 1, 1896; *El Paso Daily Times*, June 2, 1896; Cox, "Salty John Cox and Bronco Bill," 25.

16. *Deming Headlight*, June 19, 1895, *Silver City Enterprise*, May 29, and June 19, 1896; *Western Liberal*, June 19, 1896; Cox, interview by Blachly, June 7, 1952, LBBT.

17. Webb, *Handbook of Texas*, 1:858. The following December, Murray struck Louis Cabetho over the head with his revolver at Ozona's Silver Exchange Saloon, and Cabetho "took the lower route." Murray was acquitted in May 1898 (*State of Texas v. Sam Murray*, Tom Green County, case no. 1217). The following November 2, Otto Schauer and Murray shot and killed lawman Ben Cole, who had disapproved of Schauer's infatuation with Cole's daughter. Cole fired at his daughter's suitor, and Schauer's fired round unhorsed Cole. From the ground, the lawman supposedly fired at Murray, who then shot Cole between the eyes. An incessant string of continuances, reversals, changes of venues, and mistrials followed (*Ozona Courier*, quoted in the *San Angelo Standard*, January 9, 1897; *San Angelo Standard*, May 21, 28, November 5, 1898; Jeff Burton, Gosport, England, letter to authors, November 22, 2002).

18. Cox, interview by Blachly, June 7, 1952, LBBT.

19. Thornton, penal papers, requisitions, NMSRCA.

20. *El Paso Daily Times*, May 28, 1896.

21. *Deming Headlight*, reprinted from the El Paso Herald, May 29, 1896.

22. Thornton, penal papers, requisitions, NMSRCA.

23. *El Paso Daily Times*, June 2, 1896.

24. Ibid.; *Western Liberal*, June 5, 1896.

25. Cox, interview by Blachly, June 7, 1952. LBBT.

26. Ibid.; *El Paso Daily Times*, June 2, 1896

27. *El Paso Daily Times*, November 22, 1896; *Western Liberal*, November 27, 1896; *El Paso Herald* reprinted in *Silver City Enterprise*, November 27, 1896. Years later, Coleman was charged and acquitted of murder in the death of his wife. After his acquittal, he returned to western Socorro (now Catron) County, where he also faced a charge of horse rustling. In an ironic twist, on October 15, 1921, Salty John Cox, "a long, lean cattleman of the old school," led a posse of four men in an attempt to serve the warrant. Foolishly, Coleman chose to resist arrest, pulled his gun, and was dropped by a bullet fired from Cox's Mauser rifle. "One

member of the [coroner's] jury looked at Coleman's body and said he had never seen an ace in the hole that looked any prettier," Salty John recalled with pride. Having once attempted his rescue, Cox had become Henry Coleman's killer (Curry, *An Autobiography*, 287; Bryan, True Tales, 107).

Chapter 3. Strange Ways of Justice

1. Sheriff Bursum, Notice of Return (Thornton, penal papers, requisitions, NMSRCA).

2. Socorro County, Fifth Judicial District Court of New Mexico, Record Book F (1895–1898), 246, NMSRCA.

3. C. G. Dungan, Socorro, N. Mex., letter to Hon. H. B. Hamilton, judge, December 9, 1896, *Territory v. William Walters*, case no. 1571; Socorro County, Record Book F, pp. 262–63, NMSRCA; John E. Griffith, district attorney, Socorro, N. Mex., letter to Frank W. Clancy, attorney general, Albuquerque, N. Mex., December 29, 1909, Governor George Curry, penal papers, NMSRCA.

4. *Deming Headlight*, May 29, 1896.

5. *Silver City Enterprise*, August 12, 1898; Grant County District Court, Third Judicial District Court of New Mexico, Criminal Docket Book G (June 1889–December 1898), *Territory v. William Walters*, case nos. 4077 and 4084, 559 and 565, NMSRCA.

6. Only four years later, Heflin, a native of Huntsville, Texas, was shot in the Club House bar by gambler John W. Childers. The thirty-six-year-old attorney died the next afternoon, December 14, 1901 (*Silver City Enterprise*, December 17, 1901, April 29, 1902; see also Tanner and Tanner, "Silver City Shootout").

7. *Silver City Independent*, June 8, 1897; *Deming Headlight*, June 4, 1892; Grant County, Third Judicial District Court of New Mexico, *Territory v. William Walters*, case file nos. 4077 and 4084.

8. *Territory v. William Walters*, case file nos. 4077 and 4084; *Deming Headlight*, June 4, 1892. The acquittal was in case no. 4084; the prosecution had dropped the charge in case no. 4077 with leave to reinstate.

9. *Silver City Independent*, June 8, 1897; *Silver City Eagle*, quoted in Bryan, *True Tales*, 178.

10. Cox, interview by Blachly, June 7, 1952. LBBT.

11. *Arizona Daily Star*, December 10 and 11, 1897; Burton, *Dynamite and Six-shooter*, 49–52.

12. *Silver City Enterprise,* June 10, 1898.

13. Ibid., December 31, 1897.

14. Without additional explanation, Duffy signed, "Given under my hand and seal December 13, 1897, filed 18 December" (Records of the U.S. Marshal's Service, Appointments, Bonds, and Oaths of U.S. Marshals and Deputy Marshals, 1864–1912, NARA [PRLN]; William M. Griffith, Tucson, letter to Attorney General John W. Griggs, Washington, D.C., September 13, 1898, Justice file 13.065. For Milton's biography, see Haley, *Jeff Milton.*

15. *Arizona Daily Star,* December 10, 11, 15, 16, and 17, 1897; *Arizona Republican,* December 11 and 12, December, 1897; *Rio Grande Republican,* December 17, 1897; *Silver City Enterprise,* December 10, 17, 24, and 31, 1897; *Silver City Independent,* December 14, 1897; *Deming Headlight,* December 10, 17, 1897. See also Burton, *Deadliest Outlaws.*

16. W. B. Childers, Silver City, N. Mex., letter to J. N. Thacker, Tucson, Ariz. Terr., February 13, 1898, Marshals Correspondence, AHS.

17. Milton, interview by Haley, March 4, 1938, NSH. Philip Rasch, without attribution, added Scott White and Orville Cooper to the posse (Rasch, "An Incomplete Account," 5).

18. DeArment, *George Scarborough,* 196; Milton, interview by Haley, March 4, 1938, NSH; Childers to Thacker, February 13, 1898, Marshals Correspondence, AHS.

19. Lutrell, *Newspaper and Periodicals of Arizona, 1859–1911,* 33; Records of the United States Marshals Service, Arizona, Appointments, Bonds, and Oaths, Record Group 527, NARA [PRLN]; *San Diego Union,* June 22, 2003.

20. Milton, interview by Haley, December 2. 1942, NSH.

21. Ibid., March 4, 1938, and December 2. 1942, NSH. On February 16, 1898, a Grant County, New Mexico, grand jury returned two indictments against the six Steins Pass suspects (*Silver City Enterprise,* February 18, 1898; Burton, letter to the authors, July 18, 2003).

22. John W. Griggs, Washington, D.C., to William M. Griffith, Tucson, Ariz., February 16, 1898, Marshals Correspondence, AHS.

23. Ben M. Crawford, Clifton, Ariz., letter to Griffith, March 22, 1898, Marshals Correspondence, AHS.

24. *Arizona Bulletin,* "Special Edition, 1903," 45; King, *Pioneer Western Empire Builders,* 198.

25. Griffith to Griggs, September 13, 1898, Justice File 13.065.

26. Tom Ketchum and gang biographer Jeffrey Burton reached a like conclusion: "That stuff that Milton fed Haley about getting on

BB's trail after his (Milton's) return from Mexico, and being about to catch him when the call came to attend the trial in Silver City, reads almost as though designed to fit the tale he had spun Griffith—or which he and Griffith concocted between them for incorporation in the letter to [Attorney General] Griggs (Burton, letter to the authors, May 31, 2004. See also Burton, *Deadliest Outlaws*, 109–10).

27. *Rocky Mountain News*, April 27, 1901; *San Francisco Chronicle*, April 27, 1901.

28. *Western Liberal*, September 8, 1899.

29. Burton, *Dynamite and Six-shooter*, 97–109, 125–26.

30. *Santa Fe New Mexican*, August 8, 1898. On June 10, 1896, Tom and Sam Ketchum had robbed the Levi and Morris Herzstein store and post office at the little settlement of Liberty, New Mexico. During the subsequent pursuit, the Ketchums killed Levi Herzstein and Merejildo Gallegos. Although various agencies posted rewards, neither Ketchum was subsequently indicted (Burton, *Dynamite and Six-shooter*, 25–28).

31. Burton, to the authors, October 22, 2002; Burton, *Deadliest Outlaws*, 296.

32. Otero, *My Nine Years as Governor*, 111–14.

33. Hovey, "Black Jack Ketchum," 50.

34. N.M. Territorial Penitentiary, Admission Records; *Rocky Mountain News*, August 9, 1898; *Santa Fe Daily New Mexican*, August 13, 1898. "Perhaps Hovey confused Walters's arrest with that of Sam Ketchum, whose confession he does not mention" (Burton, letter to the authors, October 6, 2004).

35. Crawford to Griffith, March 22, 1898, Marshals Correspondence, AHS.

Chapter 4. Black River Toughs

1. Myrick, *New Mexico's Railroads*, 15, 32; Johnston, *Old Magdalena*, 3–5.

2. *Silver City Enterprise*, December 14, 28, 1882; February 22, and March 1, 8, 15, 22, 1883. See also Nolan, "Boss Rustler."

3. Albert Haywood Johnson, Arizona Standard Certificate of Death, May 12, 1941; William Thomas Johnson, Coryell County, Texas, Death Records, Book 1, 1903–1917; 1870 U.S. Census, McLennan County, Texas; Coryell County, Texas, Marriage Records, 1854–1956.

4. California Department of Health Services, Center for Health Statistics, "Death Index, 1940–1997," February 8, 1966; Socorro County

Deed Book 10, pp. 69–70; World War I Draft Registration Cards, 1917–1918; *Silver City Enterprise,* December 7, 1966; Johnny Longbotham, interview with Blachly, July 16, 1952, LBBT; A. J. "Jack" Stockbridge, interview with Blachly, May 1957, LBBT; headstones, Albert and Emeline Johnson, Luna Cemetery, section E. About 1930, Albert Johnson moved near Jerome, Arizona, to be near daughter Alice, living in Clarkdale. He died May 12, 1941, at Haskell Springs Ranch, Jerome (Arizona Standard Certificate of Death).

5. Ryder Ridgeway, *Graham County Courier,* May 2, 1979; Evans Coleman, Thatcher, Arizona, interview with Haley and Chesley, February 27, 1945, NSH. See also Chesley, *Adventuring with the Old-Timers,* 153–59. Coleman died at Thatcher, Arizona, on December 15, 1954 (*Arizona Republic,* December 17, 1954).

6. Coleman, interview with Haley and Chesley, February 27, 1945, NSH. The criminal docket books of Socorro and Grant counties, New Mexico, reveal no indictments returned against William Johnson.

7. Coleman, interview with Haley and Chesley, NSH.

8. Farish, *History of Arizona,* 6:294–95; Melvin Jones, "Reminiscences, as told to Mrs. George F. Kitt, January 7, 1928." MS 392, AHS, hereafter cited as Jones Reminiscences. The son of Patrick (1814–1893) and Abigail O'Dell Tuttle Coulter (1817–1898), Jim Colter told interviewer Thomas Edwin Farish that he was born in 1844 and immigrated in 1860. Other sources provide various years for his birth (Orma Phelps Udall, Papers, AHS [cited hereafter as Udall Papers]; Certificate of Death, James T. Colter, filed July 9, 1922). James D. Murray was born March 7, 1850. He died on March 26, 1902, and is buried in the Slaughter Family Cemetery, Springerville.

9. Rudd, "Eliza Catherine Rudd Tells of Early History," 200.

10. Jones Reminiscences; Udall Papers. Rosa Rudd was born March 19, 1859, at Fayetteville, Arkansas. The Colter's first child, daughter Abigail, was born December 23, 1877, and died on January 9, 1878. In addition to Abigail, the other Colter children were: Frederick "Fred" Tuttle Colter, of whom more later; Ammon Edward Colter, of whom more later; Maude Eliza Colter, born December 1, 1884, at Newton, Kans., married (first) Thomas Phelps December 26, 1898 and (second) Joseph K. Udall, died November 13, 1975, at Eagar, Ariz.; Burton "Bert" James Colter, born January 25, 1886, at Newton, Kans., of whom more later; and Harrison "Harry" Elmer Colter, born November 1,

1890, at Newton, Kans., married Joyce Udall, died November 11, 1937 (Udall Papers; United States Selective Service System, Records of the Selective Service System [World War I], Apache County, Arizona).

11. Farish, *History of Arizona,* 6:297.

12. Peterson, *Take Up Your Mission,* 32; Flake, *William J. Flake,* 83; McClintock, *Mormon Settlement,* 185; Udall Papers.

13. Socorro County, Indirect Deed Index, vol. 1, p. 46, land in San Francisco River, recorded April 1, 1880.

14. Snyder, "Alma Massacre," 2–3; "Colter Speaks on Indian Days," *Prescott Evening Courier,* September 17, 1931.

15. Farish, *History of Arizona,* 6:301; Udall Papers.

16. Socorro County, New Mexico, Deed Book 8, 99, 105; Farish, *History of Arizona,* 6:306; *Silver City Enterprise,* June 29, 1883, January 25, February 22, November 21, 1884; Udall Papers; Jones Reminiscences; *James H. Colter v. Edwin Marriage,* New Mexico Supreme Court, case no. 257, NMSRCA.

17. Jones Reminiscences.

18. Bert J. Colter, "As His Brother Knew Him," 1–6; Udall Papers; Bert J. Colter, "Autobiography (February 1963)," 1–2; Jones Reminiscences; Evans Coleman, interview with Haley and Chesley, NSH. Frederick "Fred" Tuttle Colter, who represented Apache County in the 1910 Arizona constitutional convention, went on to serve eight terms in the state senate and one term each from Apache and Maricopa counties as a state representative. In 1918, he lost the state gubernatorial election to Thomas E. Campbell by a mere 339 votes. He sought the governorship again in 1930, but lost the Democratic nomination to Governor George W. P. Hunt. Colter was struck by an automobile and died on January 8, 1944, at Phoenix (*Tucson Daily Star,* August 18, 1927; *Arizona Republic,* January 8, 1944; *Phoenix Gazette,* January 8, 1944; *St. Johns Herald-Observer,* January 15, 1944). See also Goetz, *A Prophet with Honor.*

When he was nineteen years old, Bert Colter assumed the management of his brother Fred's cow and horse outfit. He later served as an Apache County deputy sheriff, was a member of the Apache County board of supervisors, and was elected to a term in the Arizona Senate in 1941. He chose not to seek reelection, but did successfully run again in 1961. He died in 1980 (Colter, "As His Brother Knew Him"; Colter, "Autobiography").

19. Coleman, "A Little Outlaw Gang," 1.

Chapter 5. Bringing Up Red

1. Hatch, "Nancy Julia Pipkin"; William Philip Pipkin, "Aser Pipkin" and "Mary Lafentie Pipkin"; Retha Amadio, Provo, Utah, letter to the authors, May 12, 2002; General Land Office, Little Rock, Arkansas, document no. 8098, June 1, 1859; 1860 U.S. census, Prairie County, Arkansas. Born November 18, 1805, Aser Pipkin died on January 20, 1901, at Fruitland, San Juan County, New Mexico.

2. Service Record, Sergeant J. K. P. Pipkin, Witt's Regiment, Arkansas Cavalry, War Department Collection of Confederate Records, Record Group 109, National Archives and Records Administration, Washington, D.C. (NAB). See also Dirck, "Witt's Cavalry."

3. "History of the Southern States Mission," *Southern Star*, vol. 1, December 3, 1898, p. 1, published by the Southern States Mission; Amadio, letter to the authors, May 13, 2002; William Philip Pipkin, "Aser Pipkin."

4. Horace Earl Pipkin (Red Pipkin's nephew), "Story of Daniel Moroni Pipkin," MS; William Philip Pipkin, "Aser Pipkin."

5. McClintock, *Mormon Settlement*, 137–40, 142–45; Amadio, letters to the authors, May 12, and 13, 2002; 1880 U.S. census, Apache County, Arizona.

6. William C. McClellan, Sunset, Ariz., letter to Erastus Snow, Salt Lake City, Utah, December 19, 1878, and J. K. P. Pipkin, Sunset, Ariz., letter to McClellan, n.d., Sunset Order Paper, quoted in Peterson, *Take Up Your Mission*, 116.

7. Taylor, *The Last Pioneer*, 303.

8. Wilhelm and Wilhelm, *History of St. Johns Arizona Stake*, 80–81; Peterson, *Take Up Your Mission*, 23; McClintock, *Mormon Settlement*, 188.

9. Wilhelm and Wilhelm, *History of St. Johns Arizona Stake*, 82; Telling, "Ramah, New Mexico," 120; Retha Amadio, Provo, Utah, letter to the authors, May 13, 2002; Tietjen, *Ernst Albert Tietjen*, 231.

10. Tietjen, *Ernst Albert Tietjen*, 230–31; Teller, "Ramah, New Mexico," 123; Lewis, "Journal of Samuel E. Lewis," June 17, 1887, cited hereafter as Lewis, Journal. Author Gary Tietjen also revealed that a few suspected foul play.

11. Lewis, Journal, December 10 and October 26, 1888.

12. Ibid., August 21, 1890; Irving Telling, "Ramah, New Mexico," 124.

13. Lewis, Journal, October 26, 1890. Gary Tietjen provides another account of the shooting and its aftermath in *Ernst Albert Tietjen*, 231–33.

14. Teller, "Ramah, New Mexico," 124; Lewis, Journal, November 5, 1890; *Elk* (Gallup), December 5, 1890; Amadio, letter to the authors, May 13, 2002.

15. After she left James Pipkin, Vira gave birth to a daughter, Josephine, on April 5, 1891, at her parents' home in Pima, Graham County, Arizona. She divorced Pipkin and married Robert Lee McBroom at Globe, Arizona, on November 17, 1897. Sarah Levira Lewis Pipkin McBroom died on October 4, 1960 (see "Sarah Levira Lewis").

16. Coleman, "1896 Diary of Evans Coleman," July 23. 1896.

17. Ibid.; Evans Coleman, Thatcher, Ariz., letter to the editor, *St. Johns Herald-Observer*, Ariz., July 5, 1925, AHS.

18. Accomazzo, *Arizona National Ranch Histories*, 6:7; Coleman, "A Little Outlaw Gang," 1–2. Peter Eldridge Slaughter (1846–1911) and his younger brother Mason Lee "Mace" Slaughter (1863–94) were the sons of George Webb Slaughter, a cousin of Benjamin Slaughter, father of John Horton Slaughter of Cochise County renown. Arizona "Cap" Smith shot and killed Mace Slaughter near Morenci, Arizona, on July 2, 1894. Mace's nephew, Monterey "Monte" Slaughter (born in September 1874), was the oldest of Peter Slaughter's children (see Clarke, *The Slaughter Ranches*, 162–63, 193–98; *Arizona Daily Citizen*, August 7, 1894; 1900 U.S. census, Apache County, Arizona, see also Tanner and Tanner, "Revenge").

19. U.S. District Court, Second District of New Mexico. *U.S. v. James Burnett et al.*, case file no. 2009. For the activities of the High Five gang, see Tanner and Tanner, *Last of the Old-Time Outlaws*

20. Evans P. Coleman, interview with Haley and Chesley; Coleman, "A Little Outlaw Gang"; Creighton Foraker, Albuquerque, to J. E. Hurley, Las Vegas, New Mex., June 30, 1898, Misc. Letter Book of C. M. Foraker, Aug. 1897–Aug. 1898, 456, General Correspondence of the United States Marshals, New Mex., MS 322, UNM, hereafter Foraker Papers; Willson, " Little Old Arizona Cowboy."

Chapter 6. Fiasco at Grants

1. Coe, *Ranch on the Ruidoso*, 153; Pinkerton, "Highwaymen," 537; Coleman, interview with Haley and Chesley, NSH.

2. *Arizona Orb* (Bisbee), reprinted in *Holbrook Argus*, April 30, 1898; *Daily Star*, December 16, 1897.

3. *Daily Star*, December 16, 1897; Coleman, "Little Outlaw Gang," 3; Coleman, letter to *Arizona Republic*, Phoenix, December 23, 1937, AHS.

4. *Western Liberal,* April 1, 1898.

5. *Albuquerque Daily Citizen,* March 29. 1898; *Denver Evening Post,* March 30, 1898; Julyan, *Place Names of New Mexico,* 154; Tanner and Tanner, *Last of the Old-Time Outlaws,* 139–44. Unless otherwise noted, the *Albuquerque Daily Citizen,* March 29, and 30, 1898, is the source of this account of the robbery.

6. *Los Angeles Daily Times,* March 30, 1898; *Phoenix Republican* (reprinted in the *Florence Tribune,* April 9, 1898); Coleman, interview with Haley and Chesley, NSH.

7. John J. Valentine, San Francisco, letter to C. C. Lord, Los Angeles, September 7, 1898, WFB.

8. *Los Angeles Daily Times,* March 30, 1898.

9. *Holbrook Argus,* June 4, 18, and July 2, 1898. Lathrop died at Winslow, Arizona, of stomach cancer on November 10, 1948 (Certificate of Death, Judson C. Lathrop, filed November 12, 1948).

10. Tanner and Tanner, *Last of the Old-Time Outlaws,* 143; *Santa Fe Daily New Mexican,* March 30, 1898. For Fornoff's career, see Hornung, *Thin Grey Line,* 31–59.

11. *Silver City Eagle,* April 9. 1898.

12. *Los Angeles Daily Times,* March 30, 1898; *Place Names of New Mexico,* 385; "L. A. Cameron With Wells, Fargo & Co's Ex.," notebook, HR #8671, 127, WFB.

13. Zuni People, *The Zunis: Self Portrayals,* 86–90.

14. *Arizona Bulletin* (Solomonville), April 8, 1898; *Graham Guardian* (Safford. Ariz.), April 8, 1898.

15. Slaughter's active role in pursuing local rustlers had nearly cost him his life when, in May 1887, he was shot in the back by two such individuals, Joe Adkins and one Youngblood. Youngblood later surrendered and was acquitted. Adkins was convicted of larceny and sentenced in Socorro County to a one-year term at the territorial penitentiary (*Silver City Enterprise,* May 13, and July 15, 1887, May 4, 1888; N.M. Territorial Penitentiary, Admission Records, prisoner no. 330). See also Clarke, *Slaughter Ranches,* 180–92.

16. *Arizona Bulletin* (Solomonville), April 8, 1898; Creighton M Foraker, marshal, Santa Fe, telegram to U.S. Attorney General (John W. Griggs), Washington, D.C., April 9, 1898, Justice file 13.065; Miguel Otero, governor, Santa Fe, telegram to Griggs, April 9, 1898, also in file 13.065.

17. Coleman, interview with Haley and Chesley, NSH.

18. Ibid.

19. Willson, "Broncho Bill Holdups" and "Little Old Arizona Cowboy"; Coleman, "Little Outlaw Gang," 4–5.

20. Coleman, "Little Outlaw Gang," 10; Wilhelm, *History of the St. Johns Arizona Stake*, 246–48, 256, 286.

21. Coleman, "Little Outlaw Gang," 4–5.

22. Wiltbank, "Gold in Lee Valley," *White Mountain Independent*, February 14, 1980.

23. Ibid.

24. Coleman, "Little Outlaw Gang," 6.

25. Ibid.

26. *Los Angeles Daily Times*, August 8, 1898; Coleman, interview with Haley and Chesley, NSH.

27. Coleman, "Little Outlaw Gang," 6–7.

28. *Arizona Silver Belt*, April 21, 1898; *Arizona Bulletin*, April 22, 1898.

29. *Graham County Guardian*, April 22, 1898; *Arizona Silver Belt*, May 5, 1898, reprinted from the *Graham County Guardian*.

Chapter 7. Belén and Beyond

1. Marshall, *Railroad That Built an Empire*, 400–401; Myrick, *New Mexico's Railroads*, 20–25. Unless otherwise indicated, the *Albuquerque Daily Citizen*, May 24, 1898, is the source for the account of the Belén robbery.

2. *Albuquerque Daily Citizen*, May 25, 1898; *Albuquerque Morning Democrat*, May 25, 1898; *El Paso Daily Times*, May 25, 1896.

3. *Albuquerque Morning Democrat*, May 25, 1898; *Los Angles Times*, May 25, 1898; *Rocky Mountain News*, May 25, 1898; *Santa Fe Daily New Mexican*, May 24, 1898.

4. *Albuquerque Morning Democrat*, May 25, 1898.

5. Ibid.; *Albuquerque Daily Citizen*, May 25, 1898.

6. Harden, interview with Fred Martin, Sr., Socorro County, New Mexico, "Last Train Robbery, part 2"; Weinman, "Great Belen Train Robbery Loot," 4–6, 11.

7. *Albuquerque Daily Citizen*, May 28, 1898; *Albuquerque Morning Democrat*, May 25, 1898.

8. *Albuquerque Morning Democrat*, May 25, 1898; *Rocky Mountain News*, May 25, 1898; Tanner and Tanner, *Last of the Old-Time Outlaws*, 150–51; N.M. Territorial Penitentiary, Admission Records; Bursum to Haley, March 6, 1944, NSH.

9. *Albuquerque Morning Democrat,* May 25, 1898.

10. Willson, "Broncho Bill Holdups Recalled," June 25, 1950. Evans Coleman later contradicted his brother, Prime, when he wrote, "Red never participated in but one holdup with Johnson and [Walters], and that was the first [March 28, 1898] one (Evans Coleman, letter to the *Arizona Republic,* Phoenix, December 23, 1937). Notwithstanding, circumstances argue for Pipkin's participation in the Belén train robbery, if not its bloody aftermath.

11. Bryan, *Robbers,* 187–88; Brock and Cox, interview with Blachly, April 11, 1953, LBBT.

12. *Albuquerque Daily Citizen,* May 31, 1898.

13. Martin, "Train Robbers Stole More Than Money"; *Albuquerque Daily Citizen,* May 27, 1898.

14. The press later gave Wuerro's Navajo surname a Spanish spelling—Guerro or Guerra (Harden, interview with Vicente Guerro and Manuel Guerro, Alamo, New Mexico, "Last Train Robbery, part 2"; Johnston, *Old Magdalena,* 74).

15. Johnston, *Old Magdalena,* 50; Norman Cleaveland, *The Morleys,* 238; *New York Times,* February 7, 1902; Agnes Morley Cleaveland, *No Life for a Lady,* 253.

16. Coleman, interview by Haley and Chesley, February 27, 1945, NSH; Brock and Cox, interview with Blachly, April 1853, LBBT; Harden, letter to the authors, May 19, 2009.

17. Harden, "Last Train Robbery, part 2"; Harden, letter to the authors, May 29, 2006; *Rocky Mountain News,* May 27, 1898; Coleman, interview by Haley and Chesley, February 27, 1945, NSH

18. Harden, letter to the authors, May 29, 2006; *Albuquerque Daily Citizen,* May 26, 1898; *Albuquerque Morning Democrat,* May 27, 1898.

19. Coleman, interview by Haley and Chesley, February 27, 1945, NSH; Brock and Cox, interview with Blachly, April 1853, LBBT; Coleman, "Little Outlaw Gang," 9.

20. Coleman, interview by Haley and Chesley, February 27, 1945, NSH.

21. Ibid.

22. Brock, interview with Blachly, October 8, 1953, LBBT; Coleman, "Little Outlaw Gang," 9; Harden, letter to the authors, May 29, 2006. According to one of Wuerro's descendants, all agreed to never spend the money outside the Alamo reservation or the Puertocito trading post.

23. *Albuquerque Morning Democrat*, May 27, 1898.

24. *Western Liberal*, June 3, 1898.

25. Ball, *Desert Lawmen*, 212–13.

26. Bursum to Haley, March 6, 1944, NSH; *Albuquerque Daily Citizen*, May 26, 1898.

27. *Albuquerque Daily Citizen*, May 26, 28. 1898; *Albuquerque Morning Democrat*, May 27, 1898. A wooden marker, carved and maintained by his grandnephew, Hipolito Bustamante Romero, reads, "Daniel Bustamante, Born May 31, 1864, Died May 25, 1898. Daniel Bustamante and Sheriff Francisco X. Vigil both killed by 'Bronco Bill' Walters and 'Kid' Johnson. These 2 comitted [*sic*] the last known train robbery in the West."

John Cox later related that Ray Morley had Vicente Wuerro's skull and used it at the ranch house as a sugar bowl. Notwithstanding Cox's macabre tale, members of the Wuerro family confirmed to Socorro historian Paul Harden that Wuerro's remains were returned to the family at Alamo. Something of an obsession with bones continued, however. Magdalena resident Langford Johnston later insisted that, although the lawmen's bodies had been removed and buried, those of the outlaws had not been. "They had barricaded behind rimrocks on a small mesa just north of the trees, and for years people could find human bones up those rocks if they took the time and trouble to climb up to them." Because there were no dead outlaws, his account is meaningless (Brock and Cox, interview with Blachly, April 11, 1953, LBBT; Harden, "Last Train Robbery, part 2"; Johnston, *Old Magdalena*, 50).

28. *Albuquerque Daily Citizen*, May 30, 1898; Harden, "Last Train Robbery, part 2." The Vigil family marked the deputy's grave about 1901. Bustamante's grandnephew, Hipolito Bustamante Romero, aided Socorro historian Paul Harden in locating the grave in Valencia.

29. Bursum to Haley, March 6, 1944, NSH.

30. Brock and Cox, interview with Blachly, April 1853, LBBT.

31. Norman Cleaveland, *The Morleys*, 252–54.

32. Bursum to Haley, March 6, 1944, NSH. Morley died in Los Angeles in May 1932.

33. *Albuquerque Daily Citizen*, May 26, 1898. Evans, who had previously served time in Texas, first served three years and two months (October 2, 1888, to December 2, 1891) at the Territorial Penitentiary on an attempted robbery conviction. He began a second three-year New Mexico term on March 30, 1895, on a federal bigamy conviction. He had been released on September 28, 1897 (N.M. Territorial Penitentiary, Admission Records, nos. 278 and 793).

34. *Albuquerque Daily Citizen*, May 27, 1898. See the appendix for a discussion of the confusion concerning Walters and Grant "Kid" Swingle.

35. *Albuquerque Morning Democrat*, May 27, 1898.

36. *Santa Fe Daily New Mexican*, June 1, 1898; Tanner and Tanner, "'Kid' Swingle"; Rasch, "'Kid' Swingle.

37. *Albuquerque Weekly Citizen*, June 16, 1894; *Albuquerque Daily Citizen*, May 30, 1898.

38. Foraker to Griggs, June 6, 1898, Foraker Papers, file 13065. In a follow-up telegram, Foraker informed Griggs that Loomis's service would be required for no more than thirty days (Foraker to Griggs, June 6).

Chapter 8. Chase and Capture

1. Coleman, interview by Haley and Chesley, February 27, 1945, NSH; Coleman, letter to the *Arizona Republic*, December 23, 1937.

2. Coleman, interview by Haley and Chesley, February 27, 1945, NSH.

3. *Arizona Bulletin*, June 3, 1898; *St. Johns Herald*, reprinted in the *Silver City Enterprise*, June 10, 1898; *Arizona Bulletin*, June 17, 1898.

4. Coleman, interview by Haley and Chesley, February 27, 1945, NSH; *St. Johns Herald*, August 13, 1898.

5. Tanner and Tanner, *Last of the Old-Time Outlaws*, 58–63; Foraker to Joseph McKenna, U.S. attorney general, Washington, D.C., October 9, 1897, and W. B. Childers, Albuquerque, N. Mex., to McKenna, October 16, 1897, Justice file 13.065; H. W. Loomis, deposition, *U.S. v. Daniel Pipkin, et al.*, case no. 2009.

6. Foraker, Santa Fe, to Griggs, June 9, 1898, Justice file 13.065.

7. Foraker, Albuquerque, letter to J. E. Hurley, Las Vegas, N. Mex., June 30, 1898, Misc. Letter Book of C. M. Foraker, Aug. 1897–Aug. 1898, p. 456, Foraker Papers.

8. Robert E. Morrison, Prescott. Arizona, letter to William M. Griffith, Washington, D.C., July 19, 1898, Marshals' Correspondence, AHS.

9. Foraker to Hurley, June 30, 1898, Foraker Papers; Foraker, letter to Griggs, September 14, 1898, Justice file 13.065.

10. Foraker to Hurley, July 1, 1898, Misc. Letter Book, p. 463, Foraker Papers; Anderson, *History of New Mexico*, 2:629.

11. *Arizona Bulletin*, July 22, 1898; *Arizona Republic*, July 25, 1898; *Western Liberal*, August 5, 1898; Jeff Milton, "Capture of Bronco Bill," M6622-6, AHS; Mildred Taitt Milton, "Jeff Milton Goes Outlaw Hunting," 6; Burgess, *Mt. Graham Profiles*, 287–88.

12. *Arizona Bulletin*, July 22, 1898; *Graham Guardian*, July 22, 1898.

13. Mildred Taitt Milton, "Jeff Milton Goes Outlaw Hunting," 6.

14. Fox, *Ft. Thomas . . . History*, n.p.

15. *Graham Guardian* (Safford, Ariz.), July 22, 1898.

16. Milton, interview by Haley, December 25, 1939.

17. *St. Johns Herald*, reprinted in the *Albuquerque Daily Citizen*, August 2, 1898.

18. *Arizona Bulletin*, August 12, 1898. For John Thacker's role see *Arizona Bulletin*, July 22, 1898, and *Western Liberal*, August 5, 1898.

19. Smalley, *My Adventures*, 47. See also Kalt, "Epes Randolph," 131–54.

20. Milton, "Capture of Bronco Bill," 1; Milton, interview by Haley, March 4, 1938, NSH.

21. *Arizona Bulletin*, August 12, 1898; Milton, "Capture of Bronco Bill," 1.

22. Griffith, letter to Griggs, September 13, 1898, Justice file 13.065; *Arizona Bulletin*, August 12, 1898.

23. Milton, "Capture of Bronco Bill," 1; Mildred Taitt Milton, "Jeff Milton Goes Outlaw Hunting," 6.

24. Milton, interview by Haley, Tombstone, Ariz., March 4, 1938, NSH.

25. Coleman, interview by Haley and Chesley, February 27, 1945, NSH; *Arizona Bulletin*, August 12, 1898; Milton, interview by Haley, March 4, 1938, NSH. Milton later referred to the tent as a house (*Arizona Republic*, December 23, 1937). Evans Coleman, in a letter to the editor that took Milton to task for a number of his claims, countered, "And by the way, there was not a house nearer than twenty-five miles from that camp" (letter to the *Arizona Republic*, December 23, 1937, AHS).

26. J. E. Howard, Coolidge, Ariz., letter to Milton, July 24, 1945, NSH; *Arizona Bulletin*, August 12, 1898.

27. Milton, interview by Haley, March 4, 1938, NSH.

28. Brock and Cox, interview with Blachly, April 11, 1953, LBBT.

29. *Arizona Bulletin*, August 12, 1898.

30. Scott White, Tombstone, Ariz., to U.S. Marshal William K. Meade, Tucson, Ariz., April 20, 1897, Marshals' Correspondence; 1900 U.S. Census, Graham County, Arizona.

31. Howard, letter to Milton, July 24, 1945, NSH; *Western Liberal*, August 5, 1898.

32. *Arizona Bulletin*, August 12, 1898.

33. Milton, interview by Haley, March 4, 1938, NSH.

34. Ibid.

35. *Western Liberal*, September 2, 1898.

36. *Arizona Bulletin*, August 12, 1898.

37. Milton, interview by Haley, March 4, 1938, NSH.

37. *Arizona Bulletin*, August 12, 1898.

38. Ibid.

39. *Western Liberal*, reprinted in the *Albuquerque Daily Citizen*, August 6, 1898; *Arizona Bulletin*, August 12, 1898; *Arizona Republic*, December 23, 1937; Milton, interview by Haley, March 4, 1938, NSH; Haley, *Jeff Milton*, 299; Coleman, letter to the *Arizona Republic*, December 23, 1937.

40. *Arizona Bulletin*, August 12, 1898.

41. Brock, interview with Blachly, October 8, 1953, LBBT.

42. Henry Graham, interview with Blachly, July 7, 1952, LBBT; *Arizona Bulletin*, August 12, 1898; "Description of Convict," Territorial Prison at Yuma, Pipkin, no. 1695, ASL; "Description of Convict," New Mexico State Penitentiary, Pipkin, no. 4365, NMSRCA.

43. Howard, letter to Milton, July 24, 1945, NSH; Milton, interview by Haley, March 4, 1938, NSH; Milton, "My Capture of Bronco Bill."

44. Milton, "Twan't Anything!" NSH; Milton, interview by Haley, March 4, 1938, NSH; Frank King, letter to Haley, December 15, 1947, NSH; King, *Pioneer Western Empire Builders*, 199; Haley, *Jeff Milton*, 299.

45. 1910 U.S. Census, Apache County, Arizona; *St. Johns Herald*, October 20, 1900; Milton, interview by Haley, March 4, 1938, NSH; "Returns from U.S. Military Posts." See also Tanner and Tanner, *Climax Jim*.

46. Willson, "Little Old Arizona Cowboy"; Milton, interview by Haley, March 4, 1938, NSH; Graham County, Second Judicial District Court, case nos. 597, 598, 599, 600 and 602; *Arizona Bulletin*, April 7, and 14, 1899; *St. Johns Herald*, August 13, 1898.

47. Milton, interview by Haley, March 4, 1938, NSH; *Arizona Bulletin*, August 12, 1898.

48. Howard, letter to Milton, July 24, 1945, NSH; Don Hunt, Clifton, Arizona, interview with the authors, November 10, 2004.

49. Milton, interview by Haley, March 4, 1938, NSH; *Western Liberal*, August 5, 1898; *Arizona Bulletin*, August 12, 1898.

50. *Arizona Bulletin*, August 12, 1898.

51. *Arizona Bulletin*, August 12, 1898; *Arizona Republic*, August 4, 1898.

Chapter 9. Bad Days for Bad Men

1. *Arizona Bulletin,* August 12, 1898.
2. Milton, interview by Haley, March 4, 1938, NSH.
3. *Arizona Bulletin,* August 12, 1898.
4. Ibid.
5. *Western Liberal,* August 12, 1898.
6. Milton, interview by Haley, March 4, 1938, NSH; *Santa Fe Daily New Mexican,* August 8, 1898; *Western Liberal,* August 12, 1898; *Rocky Mountain News,* August 9, 1898.
7. *Santa Fe Daily New Mexican,* August 13, 1898.
8. *Silver City Independent,* August 23, 1898; *Western Liberal,* September 2, 16, 23, 1898.
9. Henry Graham, interview by Blachly, July 7, 1952, LBBT.
10. Tanner and Tanner, *Climax Jim,* 1–14; Smalley, "Reform of Climax Jim," AHS; Smalley, "Experiences of a newspaper correspondent," 4–5, AHS.
11. Coleman, interview by Haley and Chesley, February 27, 1945, NSH; Coleman, "Climax Jim," AHS; Coleman, "Little Outlaw Gang," AHS.
12. Foraker to Griggs, August 13, 1898, Justice file 13.065.
13. *Albuquerque Daily Citizen,* August 15, 1898; *Rocky Mountain News,* August 15, 1898.
14. Ibid.; *Los Angeles Daily Times,* August 15, 1898.
15. *Rocky Mountain News,* August 15, 1898; "L. A. Cameron With Wells, Fargo & Co's Ex.," notebook, HR #8671, 140, WFB; *Albuquerque Daily Citizen,* August 15, 1898; *Los Angeles Daily Times,* August 15, 1898.
16. *Rocky Mountain News,* August 15, 1898.
17. *Albuquerque Daily Citizen,* August 15, and 16, 1898; "L. A. Cameron With Wells, Fargo & Co's Ex.," notebook, HR #8671, p. 140, WFB
18. *Graham County Bulletin,* September 9, 1898.
19. Smalley, "Reform of Climax Jim," AHS.
20. *Western Liberal,* September 16, 1898.
21. Ibid., September 23, 1898.
22. *Arizona Bulletin,* December 2, 1898.
23. Foraker, Las Cruces, N. Mex., telegram to attorney general, Washington, D.C., September 13, 1898, Justice file 13.065.
24. Willson, "Little Old Arizona Cowboy," October 13, 1957.

25. *Western Liberal*, December 9, 1898; *Territory of New Mexico v. William Walters*, case nos. 1665, 1666, and 1667, Socorro County District Court Docket Book B (1898–1906), pp. 5–7; Socorro County District Court Record Book G (1898–1901), pp. 201, 207; case file nos. 1665, 1666, and 1667, Records of the New Mexico District Court for Socorro County, NMSRCA; Marshals Docket no. 714, *U.S. v. Bronco Bill, Daniel Pipkin, et al.*, case no. 2009.

26. Poldervaart, *Black Robbed Justice*, 155–64; Ball, *Elfego Baca*, 50.

27. Socorro County District Court Record Book G (1898–1901), pp. 222–23, 226–27, 230–34; Socorro County District Court file nos. 1665, 1666, and 1667.

28. *San Francisco Chronicle*, March 12, 1899; Todachinnie, "Life of Willard Butt"; Ernst, "George S. Nixon," 45; Foraker to E. J. Thacker, Tucson, Ariz., June 9, 1899, Letter Book, p. 139, Foraker Papers. Wells, Fargo dropped the comma from its name in 1898.

29. *Graham Guardian*, March 24, 1899; *San Francisco Chronicle*, March 13, 1899; *Los Angeles Daily Times*, March 13, 1899; Marshals Docket no. 714, *U.S. v. Bronco Bill, Daniel Pipkin, et al.*, case no. 2009.

30. Alias Warrant to Apprehend (Marshals Docket no. 714, *U.S. v. Bronco Bill, Daniel Pipkin, et al.*, case file 2009; *Albuquerque Daily Citizen*, March 20, 1899.

31. Graham County, Second Judicial District Court of Arizona, *Territory v. John Doe (Red Pipkin)*, case no. 674, Register of Actions, Criminal, vol. 3, p. 283, and Minute Book no. 6, p. 161, cited hereafter as *Arizona v. Pipkin*, case no. 674.

32. Socorro County, Second Judicial District Court of New Mexico, *Territory v. William Walters*, case file nos. 1691, 1692, and 1693, NMSRCA. The original case file numbers (1665, 1666, and 1667) had been renumbered when the cases were transferred to the jurisdiction of the District Court for Chaves County (nos. 193, 194, and 195). A third set of numbers (1691, 1692, and 1693) was assigned when the venue was returned to Socorro County.

33. True Bill of Indictment, September 28, 1899, and Appearance Bond, October 25, 1899, *U.S. v. Bronco Bill, Daniel Pipkin, et al.*, case no. 2009; Edward L. Bartlett, Santa Fe, N. Mex., to Miguel A. Otero, Santa Fe, November 11, 1899, Otero, penal papers, NMSRCA.

34. Socorro County, Second Judicial District Court of New Mexico, Record Book G (1898–1901), 390–91; *Western Liberal*, November 24, 1899.

35. Territorial Penitentiary, Admission Records, William Walters, no. 1282; *Santa Fe Daily New Mexican*, December 14, 1899; U.S. Department

of the Interior, Census Office, *Report of Crime, Pauperism, and Benevolence . . . 1890*, part 1. See also John Tanner, "Violence in New Mexico Territory," 32–34, 56.

Chapter 10. Stars and Bars

1. Governor M. A. Otero, Santa Fe, N. Mex., letter to Governor Nathan O. Murphy, Phoenix, Ariz., November 14, 1899, Otero, penal papers, NMSRCA.

2. Edward Bartlett, Santa Fe, N. Mex., letter to Otero, November 15, 1899, Otero, penal papers, NMSRCA.

3. B. S. Rodey, Albuquerque, N. Mex., letter to Otero, November 16, 1899, Otero, penal papers, NMSRCA.

4. Wiley E. Jones, Solomonville, Ariz., letter to Otero, November 17, 1899, and Bartlett, letter to Otero, November 22, 1899, Otero, penal papers, NMSRCA.

5. W. B. Childers, Albuquerque, N. Mex., letter to Bartlett, November 28, 1899, Otero, penal papers, NMSRCA; *Santa Fe Daily New Mexican*, November 30, 1899.

6. Foraker to J. N. Thacker, c/o Wells, Fargo, San Francisco, Cal., March.10, 1900, Letter Book, Misc. Letters Sent, 51, Foraker Papers; Tanner and Tanner, "Revenge," 2–7).

7. *U.S. v. Bronco Bill, Daniel Pipkin, et al.*, case file 2009; *Santa Fe Daily New Mexican*, April 5, 1900.

8. Territory of New Mexico, Statutes of 1887, ch. 9, p. 44, *Albuquerque Daily Citizen*, November 9, 1897; Secretary of State's Collection, Chapter II, Title IX—Crimes and Offences—Punishments Sec. 667-972 (*Compiled Laws of New Mexico, 1884*, serial number 16842); *Arizona Bulletin*, April 6, 1900.

9. Graham County, Arizona, Second Judicial District Court, *Territory v. Rufus Nephews*, case no. 715, Minute Book 6, 467; Tanner and Tanner, *Climax Jim*, 39–40.

10. Ibid., *Arizona v. Red Pipkin*, case no. 674, Minute Book no. 6, 453–59, 473; *Albuquerque Journal Democrat*, April 6, 1900.

11. *Arizona v. Red Pipkin*, case no. 674, Minute Book no. 6, p. 510; *Arizona Bulletin*, July 20, 1900.

12. *Arizona v. Red Pipkin*, case no. 674, Minute Book no. 7, pp. 79, 107; *Santa Fe Daily New Mexican*, October 23, 1900.

13. *Arizona v. Red Pipkin*, case no. 674, Minute Book no. 7, pp. 108–109.

14. Ibid., pp. 113, 119.

15. Ibid., 119; *Arizona Bulletin*, October 19, 1900.

16. *Arizona v. Red Pipkin*, case no. 674, Minute Book no. 7, pp. 189, 194–95; *Arizona Bulletin*, October 26, 1900; Records, Territorial Prison at Yuma, Arizona, Record Group 85. Daniel M. Pipkin, no. 1695, ADLAPR.

17. Merrill, "My Acquaintance with Daniel Moroni Pipkin."

18. Horace Earl Pipkin. "Story of Daniel Moroni Pipkin." Pipkin's subsequent prison record identified his wife as Katy Pipkin, then (1919) living in Prescott, Arizona. In his 1930 census enumeration he maintained that he had married at age thirty-six (ca. 1911) and was widowed (Description of Convict. Dan Pipkin, no. 4368, NMSRCA; 1930 U.S. census, McKinney County, N. Mex.).

19. *Gallup Independent*, September 5, 1918.

20. Willson, "Little Old Arizona Cowboy."

21. Brock and Cox interview by Blachly, April 11, 1953, LBBT.

22. Ibid.; Senator Joseph W. Bailey, Washington, D.C., letter to Governor George Curry, Santa Fe, N. Mex., November 26, 1909, Curry, penal papers, NMSRCA.

23. Tanner and Tanner, "The '18-carat' Black Jack," 17; Territorial Penitentiary, Conduct Record Book #1, 1898-1917, NMSRCA; J. W. Raynolds, Santa Fe, letter to Frank W. Clancy, Santa Fe, December 18, 1909, Curry, penal papers, NMSRCA; H. M. Dougherty, Socorro, N. Mex., letter to Clancy, December 22, 1909, Curry, penal papers, NMSRCA; John E. Griffith, Socorro, N. Mex., letter to Clancy, December 29, 1909, Curry, penal papers, NMSRCA; Clancy, quoted in letter to Curry, January 10, 1910, Curry, penal papers, NMSRCA.

24. Curry, letter to Bailey, Washington, D.C., January 10, 1910, Curry, penal papers, NMSRCA.

25. *Santa Fe New Mexican*, April 17, 1911; Curry, penal papers, NMSRCA; N.M. Territorial Penitentiary, Admission Records, no. 1726, NMSRCA.

26. *Albuquerque Evening Herald*, April 20, 1911.

27. *Santa Fe New Mexican*, April 17, 1911.

28. *Albuquerque Morning Journal*, April 20, 1911; *Albuquerque Evening Herald*, April 20, 1911.

29. Keleher, *Fabulous Frontier*, 215–16, 254–55; 1920 and 1930 U.S. Census, El Paso County, Texas; Cade Selvy, Los Angeles, Calif., letter to E. P. Lamborn, September 1, 1923, and L. D. Walters, Tucson, Ariz.,

letter to Lamborn, February 12, 1928, in E. P. Lamborn Papers, KSHS; *Albuquerque Morning Journal*, July 16 1910; *Arizona State Business Directory*, 254.

30. *Albuquerque Morning Journal*, April 20, 1911; *Albuquerque Evening Herald*, April 20, 1911.

31. *Albuquerque Evening Herald*, April 20, 1911.

32. *Albuquerque Morning Journal*, April 20, 1911; *Topeka State Journal*, December 19, 1905. The Santa Fe Railroad armed and county authorities deputized the special officers in 1905.

33. *Albuquerque Evening Herald*, April 20, 1911.

34. *Albuquerque Morning Journal*, April 20, 1911; N.M. Territorial Penitentiary, Admission Records, William Walters, no. 1282, NMSRCA; *Albuquerque Evening Herald*, April 20, 1911. Although there is no primary account of Walters's capture that mentions the involvement of railroad officer Jandon R. "Chief" Galusha (later Albuquerque police chief), Galusha related to journalist/historian Howard Bryan that he and Charles Mainz split the one hundred dollar reward for the arrest of Bronco Bill. The *Albuquerque Morning Journal* specifically reported that the one hundred dollar reward was destined for Mainz (Bryan, *True Tales*, 217; *Albuquerque Morning Journal*, April 20, 1911).

35. *Santa Fe New Mexican*, April 20, 1911.

Chapter 11. Last Gasps

1. Board of Parole, State of New Mexico, Parole Agreement No. 712, February 3, 1917, Governor Washington E. Lindsey, penal papers, NMSRCA.

2. William J. Barker, secretary, Santa Fe, N. Mex., to Lindsey, April 12, 1917, Lindsey, penal papers, NMSRCA.

3. Board of Parole, Parole Agreement no. 712, Lindsey, penal papers, NMSRCA; New Mexico Department of Corrections Collection, Parole Record no. 712, William Walters, Convict 1282, Parole Record Book 3, Serial Number 7240, 33, NMSRCA.

4. Coleman, "Life of a Desperado," 490–95; Cox, "Salty John Cox and Bronco Bill," 49; Parole Record no. 712, William Walters.

5. Parole Record no. 712, William Walters; Harden, interview with Fred Martin, Sr.; Harden, "Last Train Robbery, part 2"; Harden, to the authors, March 17, 2004.

6. Ibid; Jack Stockbridge, interview with Blachly, Phoenix, Ariz., March 18, 1897, LBBT; Jack Hutchinson, interview with Blachly, no

date, LBBT; Brock, interview with Blachly, October 8, 1953, LBBT; Brock and Cox, interview with Blachly, April 11, 1953, LBBT.

7. Haley, *The XIT Ranch*, 166.

8. Bryan, *Robbers*, 204–205.

9. Ibid., 205–206.

10. *New York Times*, June 29, 30, 1917.

11. Ibid., July 12, 13, 1917; *Prescott Journal Miner*, July 13, 1917; *Tucson Citizen*, July 18, 1917. See also see Byrkit, "IWW in Wartime Arizona."

12. *El Paso Labor-Advocate*, reprinted in *Carbon City News*, August 16, 1917; W. W. Risdon, Gallup, N. Mex., letter to W. E. Lindsay, governor, Santa Fe, August 5, 1917, Gov. Washington E. Lindsey Papers, folder 181, Labor Disputes in Gallup Region: Attempted Deportation, 1917, NMSRCA, cited hereafter as Lindsey Papers, folder 181; *El Paso Labor-Advocate*, reprinted in *Carbon City News*, August 16, 1917.

13. McKinley County Council of Defense, "Proclamation," Lindsey Papers, folder 181; Poldervaart, *Black-Robed Justice*, 205–206.

14. Fergusson, *Murder and Mystery in New Mexico*, 172; *Albuquerque Morning Journal*, August 1, 1917.

15. *Albuquerque Morning Journal*, August 1, 2, 1917; *Carbon City News*, August 4, 1917; Gallup *Independent*, May 22, 1919.

16. *Carbon City News*, August 4, 1917; Risdon, letter to Lindsay, August 5, 1917, Gov. Lindsey Papers, folder 181.

17. Lindsey, telegram to Judge John R. McFie, Gallup, August 1, 1917, and Lindsey, letter to McFie, August 1, 1917, Lindsey Papers, folder 181; *Carbon City News*, August 4, 1917.

18. Fred Fornoff, telegrams to Lindsey, August 3, 4, 1917; Lindsey, telegram to R. L. Roberts, Gallup, August 4, 1917; Roberts telegram to Lindsey, August 4, 1917; Gov. Lindsey Papers, folder 181.

19. *Gallup Independent*, September 5, 1918.

20. Ibid.

21. Ibid.

22. *Coconino Sun*, May 5, 1892; *Gallup Independent*, September 5, 1918.

23. *Gallup Independent*, September 5, 1918.

24. Ibid., September 12, 1918.

25. Ibid.

26. McKinley County, First Judicial District Court, Record Book C, *New Mexico v. Dan Pipkin*, case nos. 319, 320, and 321, pp. 219, 227–28.

27. *Albuquerque Morning Journal*, April 9, 29, 30 1919; *New Mexico v. Dan Pipkin*, case nos. 5666, 5667, and 5668, Bernalillo County, Second Judicial District Court, Record Book 9, pp. 262–63, 311, 361; Record Book 12, p. 156; *Gallup Independent*, April 10, 17, 1919; *Albuquerque*

Evening Herald, April 10, 1919; *Albuquerque Morning Democrat*, 10 and 11, 1919.

28. New Mexico State Penitentiary, Description of Convict, no. 4368, NMSRCA; Governor Octaviano A. Larrazolo, pardon papers, NMSRCA.

29. Brock and Cox, interview with Blachly, April 11, 1953, LBBT; Bryan, *True Tales*, 90.

30. Brock, interview with Blachly, October 8, 1953, LBBT.

31. Jack Stockbridge, interview with Blachly, Phoenix, Ariz., March 18, 1897, LBBT; Bryan, *Robbers*, 206; *Lordsburg Liberal*, June 23, 1921.

32. *Silver City Independent*, June 21, 1921.

33. *Albuquerque Journal*, August 29, 1933; Day, "Nation-wide Strikes Advance."

34. See Fergusson, *Murder and Mystery in New Mexico*, 171–93, and Stuart, *Gallup*, 14.

35. *Gallup Independent*, April 4, 1935; *Santa Fe New Mexican*, April 4, 1935; *Albuquerque Journal*, April 4, 1935.

36. *Gallup Independent*, July 6, 1938.

37. Ibid., July 7, 1938; State of New Mexico, Department of Public Health, certificate of death, Gamerco, McKinley County, no. 3281.

Afterword

1. Rhodes, "Whose Who and Why," 27; Rhodes, *Rhodes Reader*, 21.

2. *Los Angeles Times*, September 18, 1887; *Grant County News*, May 2, 1889.

3. U.S. Department of the Interior, Census Office, *Report of Crime, Pauperism, and Benevolence in the United States at the Eleventh Census: 1890*, part 1, Analysis, 128, and 140; N.M. Territorial Penitentiary, Admission Records. The 1900 census listed 255 inmates in the penitentiary. Prisoners held in safekeeping for trial, but neither convicted nor formally "admitted" to the penitentiary, explain the variance (1900 U.S. Census, Santa Fe County, New Mexico).

4. Unnumbered changes to the Arizona Penal Code as enacted March 11, 1901, Record Group 6, Secretary of the Territory, ASL.

5. Prassel, *The Great American Outlaw*, 324.

Appendix

1. Santee, *Men and Horses*, 217; Rasch, "An Incomplete Account," 1.

2. C. M. Foraker, Santa Fe, letter to attorney general, Washington, D.C., August 13, 1898, Justice file 13.065; United States District Court,

Second Judicial District of New Mexico. *U.S. v. William Raper, et al.*, case file no. 2009, NARA (RMR).

3. "Lady Cattle Rustler," 108; Marriage Certificate, County of Sierra, California; 1860 U.S. Census, Sierra County, California, p. 901.

4. 1870 U.S. Census, Carlin, Elko, Nevada, 28 June, p. 56; Record of the Nevada Orphans' Home, p. 1; "Lady Cattle Rustler," 108; Michno, *Deadliest Indian War*, 99–100; *War of Rebellion*, 1183; Elko County District Court Minute Book, *State of Nevada v. Susan Raper et al*, case nos. A21, A24, and A25; *Silver City Enterprise*, December 24, 1886.

5. 1880 U.S. census, Conejos County, Colorado; *Silver City Enterprise*, December 17, 1886; 1860 U.S. census, St. Francis County, Missouri; Socorro County, Second Judicial District Court of New Mexico, *Territory v. Susie Yonkers*, case file no. 709, NMSRCA; 1880 U. S. census, Lincoln County, New Mexico.

6. *Albuquerque Evening Democrat*, August 24, 1884; *Albuquerque Journal*, September 2, 1884; *Territory v. Susie Yonkers*, case file no. 709, NMSRCA; Socorro County, Second Judicial District Court of New Mexico, Criminal and Civil Record Book 1, p. 119, NMSRCA.

7. *Silver City Enterprise*, December 17, 1886; Sonnichsen, *Tularosa*, 33.

8. Socorro County, Second Judicial District Court of New Mexico, *Territory v. Susan Yonkers*, case file nos. 814 and 819, and *Territory v. Joe W. Raper*, case file no. 941, NMSRCA; *Rio Grande Republican*, December 12 and 19, 1885; *Silver City Enterprise*, December 17, 1886.

9. Grant County, Third Judicial District Court of New Mexico, *Territory v. Susan Yonkers*, case no. 2106, NMSRCA; *Silver City Enterprise*, December 17, 1886.

10. *United States v. William Raper, et al.*, case no. 2009, NARA (RMR).

11. *Albuquerque Daily Citizen*, May 26, 1898.

12. Christopher Swingle, DO, Scottdale, Georgia, letter to the authors, January 24, 2004; 1870 U.S. Census, Polk County, Missouri; *Socorro Bullion*, April 8, 1888; Elmer Swingle, "Grant Swingle." See also Tanner and Tanner, "'Kid' Swingle."

13. *St. Johns Herald*, August 18, 1887, from the *Clifton Clarion*; Flake, "Some Reminiscences," AHS.

14. *Silver City Enterprise*, October 24, 1887; *Albuquerque Morning Democrat*, October 6, 1887; *Arizona Silver Belt*, October 8, 1887; *St. Johns Herald*, November 3, 10, 17, 1887; *Arizona Champion*, November 5, 1887, from the *Journal Miner* (Prescott, Ariz.). Identified by the press only as Walters, the driver was almost certainly St. Johns resident Joseph W.

Walters, a thirty-four-year-old native of Utah (Apache County, 1886 Great Register; *Arizona 1890 Great Registers*, p. 338).

15. *St. Johns Herald*, February 2, 1888, from the *Clinton Democrat* (Missouri); Christopher Swingle, letter, January 24, 2004.

16. State of California, "Register and Descriptive List of Convicts under Sentence of Imprisonment in the State Prison at Folsom," pp. 171–72, California State Archives; *San Francisco Chronicle*, June 28, 1893; McKinney, letter to Lamborn, March 31, 1933, KSHS.

17. *Los Angeles Times* August 8, 1898. Coleman, "Little Outlaw Gang," 2, AHS; Coleman, interview with Haley and Chesley, February 27, 1945, NSH; Willson, "Broncho Bill Holdups Recalled" and "Little Old Arizona Cowboy."

18. Bob Beverly, Lovington, N. Mex., interview with Haley and Chesley, March 24, 1945, NSH; Beverly, "Horse Race at Seymour," 237–39. For an account of the 1896 killing of Guyse, see *Santa Fe Daily New Mexican*, April 28, 1896; *Albuquerque Morning Democrat*, May 2, and 5, 1896.

19. Beverly, interview with Haley and Chesley, March 24, 1945, NSH; Chesley, *Trails Travelled*, 119.

20. *Silver City Enterprise*, October 24, 1890; Beverly, interview with Haley, June 23, 1946, NSH.

21. Coleman, "Life of a Desperado," 484–95; Coleman, *From Mustang to Lawyer*, 21, 72; Coleman, "Dumb Heroes," 122–24.

22. *Arizona Bulletin*, August 12, 1898; N.M. Territorial Penitentiary, Admission Records, William Walters, no. 485; 1910 U.S. census, Santa Fe County, New Mexico Territory; *Santa Fe New Mexican*, April 17, 1911.

23. Susan Eason, director, Catholic Archives of Texas, Austin, letter to the authors, August 27, 2002; 1870 and 1880 U.S. census, Harris County, Texas; Lisa May, archivist, Diocese of Galveston-Houston, Houston, Tex., letter to the authors, April 8, 2003. Mary Jane Walters and Jonathan Busley had married on March 4, 1870 (no. 1373, Harris County, Texas, Marriage Book, vol. F, p. 186).

24. J. W. Bailey, Washington, D.C., letter to George Curry, Santa Fe, N. Mex., November 26, 1909, Curry, penal papers, NMSRCA; Rachel Roberts, archives director, Dallas, letter to the authors, March 29, 2002; Coleman, interview with Haley and Chesley, February 27, 1945, NSH; *Silver City Enterprise*, February 20, 1891.

25. N.M. Territorial Penitentiary, Admission Records, William Walters, no. 485; H. O. Bursum, Socorro, N. Mex., letter to Haley, March 6, 1944, NSH; Walter Birchfield, El Paso, Tex., letter to Haley, November 2, 1939, NSH.

26. Walters, *Tombstone's Yesterday,* 217; Adams, *Burs under the Saddle,* 526–33; *Albuquerque Evening Herald,* April 20, 1911.

27. Chesley, *Trails Travelled,* 125; Barrington, *Celebrating 100 Years,* 27.

28. Kemp, *Cow Dust,* 92, 94.

29. Ibid., 91–92.

30. Rasch, "Death of a Bank Robber," 50–52. In December 1885, several years before Walters's alleged appearance at the V+T, several burglars robbed the store of J. F. Habernigg of about $400 worth of clothing (*Socorro Bullion,* December 12, 1885). The burglary does not fit the circumstances of the robbery as described by Kemp.

31. Barrington, *Celebrating 100 Years,* 135; Cole Railston, interview with Haley and Chesley, February 26, 1945, NSH.

32. Julyan, *Place Names,* 331.

33. *Santa Fe Daily New Mexican,* April 3, 1896; *Southwest Sentinel,* October 21, 1890.

34. *Albuquerque Morning Journal,* April 20, 1911.

Bibliography

Manuscripts

"Bronco Bill." Ephemera File. Arizona Historical Society, Tucson.

Blachly, Louis Bradley. Transcripts of Oral Interviews. MSS 123 BC, Pioneers Foundation Oral History Collection. Center for Southwest Research, University of New Mexico, Albuquerque.

Coates, Morris. "Mogollons of the Early Days" [online]. Transcript of interview by Frances Totty, July 5, 1938. Manuscripts from the Federal Writers' Project, 1936–1940. Library of Congress, Washington, D.C. Available from World Wide Web (accessed September 8, 2007).

Coleman, Evans P. "A Little Outlaw Gang"; "Climax Jim"; "1896 Diary of Evans Coleman"; "Reminiscences of an Arizona Cowboy." MS 0162. Arizona Historical Society, Tucson.

Colter, Bert J. "As His Brother Knew Him—Fred Tuttle Colter (July 27, 1963)," Udall Papers, Arizona Historical Society; "Autobiography (February 1963)," Biofile, AHS.

Flake, Osmer D. "Some Reminiscences of the Pleasant Valley War and Causes that Led Up to It." Special Collections, University of Arizona, Tucson.

International Genealogical Index (IGA), North America. Batch no. M591612, dates: 1874–1885, source call no. 0984711. Vol. 5.0. Church of Jesus Christ of Latter-day Saints, Salt Lake City, Utah.

Jones, Melvin. "Reminiscences, as told to Mrs. George F. Kitt, January 7, 1928." MS 392. Arizona Historical Society, Tucson.

Lamborn, E. P., Papers, 1913–1970. Manuscript Collection No. 156. Kansas State Historical Society, Topeka.

Lewis, Samuel E. "Journal of Samuel E. Lewis Missionary Work" [online]. Available from World Wide Web (accessed December 1, 2002): www.surnames.com/arminta/samuel_edward_lewis_.htm.

Merrill, Bob. "My Acquaintance with Daniel Moroni Pipkin," n.d. MS. Photocopy provided to the authors by Mrs. Retha Amadio, Provo, Utah.

Milton, Jeff. "And I Went on About My Business," August 22, 1938. MS. J. Evetts Haley Interviews. Nita Stewart Haley Memorial Library and J. Evetts Haley History Center, Midland, Texas.

———. "Twan't Anything: Anybody Could Have Done It," Christmas 1939. MS. J. Evetts Haley Interviews. Nita Stewart Haley Memorial Library and J. Evetts Haley History Center, Midland, Texas.

Milton, Jeff. As told to Edith Kitt. "The Capture of Bronco Bill," n.d. MS 6628. Arizona Historical Society, Tucson.

Milton, Mildred Taitt. "Jeff Goes Outlaw Hunting and a Rattlesnake saves his Bacon," n. d. MS 500. Arizona Historical Society, Tucson.

Peck, Arthur (Artisan) Leslie, Sr. "In the Memory of Man," n.d. MS 652. Arizona Historical Society, Tucson.

Pipkin, Horace Earl (nephew). "The Story of Daniel Moroni Pipkin, better known as Red Pipkin, as told to me by my father James Knox Pipkin [Jr.]," April 11, 1980. MS. Photocopy supplied to the authors by Mrs. Retha Amadio, Provo, Utah.

"Sarah Levira Lewis" [online]. Available from World Wide Web (accessed December 1, 2002): www.surnames.com/arminta/sarah_levira_lewis.htm.

Smalley, George H. "Climax Jim: Cattle Rustler"; "Climax Jim: My Favorite Outlaw"; "Experiences of a newspaper correspondent in Arizona during the turbulent 90's." Smalley Papers, 1862–1954. MS 0305. Arizona Historical Society, Tucson.

Snyder, Agnes Meader. "The Alma Massacre" [online]. Transcript of interview by Frances Totty, December 3, 1937. Manuscripts from the Federal Writers' Project, 1936–1940. Library of Congress, Washington, D.C. Available from Word Wide Web (accessed September 8, 2007).

Swingle, Elmer (nephew). "Grant Swingle, or Charlie Williams," MS. Photocopy provided to the authors by Christopher A. Swingle, DO, Scottdale, Georgia.

Udall, Orma Phelps. Papers. MS 814. Arizona Historical Society, Tucson.

Government Documents

Apache County, Arizona Territory. 1886 Great Register.

———. Third Judicial District Court. *Territory of Arizona v. Isaac Aldridge and William Johnson*, case file no. 215. *Territory of Arizona v. V. A. Word*, case file no. 236.

Arizona, State of. Certificates of Death. James T. Colter, filed July 9, 1922; George C. Felshaw, filed April 9, 1937; Fred T. Colter, filed January 10, 1944; Albert Haywood Johnson, filed May 13, 1941; Judson C. Lathrop, filed November 12, 1948. Arizona Department of Library, Archives and Public Records, Phoenix.

Arizona, Territory of. Records, Secretary of the Territory. Benjamin J. Franklin, Proclamation of Commutation of Sentence, September 2, 1896. Record Group 6. Arizona Department of Library, Archives and Public Records, Phoenix.

———. Records, Territorial Prison at Yuma. Record Group 85. Arizona Department of Library, Archives and Public Records, Phoenix.

———. Statutes. House Bill no. 2, "An Act defining certain offenses Against the Public Peace," February 28, 1889. Arizona Department of Library, Archives and Public Records, Phoenix.

Bernalillo County, New Mexico Territory. Second Judicial District Court. Record Book 9. Records of the United States Territorial and New Mexico District Courts. New Mexico State Records Center and Archives, Santa Fe.

California Department of Health Services, Center for Health Statistics. "Death Index, 1940–1997," February 8, 1966.

California, State of. Sierra County Certificate of Marriage, Thomas Raper to Susan Warfield, March 6, 1860.

———."Register and Descriptive List of Convicts Under Sentence of Imprisonment in the State Prison at Folsom." California State Archives, Sacramento.

Chaves County, New Mexico Territory. Fifth Judicial District Court. *Territory of New Mexico v. William Walters*, criminal case files, box 1, nos. 193 (1665/1691), 194 (1666/1692), and 195 (1667/1693). Records of the United States Territorial and New Mexico District Courts. New Mexico State Records Center and Archives, Santa Fe.

Cochise County, Arizona Territory. First Judicial District Court. Minutes, vol. 9, 291, *Territory of Arizona v. William Downing*, case no. 745A. Arizona Department of Library, Archives and Public Records, Phoenix.

Coryell County, Texas. Death Records, Book 1, 1903–1917; Marriage Records, 1854–1956.

Elko County, State of Nevada. District Court Minute Book, vol. 1. *State of Nevada v. Susan Raper et al*, case no. A21, and *State of Nevada v. Susan Raper*, case nos. A24 and A25.

Graham County, Arizona Territory. Demand on the County Treasury, no. 31D. Sheriff Fees, filed November 9, 1900. Kevin and Bev Mulkins Collection, Tucson.

———. Demand on the County Treasury, no. 40D. Purchased Jurors Certificates, filed November 12, 1900. Kevin and Bev Mulkins Collection, Tucson.

———. Second Judicial District Court. *Territory of Arizona v. John Thomas, alias Climax Jim*, case file no. 647. Kevin and Bev Mulkins Collection, Tucson, Ariz.

———. Second Judicial District Court. Minute Books 5, 6, 7 and 10.

———. Second Judicial District Court. Register of Actions—criminal, vol. 3.

Grant County, New Mexico Territory. Register of Prisoners Confined in the County Jail 1877–1895. New Mexico State Records Center and Archives, Santa Fe.

———. Third Judicial District Court. Criminal Docket Book G (June 1889–December 1898). Records of the United States Territorial and New Mexico District Courts. New Mexico State Records Center and Archives, Santa Fe.

———. Third Judicial District Court. Journal L (June 1889–May 1891), Journal M (May–July 1891), and Journal O (May 1895–December 1897). Records of the United States Territorial and New Mexico District Courts. New Mexico State Records Center and Archives, Santa Fe.

———. Third Judicial District Court. *Territory of New Mexico v. William Walters*, case files nos. 4077 and 4084. Records of the United States Territorial and New Mexico District Courts. New Mexico State Records Center and Archives, Santa Fe.

Harris County, Texas. Marriage Book F.

McKinley County, New Mexico Territory. First Judicial District Court. Record Book C. Records of the United States Territorial and New Mexico District Courts. New Mexico State Records Center and Archives, Santa Fe.

Nevada, State of. Record of the Nevada Orphans' Home. Nevada State Library and Archives, Carson City.

New Mexico, State of. Certificate of Death, Daniel M. Pipkin, McKinley County, no. 3281. Department of Public Health.

———. Department of Corrections Collection. Parole Board Record Book 3 (1916–1919), serial number 7240. New Mexico State Records Center and Archives, Santa Fe.

———. Governor's Papers. Governor Octaviano A. Larrazolo, pardons, Dan Pipkin, file no. 4368. Governor Washington E. Lindsey, folder 181, Labor Disputes in Gallup Region: Attempted Deportation, 1917. Governor Washington E. Lindsey, box 11, folder 312. New Mexico State Records Center and Archives, Santa Fe.

———. Penal Papers. Governor Washington E. Lindsey, box 11, folder 312. New Mexico State Records Center and Archives, Santa Fe.

New Mexico, Territory of. Governor's Papers. Governor Edmund G. Ross, Journal Book, TANM roll 162; Governor George Curry, Letters Received, September–November 1909, TANM, roll 171. New Mexico State Records Center and Archives, Santa Fe.

———. Legislative Assembly Papers. Report of the Special Standing Committee of the Council on Penitentiary. February 23, 1887, TANM roll 6. New Mexico State Records Center and Archives, Santa Fe.

———. Penal Papers. Governor Miguel A. Otero, TANM rolls 154 and 155. Governor George Curry, TANM roll 179. Governor William J. Mills, TANM roll 189. New Mexico State Records Center and Archives, Santa Fe.

———. *James H. Colter v. Edwin Marriage*, no. 257. United States Territorial and New Mexico Supreme Court Records, box 24. New Mexico State Records Center and Archives, Santa Fe.

———. Territorial Census of 1885, TANM roll 40. New Mexico State Records Center and Archives, Santa Fe.

———. Territorial Penitentiary. Admission Records (Record of Convicts). Conduct Record Book #1 (1898–1917). New Mexico State Records Center and Archives, Santa Fe.

Pinal County, Arizona Territory. Second Judicial District Court. *Territory of Arizona v. Frans Oscar Torén* (indicted as Oscar Rogers), case file no. 132. Arizona Department of Library, Archives and Public Records, Phoenix.

Socorro County, New Mexico Territory. Deed Books 8 and 10.

———. Direct Deed Index Book, volume 1.

———. Fifth Judicial District Court. Criminal and Civil Docket Book 2, *Territory v. William Johnson*, no 693. Records of the United States

Territorial and New Mexico District Courts. New Mexico State Records Center and Archives, Santa Fe.

———. Fifth Judicial District Court. Record Books F (1895–1898) and G (1898–1901). Records of the United States Territorial and New Mexico District Courts. New Mexico State Records Center and Archives, Santa Fe.

———. Fifth Judicial District Court. *Territory of New Mexico v. William Walters*, case file nos. 1517, 1665 (1691), 1666 (1692), and 1667 (1693). Records of the United States Territorial and New Mexico District Courts. New Mexico State Records Center and Archives, Santa Fe.

———. Fifth and Second Judicial District Courts. Criminal Docket Books A (1886–1898) and B (1898–1906). Records of the United States Territorial and New Mexico District Courts. New Mexico State Records Center and Archives, Santa Fe.

———. Indirect Deed Index Book, volume 1.

———. Second Judicial District Court. Criminal and Civil Record Book 1, *Territory v. Susie Younkers*, no. 709. Records of the United States Territorial and New Mexico District Courts. New Mexico State Records Center and Archives, Santa Fe.

———. Second Judicial District Court. *Territory v. Susie Younkers*, case file nos. 709, 814 and 819; *Territory v. Joe W. Raper*, case file no. 941. Records of the United States Territorial and New Mexico District Courts. New Mexico State Records Center and Archives, Santa Fe.

Tom Green County, Texas. District Court. *State of Texas v. Sam Murray*, case no. 1217.

United States Army. "Returns from U.S. Military Posts, 1800–1916." National Archives Microfilm Publications, M617, roll 34. National Archives Building, Washington, D.C.

United States Department of Commerce. Bureau of the Census. Census enumerations for: Arizona, (1910); New Mexico (1910, 1920, 1930); Texas (1920, 1930).

United States Department of the Interior. Census Office. Census enumerations for: Arizona (1880, 1900); Arkansas (1860, 1870, 1880); California (1860); Colorado (1880); Iowa (1880); Kansas (1880); Missouri (1870, 1880); Nevada (1870); New Mexico (1880, 1900); Texas (1870, 1880, 1900).

———. *Report of Crime, Pauperism, and Benevolence in the United States at the Eleventh Census: 1890*, part 1, Analysis. Washington D.C.: Government Printing Office, 1896.

United States Department of Justice. File 13.065. The Black Jack Gang. Confidential Correspondence, 1896–1898. Central Files. Record Group 60. National Archives and Records Administration at College Park, Md.

United States Criminal Code. The Federal Penal Code Enforce January 1, 1910. Boston: Little Brown, and Co., 1910.

United States Department of State. "List of U. S. Consular Officers, 1789–1939," National Archives Microfilm Publications, M587, roll 14. National Archives Building, Washington, D.C.

United States District Court. New Mexico, Territory of. *U.S. v. Daniel Pipkin, Edward Coulter, James Burnett, William Raper, and William Johnson*, case file no. 2009. Record Group 21. National Archives and Records Administration, Rocky Mountain Region (Denver).

United States General Land Office. Register of the Land Office, Little Rock, Arkansas. Land Patent to Aser Pipkin, June 1, 1859, no. 8098. Record Group 69. National Archives and Records Administration at College Park, Md.

United States Marshals Service. Appointments, Bonds, and Oaths of U.S. Marshals and Deputy Marshals, 1864–1912. Records of the United States Marshals Service, Arizona. Record Group 527. National Archives and Records Administration, Pacific Southwest Region (Laguna Niguel, Calif.).

———. General Correspondence of the United States Marshals, Arizona, MS 820. Arizona Historical Society, Tucson.

———. General Correspondence of the United States Marshals, New Mexico, MS 322. Creighton Foraker Papers (August 1, 1897–January 17, 1911). Center for Southwest Research, University of New Mexico, Albuquerque.

United States Post Office Department. *Annual Report of the Postmaster General, 1897 [3639-4]*. Washington, D.C.: U.S. Government Printing Office, 1897.

———. *Annual Report of the Postmaster General, 1898*. Washington, D.C.: U.S. Government Printing Office, 1898.

———. Records of the Division of Postmasters, Post Office Appointments, New Mexico. National Archives Microfilm Publication M841, roll no. 84. Record Group 28. National Archives Building, Washington, D.C.

United States Selective Service System. Records of the Selective Service System (World War I). National Archives Microfilm Publication

M1509A. Record Group 163. National Archives Building, Washington, D.C.

———. Draft Registration Cards, 1917–1918. National Archives and Records Administration, Washington, D.C. M1509.

United States War Department. War Department Collection of Confederate Records. Service Record, Sergeant J. K. P. Pipkin, Witt's Regiment, Arkansas Cavalry. Record Group 109. National Archives Building, Washington, D.C.

Yavapai County, Arizona Territory. Third Judicial District Court. *Territory of Arizona v. Daniel M. Harvick, John Halford, William Stiren, and J. J. Smith,* case file no. 36. Arizona Department of Library, Archives and Public Records, Phoenix.

Newspapers

Arizona

Arizona Bulletin (Solomonville)
Arizona Champion (Flagstaff)
Arizona Daily Citizen (Tucson)
Arizona Daily Gazette (Phoenix)
Arizona Daily Star (Tucson)
Arizona Republican (later *Republic*) (Phoenix)
Arizona Silver Belt (Miami)
Arizona Weekly Journal-Miner (Prescott)
Arizona Weekly Star (Tucson)
Coconino Sun (Flagstaff)
Copper Era (Clifton)
Epitaph (Tombstone)
Florence Tribune
Graham County Courier
Graham County Guardian
Holbrook Argus
Prospector (Tombstone)
Prescott Evening Courier
St. Johns Herald
St. Johns Herald-Observer
Tombstone Prospector
Weekly Phoenix Herald
White Mountain Independent (Show Low)

California

Los Angeles Daily Times
San Francisco Chronicle

Colorado

Denver Evening Post
Rocky Mountain News (Denver)

Kansas

Topeka State Journal

Missouri

St. Louis Globe-Democrat

New Mexico

Albuquerque Daily Citizen
Albuquerque Weekly Citizen
Albuquerque Evening Herald
Albuquerque Journal
Albuquerque Morning Democrat
Albuquerque Morning Journal
Bullion (Socorro)
Carbon City News (Gallup)
Carbon City News and McKinley County Republican (Gallup)
Deming Headlight
Elk (Gallup)
Gallup Independent
Herald (Silver City)
Rio Grande Republican (Las Cruces)
Santa Fe Daily New Mexican
Santa Fe New Mexican
Silver City Eagle
Silver City Enterprise
Silver City Independent
Socorro Chieftan
Southwest Sentinel (Grant County)
Western Liberal (Lordsburg)

New York

New York Times

Ohio

Cincinnati Daily Times

Oregon

Grant County News (John Day)

Tennessee

Southern Star (Chattanooga)

Texas

El Paso Daily Times
San Angelo Standard

Books and Articles

Accomazzo, Betty, ed. *Arizona National Ranch Histories of Living Pioneer Stockman* [*sic*]. Phoenix: Arizona National Livestock Show, 1978.

Adams, Ramon F. *Burs under the Saddle: A Second Look at Books and Histories of the West.* Norman: University of Oklahoma Press, 1964.

Alexander, Bob. *Sheriff Harvey Whitehill: Silver City Stalwart.* Silver City, N. Mex.: High-Lonesome Books, 2005.

Anderson, George B. *History of New Mexico: Its Resources and People,* vol. 2. Los Angeles: Pacific States Publishing Co, 1907.

Apache County Centennial Committee. *Lest Ye Forget.* Arizona: Apache County Centennial Committee, 1980.

Arizona 1890 Great Registers. Compiled by Barbara Baldwin Salyer. Mesa: Arizona Genealogical Advisory Board, 2001.

Arizona State Business Directory: Including El Paso, Texas: 1917 and 1920. Denver, Colo.: Gazetteer Publishing and Printing Co., 1917 and 1920.

Ball, Larry D. *Desert Lawmen: The High Sheriffs of New Mexico and Arizona, 1846–1912.* Albuquerque: University of New Mexico Press, 1992.

———. *Elfego Baca in Life and Legend.* El Paso: University of Texas Press, 1992.

———. *The United States Marshals of New Mexico and Arizona Territories, 1846–1912.* Albuquerque: University of New Mexico Press, 1978.

Banta, Albert Franklin. *Albert Franklin Banta: Arizona Pioneer.* Edited by Frank D. Reeve. Publications in History, vol. 14. Albuquerque: Historical Society of New Mexico, 1953.

Barrington, Jacky, ed. *Celebrating 100 Years of Frontier Living.* Magdalena, N. Mex.: privately printed, 1984.

Bartholomew, Ed. *Black Jack Ketchum: Last of the Holdup Kings.* Houston: Frontier Press of Texas, 1955.

Beverly, Bob. *Hobo of the Rangeland,* Lovington, N. Mex.: n. p., 1940.

———. "Horse Race at Seymour in 1890." *Frontier Times* 12, no. 6 (March 1935): 237–39.

Bryan, Howard. *Robbers, Rogues, and Ruffians: True Tales of the Wild West.* Albuquerque: Clear Light Press, 1991.

———. *True Tales of the American Southwest: Pioneer Recollections of Frontier Adventures.* Albuquerque: Clear Light Press, 1991.

Byrkit, James W. "The IWW in Wartime Arizona," *Journal of Arizona History* 18 (Summer 1977): 149–70.

Burgess, Glenn, ed. *Mt. Graham Profiles,* vol. 1. Graham County, Ariz.: Graham County Historical Society, 1977.

Burton, Jeff. *The Deadliest Outlaws.* Portsmouth, England: Palomino Books, 2007.

———. *Dynamite and Six-shooter.* Santa Fe, N. Mex.: Palomino Press, 1970.

Chesley, Hervey E. *Adventuring with the Old-Timers, Trails Travelled—Tales Told.* Midland, Tex.: Nita Stewart Haley Memorial Library, 1979.

Clarke, Mary Whatley. *The Slaughter Ranches and Their Makers.* Austin: Jenkins Book Publishing Co., 1979.

Cleaveland, Agnes Morley. *No Life for a Lady.* Boston: Houghton Mifflin Company, 1941.

Cleaveland, Norman, with George Fitzpatrick. *The Morleys—Young Upstarts on the Southwest Frontier.* Albuquerque: Calvin Horn Publisher, 1971.

Coe, Wilbur. *Ranch on the Ruidoso: The Story of a Pioneer Family in New Mexico, 1871–1968.* New York: Alfred A. Knopf, 1968.

Coleman, Max. "Dumb Heroes of the West." *Frontier Times* 8 (December 1930): 120–25.

———. "Life of a Desperado." *Southwest Review* 16 (Summer 1931): 484–95.

Compiled Laws of New Mexico, 1884, serial no. 16842. Santa Fe: New Mexico Printing Company, 1885.

Cox, John T. "Salty John." "Salty John Cox and Bronco Bill," transcribed by Eve Ball. *True West* 24 (June 1977): 24–25; 48–49.

Curry, George. *An Autobiography, 1861–1947.* Albuquerque: University of New Mexico Press, 1958.

Day, Dorothy. "Nation-wide Strikes Advance," *Catholic Worker* (November 1933).

DeArment, Robert K. *George Scarborough: The Life and Death of a Lawman on the Closing Frontier.* Norman: University of Oklahoma Press, 1992.

Dirck, Brian. "Witt's Cavalry: An Arkansas Guerrilla Unit" [online]. Available from World Wide Web (accessed September 8, 2007): www.faulknerhistory.com/articles/WittsCavalry.htm

Dykstra, Robert R. *The Cattle Towns: A Social History of the Kansas Cattle Trading Centers.* New York: Alfred A. Knopf, 1968.

Eden, M. C. "America's First Train Robbery." *Tally Sheet* (English Westerners) 21 (October 1974): 3–8.

Ernst, Donna B. "George S. Nixon, More Than One Run-in with Outlaws," *Journal* (Western Outlaw-Lawman History Association) 10 (Summer 2001): 43–48.

Farish, Thomas Edwin. *History of Arizona,* 8 vols. San Francisco: Filmer Bros., 1915–18.

Fergusson, Erna. *Murder and Mystery in New Mexico.* Albuquerque: Merle Armitage Editions, 1948.

Flake, Osmer D. *William J. Fluke: Pioneer Colonizer.* N.p., ca. 1950s.

Fox, Sharon Jeanne Hinton. *Ft. Thomas, Camp Thomas, Camp Goodwin, Geronimo, Maxey, Emery, Ashurst History; Newspaper Articles, Publications, Private Parties Stories, Pictures and etc.* Central, Ariz.: The Fox Run, 1997.

Goetz, Charles E. *A Prophet with Honor: The Fred Tuttle Colter Story.* N.p.: privately printed, 1965.

Haley, J. Evetts. *Jeff Milton: A Good Man with a Gun.* Norman: University of Oklahoma Press, 1948.

———. *The XIT Ranch of Texas and the Early Days of the Llano Estacado.* Chicago: Capitol Reservations Lands, 1929. Reprinted with new introduction by J. Evetts Haley. Norman: University of Oklahoma Press, 1953.

Hampton, Wade. "Brigandage on our Railroads" *North American Review* 159 (December 1894): 665–68.

Harden, Paul. "The Last Train Robbery," *El Defensor Chieftain* (Socorro, N. Mex.), November 1 (part 1), and December 6 (part 2), 2003.

Harlow, Alvin F. *Old Waybills: The Romance of the Express Companies.* New York: D. Appleton-Century Co., 1934.

Harvick, Dan, as told to William Sparks. "Canyon Diablo Train Robbery, *Frontier Times* 45 (January 1971): 8–11, 48–51.

Hatch, Lelia Kirk. "Nancy Julia Pipkin" [online]. Available from World Wide Web (accessed September 8, 2007): .

———. *A Hundred Years of Horse Tracks: The Story of the Gray Ranch.* Silver City, N. Mex.: High-Lonesome Books, 1996.

Hornung, Chuck. "Cipriano Baca—New Mexico Peace Officer," *The Journal* of the Western Outlaw-Lawman History Association 5 (Spring–Summer 1996): 42–47.

———. *The Thin Gray Line—The New Mexico Mounted Police.* Fort Worth, Tex.: Western Heritage Press, 1971.

Hovey, Walter C. "Black Jack Ketchum Tried to Give Me a Break!" *True West* 19 (March–April 1972): 6–11, 48–52.

Hume, James B., and John N. Thacker. *Report of Jas. B. Hume and Jno. N. Thacker, Special Officers, Wells, Fargo & Co's Express, Covering a Period of Fourteen Years Giving Losses by Train Robbers, Stage Robbers and Burglaries and a Full Description and Record of All Noted Criminals Convicted of Offenses Against Wells, Fargo & Company since November 5th, 1870,* San Francisco: H. S. Crocker & Co., Stationers and Printers, 1885.

Johnston, Langford Ryan. *Old Magdalena Cow Town.* Magdalena, N. Mex.: Bander Log, n.d.

Julyan, Robert. *The Place Names of New Mexico,* rev. ed. Albuquerque: University of New Mexico Press, 1998.

Kalt, William D., III. "Epes Randolph: Railroad Man of the Southwest," *Journal of Arizona History* 47, no. 2 (Summer 2006): 131–54.

Keleher, William A. *The Fabulous Frontier.* 1945. Reprint, Albuquerque: University of New Mexico Press, 1982.

King, Frank M. *Pioneer Western Empire Builders; A True Story of Pioneer Men and Women.* Pasadena, Calif.: Trail's End Publishing Co., 1946.

Klasner, Lily. *My Girlhood among Outlaws,* edited by Eve Ball. Tucson: University of Arizona Press, 1972.

Kemp, Ben W., with J. C. Dykes. *Cow Dust and Saddle Leather.* Norman: University of Oklahoma Press, 1968.

Knight, John T. "How to Repel Train Robbers," *North American Review* 160 (February 1895): 254–56.

"Lady Cattle Rustler." *Pioneer Nevada.* Reno, Nev.: Harolds Club, 1951.

Lutrell, Estelle. *Newspapers and Periodicals of Arizona, 1859–1911,* University of Arizona General Bulletin no. 15. Tucson: University of Arizona, 1949.

McClintock, James H. *Mormon Settlement in Arizona.* Phoenix: Manufacturing Stationers, 1921.

Marshall, James. *Santa Fe: The Railroad That Built an Empire.* New York: Random House, 1945.

Martin, Bob. "Train Robbers Store More Than Money" [online]. Available from World Wide Web (accessed May 20 2009): www.krqe.com/dpp/news/news_13_digs/crime_krqe_belen_train_robbers_stole _more_than_money_200905200045.

Meadows, John P. *Pat Garrett and Billy the Kid as I Knew Them: Reminiscences of John P. Meadows*, edited by John P. Wilson. Albuquerque: University of New Mexico, 2004.

Michno, Gregory. *The Deadliest Indian War in the West: The Snake Conflict, 1864–1868.* Caldwell, Id.: Caxton Press, 2007.

Miller, Joseph, ed. *The Arizona Story.* New York: Hastings House, 1952.

Myrick, David F. *New Mexico's Railroads, A Historical Survey*, rev. ed. Albuquerque: University of New Mexico Press, 1990.

Nolan, Frederick. *Bad Blood: The Life and Times of the Horrell Brothers.* Stillwater, Okla.: Barbed Wire Press, 1994.

———. "'Boss Rustler:' The Life and Times of John Kinney, Parts 1 and 2." *True West* 43 (September 1996): 14–21; 43 (November 1996): 12–19.

Otero, Miguel Antonio. *My Nine Years as Governor of the Territory of New Mexico, 1897–1906.* Albuquerque: University of New Mexico Press, 1940.

"The Modern Dick Turpin," *Harper's Weekly* 36 (January 16, 1892): 63.

Peterson, Charles S. *Take Up Your Mission: Mormon Colonizing along the Little Colorado River, 1870–1900.* Tucson: University of Arizona Press, 1973.

Pinkerton, William A. "Highwaymen of the Railroad," *North American Review* 157 (November 1893): 530–40.

———. *Train Robberies and Train Robbers.* 1907. Reprint, Fort Davis, Tex.: Frontier Book Co., 1968.

Pipkin, William Philip. "Aser Pipkin, 1805–1901" [online]. Available from World Wide Web (accessed December 1, 2002): .

———. "Mary Lafentie Pipkin, 1869–1909" [online]. Available from World Wide Web (accessed December 1, 2002): .

Poldervaart, Arie W. *Black-Robed Justice.* Santa Fe: Historical Society of New Mexico, 1948.

Prassel, Frank Richard. *The Great American Outlaw: A Legacy of Fact and Fiction.* Norman: University of Oklahoma Press, 1993.

Rasch, Philip J. "An Incomplete account of 'Bronco Bill' Walters." *The Brand Book* of the English Westerners' Society 19, no. 2 (January 1973): 1–12.

———. "Death of a Bank Robber," *Quarterly* (National Association for Outlaw and Lawman History) (Summer 1982), reprinted in *Desperadoes of Arizona Territory*, pp. 50–52.

———. "'Kid' Swingle: A Forgotten Highwayman," *Quarterly* (National Association and Center for Outlaw and Lawman History) 9, no. 3 (Winter 1985): 6–7.

Revised Statutes of Arizona (1913), Penal Code, complied by Samuel L. Pattee. Phoenix: The McNeil Co., 1913.

Rhodes, Eugene Manlove. "Whose Who and Why," *Saturday Evening Post* 190, no. 15 (October 13, 1917): 27.

———. *The Rhodes Reader: Stories of Virgins, Villains, and Varmints,* selected by W. H. Hutchinson. Norman: University of Oklahoma Press, 1957.

Rudd, Elizabeth Catherine. "Eliza Catherine Rudd Tells of Early History," *White Mountain Roundup* (July 1970), reprinted in Apache County Centenniel Committee, *Lest We Forget.* Apache County, Ariz., 1980.

Santee, Ross. *Men and Horses.* New York: The Century Company, 1926.

Secrest, William B. *Perilous Trails, Dangerous Men: Early California Stagecoach Robbers and their Desperate Careers, 1856–1900.* Clovis, Calif.: Quill Driver Books, 2001.

Smalley, George Herbert. *My Adventures in Arizona,* edited by Yndia Smalley Moore. Tucson: Arizona Pioneers' Historical Society, 1966.

———. "The Reform of Climax Jim, Cattle Rustler," *Los Angeles Herald Illustrated Magazine* (ca. January 23, 1902).

Sonnichsen, C. L. *Tularosa: Last of the Frontier West.* 1960. Reprint, Albuquerque: University of New Mexico, 1980.

Stephens, Robert W. *Mannen Clements, Texas Gunfighter.* Dallas: privately printed, 1996.

Stuart, Gary L. *The Gallup 14.* Albuquerque, University of New Mexico Press, 2000.

Tanner, John D., Jr. "Violence in New Mexico Territory: A Penitentiary Analysis," *The Journal* of the Western Outlaw-Lawman History Association 12 (Summer 2003): 32–34, 56.

Tanner, Karen Holliday, and John D. Tanner, Jr. *Climax Jim: The Tumultuous Tale of Arizona's Rustling Cowboy.* Tucson: Arizona Lithographers, 2005.

———. "The Great Grant's Robbery," *True West* 45 (August 1998): 12–17.

———. "'Kid' Swingle: Southwestern Rustler, Robber, and All Around Rascal," *Quarterly* of the National Association for Outlaw and Lawman History 40, no. 4 (October–December 2006): 43–52.

———. *The Last of the Old-Time Outlaws: The George West Musgrave Story.* Norman: University of Oklahoma Press, 2002.

———. "The Lowdown on 'Quarrelsome' Bill Downing," *Wild West* 21, no. 5 (April 2009): 40–45.

———. "Red Pipkin, Outlaw from the Black River Country," *Wild West* 16, no. 3 (October 2003): 30–36, 71.

———. "Revenge: The Murder of Ed Beeler," *Journal* (Western Outlaw-Lawman History Association) 13 (Summer 2004): 2–7.

———. "Rewards and Justice Did Not Mix: The Logan, New Mexico, Train Robbery," *Journal of the Wild West History Association* 1, no. 1 (February 2008): 13–28, 50.

———. "Scott White: Arizona Lawman," *Journal of Arizona History* 49, no. 1 (Spring 2008): 1–26.

———. "Silver City Shootout: 'Why Did He Shoot Me, We Were Good Friends?'" *Wild West* 17, no. 9 (October 2005): 38–44.

———. "Susie Raper—Female Buccaneer of the Sagebrush," *Wild West,* forthcoming.

———. *"Up Goes Your Hands!" Holdup at Maricopa.* Tucson: Arizona Lithographers, 2009.

Taylor, Samuel W. *The Last Pioneer: John Taylor, a Mormon Prophet.* Salt Lake City, Utah: Signature Books, 1999.

Telling, Irving. "Ramah, New Mexico, 1876–1900: An Historical Episode with Some Value Analysis," *Utah Historical Quarterly* 21, no. 2 (April 1953): 117–36.

Thorp, N. Howard (Jack), as told to Neil McCullough Clark. *Pardner of the Wind.* Caldwell, Idaho: Caxton Printers, 1945.

Tietjen, Gary. *Ernst Albert Tietjen.* Bountiful, Utah: Family History Publishers, 1992.

Todachinnie, Howard. "Life of Willard Butt." [online]. Available from World Wide Web (accessed October 1, 2007):

Walters, Lorenzo D. *Tombstone's Yesterday: True Chronicles of Early Arizona, 1877–1887.* 1928. Reprint, Glorieta, N. Mex.: Rio Grande Press, 1968.

The War of Rebellion: A Compilation of Official Records of the Union and Confederate Armies, 1861–1865, ser. 1, vol. 50, pt. 2. Washington, D.C.: Government Printing Office, 1897.

Webb, Walter Prescott. *The Handbook of Texas,* 2 volumes. Austin: Texas State Historical Association, 1952.

Weinman, Ken. "The Finding of the Great Belén Train Robbery Loot." *Gold and Treasure Hunter* (March–April 1987): 4–6, 11.

White, Scott, as told to John Edwin Hogg. "Bad Man's Nemesis: The adventures and experiences of an Arizona sheriff, in a land and a time when a man often wore a mustache, but always wore a gun," *Touring Topics* 23, no. 4 (April 1931): 22–26, 36–37.

Wilhelm, C. Leroy and Mary R. *A History of the St. Johns Stake: The Triumph of Man and His Religion over the Perils of a Raw Frontier.* Orem, Utah: Historical Publications, 1982.

Williams, Michael. "Real Men of Arizona: The Story of Two Famous Arizona Gunfights—The Fights of Jeff Milton who is a Gun-fighter of the Very First Grade." *Pearson's Magazine* (September 1912): 119–24.

Willson, Roscoe G. "A Little Old Arizona Cowboy Enjoys Excitement of Banditry," *Arizona Days and Ways* (*Arizona Republic* [Phoenix]), October 13, 1957.

———. "Broncho Bill Holdups Recalled by Pioneer." *Arizona Days and Ways* (*Arizona Republic* [Phoenix]), June 25, 1950.

———. *Pioneer Cattleman of Arizona.* Phoenix: McGrew Commercial Printery, 1951.

———. *Pioneer and Well Known Cattleman of Arizona.* Phoenix: McGrew Commercial Printery, 1956.

Winfield, Craig. "Broncho Bill Walters: Last of the Old-Time Train Robbers." *Oldtimers Wild West* (December 1977): 8, 45–48.

———. "Broncho Bill Walters: Texas Badman," *Real West* 12 (October 1969): 10–12, 70–71.

The Zuni People. *The Zunis: Self Portrayals,* Avina Quam, translator. Albuquerque: University of New Mexico Press, 1972.

Index